A Charismatic Catholic shares treasures from the storehouse of the Catholic Church.

Speaking to non-Catholics and Catholics alike, Judith Tydings pushes aside tradition-bound walls to illumine the lives of the canonized Saints of the Catholic Church.

Healing and understanding flow as she shares with humility, love, and humor the insights she has gained in study of the lives of those exemplary—but also human—Christians singled out for recognition during nearly two thousand years of Christian history.

Mrs. Tydings does not hide nor excuse the incongruities and abuses to which the system of honoring the Saints has occasionally been subjected, but she focuses primarily on the Saints themselves, those persons in whose lives can be seen a reflection of the care of God for His people throughout the ages.

In this book, history grants inspiration and encouragement for today for Christians of all denominations.

Gathering a People

Catholic Saints in Charismatic Perspective

Judith Tydings

Gathering a People

Judith Tydings

Logos International
Plainfield, New Jersey

Nihil Obstat:
Reverend Ernest E. Larkin, O. Carm.
Censor Librorum

Imprimatur:
William Cardinal Baum
Archbishop of Washington

Father, you are holy indeed,
and all creation rightly gives you praise.
All life, all holiness comes from you
through your Son, Jesus Christ our Lord,
by the working of the Holy Spirit.
From age to age you gather a people to yourself,
so that from east to west
a perfect offering may be made
to the glory of your name.

Eucharistic Prayer III

TABLE OF CONTENTS

SOME SAINTS

St. Paul	d.c.	67
St. John the Divine	d.c.	100
St. Ignatius of Antioch	d.c.	107
St. Polycarp of Smyrna	d.c.	155
The Martyrs of Lyons	d.	177
St. Antony of Egypt	c.	251-356
St. Alban, martyr	d.c.	287
St. Pachomius	c.	290-346
St. Athanasius	c.	296-373
St. Agnes	d.c.	304
St. Basil	c.	330-379
St. Monica		331-387
St. Ambrose	c.	334 or 340-397
St. Jerome	c.	342-420
St. Paula		347-404
St. Augustine		354-430
St. Simeon the Stylite	c.	390-459
St. Scholastica	c.	480-543
St. Benedict	c.	480-547
St. Gregory the Great, pope	c.	540-604
St. Hilda of Whitby		614-680
St. John Climacus	d.c.	649
St. Aidan	d.	651
St. Fiacre	d.c.	670
St. Boniface	c.	675-754 or 755
St. Lioba	c.	700-780
St. Benedict of Aniane	c.	750-821
St. Anskar		801-865
St. Meinrad, hermit	d.	861
The Cluny Saints		910-1157
St. Symeon the New Theologian		949-1022
St. Romuald, abbot	c.	950-1027

St. Peter Damien		1007-1072
St. Bernard of Clairvaux		1090-1153
St. Dominic		1170-1221
St. Francis of Assisi		1181-1226
St. Clare of Assisi		1193-1253
St. Anthony of Padua		1195-1231
St. Bonaventure		1221-1274
St. Thomas Aquinas		1225-1274
St. Elizabeth of Portugal		1271-1336
St. Gregory Palamas	c.	1296-1359
St. Bridget of Sweden	c.	1303-1373
St. Catherine of Siena		1347-1380
St. Colette of Corbi		1381-1447
St. Joan of Arc		1412-1431
St. Catherine of Genoa		1447-1510
St. Angela Merici		1474-1540
St. Ignatius Loyola		1492-1556
St. Peter of Alcantara		1499-1562
St. Teresa of Avila		1515-1582
St. Philip Neri		1515-1595
St. John of the Cross		1542-1591
St. Robert Bellarmine		1542-1621
Bl. Mary of the Incarnation: Mme. Acarie		1566-1618
St. Francis de Sales		1567-1622
St. Martin de Porres		1579-1639
St. Vincent de Paul		1585-1660
St. Louise de Marillac		1591-1660
St. Joseph of Cupertino		1603-1663
St. Alphonsus Liguori		1693-1787
St. Benedict Labre		1748-1783
St. Julie Billiart		1751-1816
Bl. Anna Maria Taigi		1769-1837
St. Elizabeth Seton		1774-1821

Bl. Anne-Marie Javouhey	1779-1851
St. Madeleine Sophie Barat	1779-1865
St. John Vianney: The Cure d'Ars	1786-1859
John Henry Cardinal Newman*	1801-1890
St. Catherine Laboure	1806-1876
St. John Bosco	1815-1888
St. Pius X, pope	1835-1914
St. Bernadette	1844-1879
St. Frances Xavier Cabrini	1850-1917
Charles de Foucauld*	1858-1916
St. Therese of Lisieux	1873-1897
Elizabeth of the Trinity*	1880-1906
John XXIII, pope*	1881-1963

Butler's *Lives of the Saints* lists some twenty-five hundred Saints. *The Roman Martyrology* includes some forty-five hundred names and is not exhaustive.

Abbreviations for Table of Saints

c. *circa*, about (with a date)
d. died
* cause pending, but not yet canonized or beatified

ACKNOWLEDGMENTS

Grateful acknowledgment is made to the publishers, authors and copyright owners of works quoted in this book for permission to reprint excerpted materials.

Excerpts from LETTERS FROM THE SAINTS arranged and selected by a Benedictine of Stanbrook Abbey reprinted by permission of Hawthorn Books, Inc. Copyright © 1964 by Burns and Oates, Ltd. All rights reserved.

Excerpts from THE SPIRITUAL EXERCISES AND THE IGNATIAN MYSTICAL HORIZON by Harvey D. Egan, SJ, reprinted by permission of The Institute of Jesuit Sources. © 1976 by The Institute of Jesuit Sources.

Excerpts from COME, SOUTH WIND: A COLLECTION OF CONTEMPLATIVES ed. M.L. Shrady reprinted by permission of Pantheon Books, Inc. Copyright © 1957 by Pantheon Books, Inc.

Excerpts from "The Role of the Holy Spirit and the Gifts of the Spirit in the Mystical Tradition" by Vinson Synan used by permission of *One in Christ: A Catholic Ecumenical Review* in which the article originally appeared.

Excerpts from DON BOSCO by Edna Beyer Phelan used by permission of Doubleday & Company, Inc. Copyright © by Edna Beyer Phelan.

Excerpts from THE WOMAN GOD LOVED by Glenn D. Kittler used by permission of Doubleday & Company, Inc. Copyright © 1959 by Glenn D. Kittler.

Excerpts from "Pentecostalism and the Doctrine of Saint Teresa and Saint John of the Cross," by Teresa Del Monte Sol used by permission of *Spiritual Life: A Quarterly of Contemporary*

INTRODUCTION

When I first began to write this book several years ago, my intention was to share with anyone, who might be interested, my love and understanding of Saints [1] of the Catholic Church. That hasn't changed. I was, and still am, writing primarily for those who witness to having been baptized in the Spirit, [2] whether that *experience* be understood as the actualization of one's baptismal and/or confirmation graces, or the release of the Spirit, or some other formulation. I felt that we needed the example of the holy lives lived by Saints. Reading through Church history, I had come across many examples of people who seemed charismatic without being especially distinguished for holiness. On the other hand, I never found holiness without evidence also of charisms. [3] I wanted Catholic theologians, concerned about the newness and "differentness" of the charismatic renewal or the Catholic Pentecostal movement, to see it as continuous and completely in harmony with Catholic tradition and classical spiritual theology, which, after all, is a distillation of the wisdom contained in Saints' lives.

All these concerns are still with me but I realize now how myopic I was until the Lord began to stretch my vision. I had seen Saints chiefly as models of holiness. This is true, but their significance is far greater than that! I had felt that people interested in Saints would, for the most part, be Catholics. I have found that is not the case. I have discovered that many Christians, who have been touched by this marvelous outpouring of the Holy Spirit in our day, and who are not Roman Catholic, are curious about and are sometimes edified by "our" Saints! In a paper presented in Rome in 1973, in connection with the official dialogue between Pentecostal Christians and the Roman Catholic Church, Dr. Vinson Synan, a pastor and the General Secretary of the Pentecostal Holiness Church, expressed this very thing:

> . . . the experience and teachings of St. Francis of Assisi, St. Teresa of Avila, St. John of the Cross, St. Francis Xavier, St. Bernard, and St. Catherine of Genoa, to name a few, have

convinced me that we are on most points indeed soul-brothers.[4]

Dr. Synan concluded by making the suggestion that modern Pentecostals and charismatics seriously study great Catholic Saints of the "mystical tradition." He counseled that it be done "with at least as much interest in those who were canonized as in those who were excommunicated or burned at the stake." [5]

As work progressed on this book, I felt the Lord was telling me that He wanted to invite His people to begin to understand their past, to let Him heal the hurts and the bad memories, and to have His people discover all the ways throughout the ages that He has provided for them despite man's unfaithfulness. Saints are a significant way that God has cared for His people. I felt that the Lord was saying that it is principally Saints, living and dead, who will bring about the union of His body.

A non-Christian looking at the history of Christianity sees Jesus, Pentecost, Christian communities, the ascetic movement, monasticism, Church councils, religious orders, the Papacy, the Protestant Reformation, Saints, the World Council of Churches, Vatican II and so on. In other words, to a non-Christian there is such a thing as a body of knowledge called the history of Christianity. Perhaps we Christians have yet to understand that we are sharers in a common Christian history. The history of all parts of Christ's body is my history because I am a Christian. Tent meetings, dancing in the Spirit and the Book of Common Prayer might not be part of my Catholic tradition, but they are a part of my history because they are part of the common Christian heritage. In the same way, relics, rosaries, novenas, pilgrimages and the custom of canonizing Saints belong to Lutherans, Baptists, Methodists,[6] Pentecostals and all Christians and not just Catholics. So "my" Saints are really "our" Saints.

A saintly and learned Anglican, Edward Bouverie Pusey (1800-1882) pointed in this direction. He remarked when John Henry Newman (1801-1890), later a renowned cardinal and finally a candidate for canonization, left the Anglican Church to become a Catholic:

> He seems to me not so much gone from us, as transplanted into another part of the Vineyard. . . . And who knows what in the mysterious purposes of God's good Providence may be the effect of such a person among them. . . . As each, by God's grace, grows in holiness, each Church will recognize more and more, the Presence of God's Holy Spirit in the other, and what now hinders the union of the western Church will fall off.[7]

For the past ten years or so Protestants and Catholics who have been baptized in the Spirit have been joining with classical Pentecostals in order to all praise the Lord together. Dr. Synan puts it this way:

> There always seems to be a special spiritual dynamic when charismatic Catholics, neo-pentecostals, and classical pentecostals join hearts and voices in prayer, praise and worship, giving common witness to the magnificent work of the Holy Spirit in the body of Christ.[8]

What I am sensing is that the Lord is calling us to take another step. It is not enough to have joined voices and hearts. I believe He is calling us to begin to be of one mind. The body of Christ will never be truly one until we are of one mind and one heart.

As a preparation for this work of union, with the power and guidance of the Holy Spirit, I think the Lord is calling us to go back into our past—our common past—first alone, and then with each other. As we do this, the Lord will, I think, grant us a gigantic healing of the memories. The Lord wants all of us to come to grips with what each denomination and part of His body would rather put under the rug. Together we must share the guilt and hurt and pain we have caused one another. Together we must face things like the persecution of recusant Catholics in England, or the Inquisition from which, by the way, some Saints canonized by the

Catholic Church suffered also. The Lord wants us to look at how we have sinned against one another. Then He wants us to seek and receive forgiveness, first from Him, for it is His body that we have injured, and then from each other.

That is perhaps only half of the healing work the Lord wants to do with us. We could call it the "binding up the wounds" aspect. The other dimension of this healing work of the Lord could be said to be "sharing treasures from the storehouse." All of us have received riches and blessings from the Lord and I believe He wants us to share them with one another. Saints are treasures to be shared. Already we are sharing some treasures, but unfortunately we are not always aware of it. How many Catholics attending Sunday Mass, and opening their *Peoples Mass Book* [9] to page 475 to join in singing "A Mighty Fortress is Our God," notice that the hymn is attributed to Martin Luther whose name appears on the page!

When I say we are to go back into the past, first alone, then with each other, I mean that each of us, each different part of Christ's body, has to have an individual and a denominational historical consciousness before we can share together in a common Christian historical consciousness. At the level of the individual, after baptism in the Spirit it is common for a person to take a fresh look at his or her past. If the person is situated in a healthy Christian environment, this look backwards will result in strength being drawn from treasured memories. Hurts will be healed over by the love of Christ. The past then becomes integrated into the personality in a happy, healthy way. Then, and only then, is the person able to go on to restoring or establishing relationships with others.

I believe the Lord wants this to happen on a denominational level. Some people will need healing or may be led to repent regarding their personal relationship to their own denomination or grouping. That happened to me. Then each of our Christian groupings needs to go back to its origins. We need to understand our past, all of it, the bad as well as the good. We need to comprehend the riches as well as the sorrows of our own traditions. Then, and only then, will the Lord reveal to us His plan about right ways of relating to one another so that we may become His strong, vigorous body, full of compassion, reaching out in love and power to the entire world.

In his introduction to *Charismatic Bridges* in 1974, Dr. Synan observed a trend in the charismatic renewal towards the building of "charismatic walls." He pointed out that there was a "Catholic Charismatic Renewal" and a "Lutheran Charismatic Renewal," and he exhorted us to pray earnestly for unity in the Spirit. Without in any way lessening the prayer for unity, I want to suggest that this trend, which looks like the building of walls, perhaps indicates a time of waiting, is a good thing, and is only temporary.[10] I think we are in a temporary period of withdrawal to do precisely what I have been describing. Many Christians are now being led to begin to understand their traditions. I believe the Lord wants Catholics to examine their roots to see whence they came and so to better understand where they are. I believe the Lord asks the same of all other Christian denominations or groupings. When each part of the body of Christ emerges from this time with an integrated personality, a healthy self-understanding and a continuity with the past, then we can get on with the collective healing of the memories that the Lord is yearning to grant us.

Cardinal Suenens, in *A New Pentecost?*, spoke of the need for understanding our past in his chapter on "The Holy Spirit and Ecumenical Hopes."

Ignorance of the factors that gave rise to our present situation is a block to the development of ecumenical dialogue. We ignore the past at our cost: it is the key to understanding the present. History is made up of a series of chain reactions. It is indispensable, if we are to understand the reasons for schisms and rifts. . . . History is a school in which we acquire a healthy relativity. . . . It teaches us humility—we all have to admit our faults—and the forebearance of God, in His dealings with us.[11]

Ecumenism proceeds on a variety of levels. There are official dialogues conducted by theologians and commissioned by the participating Church bodies. Another significant present-day form of ecumenism is that which is exemplified by Christian communities such as The Word of God, in Ann Arbor, Michigan, where men and women belonging to a variety of Christian denominations live and love and serve one another as brothers and sisters in the Lord. The sharing of history and tradition by Christians who are not professional theologians might be said to pertain to the "Living Room Dialogues" [12] level of ecumenism. A sense of history, however, is necessary to all ecumenism.

Much ecumenism of the future may be an ecumenism rising out of need, in which all divisions fall away in the face of a common effort. In the last quarter of the twentieth century the world is growing progressively darker. As those who bear the light of Christ draw together in spiritual combat against the forces of evil that pervade the earth, they will find themselves united under the banner of Jesus Christ.

Gathering A People is a product of my own denominational healing of the memories. It is a sign of my gratitude to the Lord for His goodness to me and it is an attempt to share some of the fruits of this healing. Most of the book will deal with the "sharing the treasures from the storehouse" aspect of the healing I received. That was my discovery of canonized Saints and what I believe they mean for the body of Christ. The other aspect of the healing, the "binding up the wounds," was brought about by the discovery of a simple formula for describing the dynamics of the Church. Only one chapter will be devoted to that subject but the theme can be seen throughout the book.

While sharing some insights, this book is mainly an attempt to point directions. An annotated bibliography accompanies the text in the hope that it will serve those who might wish to pursue their own inquiry into Saints. I would exhort readers to consult the footnotes and the glossary to get the exact meaning of unfamiliar terms or to gain an understanding of how I may be using a word or an expression.

By concentrating on canonized Saints of the Catholic Church I don't mean to suggest that saintly Christians only appear within Roman Catholicism. That would be just as untrue as it would be to suggest that the handful of people the Church has canonized represents the only holiness there is in the Catholic Church. I have no difficulty imagining Jessie Penn-Lewis engaged in spirited dialogue with Ignatius Loyola. George Mueller and John Vianney, would have similar notes to compare on the care of orphans.

Sharing history and tradition [13] with one another will have to be done with a lot of humility, a lot of love, and a sense of humor. I have tried to write about Saints of the Roman Catholic Church and the custom of canonizing them, with humility, love and humor. I think it was Chesterton who once wrote about it being necessary to be grounded as upon rock in one's denomination in order to engage fruitfully in what we now call "ecumenical dialogue." The line went something like: "One can dance on a rock more easily than upon a tightrope." Some Catholic readers may feel I have done too much dancing. Some readers who are not Catholic may feel I haven't danced enough and am too proud of my own tradition. A good sense of humor requires a healthy sense of perspective enabling one to perceive the incongruous. Some readers may not agree with my perspective. Whatever the deficiencies, I offer this book in love to all who may read it, with the prayer that in some way it will assist the Lord's work of gathering us, His people, together.

Feast of St. Bridget of Sweden
July 1976

NOTES TO INTRODUCTION

1. All Christians could be called "saints" following the custom of St. Paul. In Roman Catholic usage a "Saint" is a deceased man or woman whose holiness and heroic virtue have been recognized and confirmed by the Church's official processes of beatification and canonization or by the continued existence of veneration and a feast approved by the Church. See Chapter 3.

2. "The term, *baptism in the (Holy) Spirit*, originates from the words of Christ just before His ascension: 'John baptized with water, but before many days, you shall be baptized with the Holy Spirit' (Acts 1:5). (Cf. Luke 24:49; Matt. 3:11; Mark 1:8; I Cor. 12:13). Thus the baptism in the Spirit is substantially that which happened to the 120 disciples when the Holy Spirit descended on them on that first Christian Pentecost. It is from the renewal of this same experience that the Pentecostal movement gets both its name and its dynamism.

> . . . To be baptized in the Holy Spirit does not mean to receive the sacrament of baptism, through the pouring of water over one's head. This is certainly not what happened to the apostles on Pentecost day. If they were baptized with water, this occurred sometime previously. Their baptism in the Holy Spirit was an interior experience of the power of the Holy Spirit filling and transforming them. So it happens also with most people today." (Edward O'Connor, C.S.C., *The Pentecostal Movement in the Catholic Church*, Ave Maria Press, Notre Dame, Indiana, 1971. pp. 131-132.)

3. Chapters nine, ten and eleven deal specifically with Saints and charisms. It is my view that the essence of the charismatic renewal is of the essence of the Christian life even more than the essence of the liturgical renewal was of the essence of the Christian life, if that's possible. Some might agree with Robert Wild (*Enthusiasm in the Spirit*, Ave Maria Press, Notre Dame, Indiana, 1975, p. 15) that a Saint like Therese of the Child Jesus, the Little Flower, would not qualify today as a charismatic. I would disagree as does one of Therese's present-day counterparts. Carmelite sister Therese Del Monte Sol writes: "God never raises a person to great holiness in isolation from others, no matter how humble, unimportant or hidden his role in life, and since the gifts [charisms] are given to us for others, in every case of genuine holiness there will be spiritual gifts in evidence. An example of this is Saint Therese. Hers was a hidden life, but in spite of the fact that some authors like to emphasize that she did not possess extraordinary gifts, she *did* possess a very extraordinary gift of teaching, so extraordinary, in fact, that she was given a special mission of teaching her way of spirituality to the whole world." (*Spiritual Life*, Spring, 1971, p. 26.)

4. Vinson Synan, "The Role of the Holy Spirit and the Gifts of the Spirit in the Mystical Tradition," in *One in Christ*, 1974, Vol. X, No. 2, p. 202.

5. *Ibid.*

6. A Methodist minister of Bath, England, J. Neville Ward, wrote a book on the rosary (*Five for Sorrow, Ten for Joy*, Doubleday and Company, Inc., Garden City, New York) which was published in 1973. In his preface Rev. Ward wrote: ". . . In Methodism the silence about the Mother of Jesus is positively deafening. I have begun to wonder what anxiety is behind this surprising mental hang-up." Admitting initial nervousness, Rev. Ward tells us how he overcame it and he shares with his readers his beautiful meditations.

7. Henry Parry Liddon, *Life of Edward Bouverie Pusey, D.D.* Second Edition. London, 1893, Vol. II, p. 461 as quoted by Philip Boyce, O.D.C. in "Gleanings from the Newman Symposium in Rome" in *The Clergy Review*, December 1975.

8. Vinson Synan, *Charismatic Bridges*, Word of Life, Ann Arbor, Michigan, 1974, p. xi.

9. *Peoples Mass Book*, World Library of Sacred Music, Inc., Cincinnati, Ohio, 1966.

10. Fr. Kilian McDonnell in *Catholic Pentecostalism: Problems in Evaluation*, Dove Publications, Pecos, New Mexico, 1970, mentions this tendency in relation to political and social processes and I would suggest that the same interpretation applies here to ecumenical processes. "Field research has shown that the initial reaction of Pentecostals to the prophetic gifts is to withdraw temporarily from social involvement. This would follow the general pattern of the classical mystical and ascetical tradition" (pp. 36-37).

11. Leon Joseph Cardinal Suenens, *A New Pentecost?*, The Seabury Press, New York, 1974, p. 182.

12. The Living Room Dialogues program was started in 1965 by the Division of Christian Unity of the National Council of Churches and the Apostolate of Good Will of the Confraternity of Christian Doctrine of the Roman Catholic Church. The plan of the Living Room Dialogues was to have twelve to fifteen people—Catholic, Orthodox and Protestant, men and women, married and single, of different nationalities and races—meet in their homes once a month for Scripture reading, prayer and discussion. The purpose of this was to aid individual Christians to become personally concerned about Christian unity and to pray for the reunion of all Christians.

13. For a theological confirmation of the prophetic thrust of this Introduction see the paper by Francis Sullivan, S.J., given at the theological conference on the charismatic renewal at Glenview, Illinois, in October 1976, soon to be published with the other papers from this conference. From the institutional side there is support from Bishop Paul Anderson of Duluth, Minnesota. (Homily at Atlantic City Eastern Regional Conference, 25 October 1976.)

CHAPTER 1

Binding Up Wounds

For many years I had a faulty concept of the Catholic Church. Until I was baptized in the Spirit and for some time thereafter I understood the Church to be an institution or an organization composed of bishops and priests and a pope. These administrators dispensed sacraments which in turn dispensed something called grace which was needed for salvation. All initiative came from above and the Holy Spirit acted only through the hierarchy. After I was baptized in the Spirit I knew the Lord had entered my life. I knew also that I belonged to the people of God and I very gradually and somewhat vaguely began to feel like I was a part of the Church.

It was in the reading of lives of canonized Saints of the Catholic Church that I began to see that my concept of the Church and how God dealt with His people was deficient. I read about an illiterate dyer's daughter, St. Catherine of Siena (recently proclaimed a Doctor of the Church), who chastised a pope for the unholy life he was leading. Then I found out that she wasn't the only one who had done such a thing [1] or had had such a close, intimate relationship with the Lord. I began to see that the Saints were not, to quote a respected Roman Catholic theologian Karl Rahner: ". . . success-ful products of the Church in her role as an institutional establish-ment of salvation, products who—brought to maturity by instruction and education, direction and means of grace—are, as it were, handed over as the completed end-result to the 'triumphant' Church." [2]

I also began to see that there was another dimension to the Church.

Until I was thirty, for me the person of Jesus and the possibility of a relationship with Him were covered over to some extent by layers of custom, Church laws, rote catechism answers and pious practices. The Church had provided me with excellent instruction, good formation and needed discipline. But in my case this strong and sturdy house had been built on an inadequate foundation which presupposed that there had been evangelization and initiation.

Before I was thirty, had someone asked me what the Moravian pastor asked John Wesley, "Do you know Jesus Christ?", I would have given the same answer Wesley did, "I know He is the Savior of the world." The pastor's response, "True, but do you know He has saved *you*?" would have left me in complete disarray.

After I "met the Lord" in 1966 and was baptized in His Spirit, the thought that I hadn't known the Lord very well for perhaps half my life,[3] plus my inadequate concept of what constituted the Church, conspired to create in me some resentment towards "the Church" for seemingly keeping the Good News from me for so long. My reaction was: "How could the Church do this to me?" But while asking that question, there was the gnawing sense that in some way I too was "the Church." I didn't know how that could be, yet I somehow knew I couldn't just blame everything on the hierarchy.

Three and a half years after I was baptized in the Spirit, I was asked to teach religion in a girls' Catholic high school. I yearned to share with my students the joy of knowing Jesus Christ, but when I mentioned Jesus the reaction was, "We've heard about Him for years. Can't you pick a more interesting subject?" The only Jesus they knew was Jesus the model Christian who lived two thousand years ago. Most of the girls were apathetic about religion and casual in their practice of Catholicism. If they went to Sunday Mass at all it was because their parents insisted that they attend. There were a few, however, who reminded me very much of myself when I was a high school student. They were "model Catholics" and they listened to me with a condescending attitude. After all, they had studied religion so many years they knew it all. And they knew they were good. The way they lived and defined Christianity resembled very much the American Boy Scout Code. They were "brave, thrifty, clean and reverent."

My generation hadn't known the real Jesus either, but we did know some basic theology. When I was baptized in the Spirit, the whole Baltimore catechism came alive and I was more than grateful to Sister Basil and all the other sisters who had drilled it into my head. But these students of mine in 1970 not only had no personal relationship with Jesus, they didn't even know any doctrine! They didn't know what the Trinity was and they didn't know that Catholics are supposed to believe in the second coming.[4] I asked over and over: "How can this have happened?"

It was then that I came across the writings of an English Catholic layman, Baron Friedrich von Hugel [5] (1852-1925). How I discovered him was just one of those many "happy coincidences" people experience in their walk with Jesus.[6] His writings taught me a formula which has helped me over the years much the same way that $F = ma$ helps people with physics. This formula helped me to put what I was learning about Saints and what I was beginning to experience as one of "the people of God" into perspective. I share it because it was the instrument that God used to bring about the "denominational healing" that I needed and also because it might help someone else the way it did me.

Baron von Hugel taught that there are three elements in a full and fruitful religion. These elements are the institutional, the intellectual and the mystical. All three elements are necessary and they will always be in creative healthy tension.

Dr. Douglas V. Steere,[7] the Quaker observer at Vatican II, is an authority on von Hugel. He explains the formula (to which von Hugel devotes thirty-two pages) this way:

> . . . a full and fruitful religion is described as containing a creative tension between the mystical or emotional element, the historical or institutional element, and the intellectual or scientific element. If religious practice attempts to delete or to neglect the critical scrutiny of the intellectual . . . element of religion, it not only weighs itself down with superstitious accretions, outdated cultural patterns, and often with un-criticized ethical practices of a spurious character, but it is powerless to engage fully with the thought of the generation in which it lives in order to express to them in viable terms the truth it longs to share.
>
> If religious practice should seek to omit or write off as "enthusiasm" the mystical and emotional element in religion, in favor of some rigid intellectual or ethical formula or in an effort to preserve intact some set of traditional institutional forms, then the elegant heating plant stands as frigid and useless as an automatic oil furnace when a storm has cut off the current.
>
> If in the burst of an enlightenment period, religious practice seeks to live on intellect or science alone, or in a romantic age to exist on an exclusive inward focus upon the mystical and emotional element of religion, scorning the historical element . . . and turning its back on its institutional counterpart, the Church, then once again impoverishment results.[8]

This simple formula (theologians call it a "construct") of three elements—intellectual, institutional and mystical—made wonderful sense to me. The frigid heating plant reminded me of David du Plessis' famous illustration in which he likened the Word to a T-bone steak. If, he said, you put it in front of someone while it is still frozen, you can discuss it in terms of the number of calories it contains, how much it weighs, and its vitamin content, but the person can't eat it and will remain hungry. People not baptized in the Spirit have the Word "on ice." [9] Von Hugel wrote about the temptation of the mystical element to sweep aside the institutional element as so much oppressive ballast and the intellectual element as so much hair-splitting. I could see the tendencies connected with the mystical element (hopefully not to any great or unhealthy degree) in myself and in the Pentecostal movement or charismatic renewal. In applying von Hugel's construct to the Catholic Church, and granting the fact that there is a charism of office, it seemed possible to say that the hierarchy, bishops, priests and other officials constituted the *institutional element* of the Church. The *intellectual element* included theologians, living and dead, and such areas of interest as psychology of religion or any discipline which would assist the institutional or hierarchical element of the Church as well as the mystical/charismatic element of the Church. It then was obvious to me that I belonged to the *mystical/experiential/emotional/charismatic* element of the Church.

It is impossible to describe what a revelation that was and the healing it brought. While reverencing the office and person of the Holy Father, I came to realize that Jesus, not the pope, was the head of the Church [10]—the people of God—and I was one of those people. Relevant here might be something written by Fr. Edward O'Connor and quoted by Walter J. Hollenweger in *New Wine in Old Wineskins*. [11] Hollenweger says that, in answering the question "whether it is thinkable that the Holy Spirit be more at work in the classical Pentecostal churches than in that church which generally has been accepted to be the most authentic church," Fr. O'Connor says:

5

This may be God's way of demonstrating to members of the Church that he alone is sovereign Lord, and that all institutions and hierarchs on earth, even in the Church, are nothing but instruments and ministers. . . . We need to have it demonstrated for us that God's action transcends the action of the Church. . . .

As this new understanding of the nature of the Church began to take hold I began to feel squarely upon my shoulders the burden of teaching those high school girls. I discarded the attitude that their ignorance was the hierarchy's fault or the Church's fault. If I was part of the Church it was my fault as much as anybody's. I came to feel that in some way I had a share in all the sins of the Church. The Lord then led me to repentance. I asked His forgiveness for any resentment I had harbored in my heart towards those who were His official ministers. The Lord then filled me with an immense love for His body on earth. That love has increased over the years just as my understanding of what constitutes the body of Christ has expanded.

The next book to cross my path was Karl Rahner's *The Dynamic Element in the Church*,[12] which includes a section dealing with "The Charismatic Element in the Church." That book completed for me what I had learned from von Hugel. Although Rahner speaks of two elements, institutional and charismatic, not three, I did not see any contradiction. For me, Rahner was the living personification of von Hugel's intellectual element and his book gave me a reverence for theology. Reverence for authority and institution were not long in coming. My contact with leaderless prayer meetings and with charismania were limited but sufficient to show me that charisms need to be regulated and discerned.

The little construct of von Hugel, despite its limitations, taught me how to apply what I was learning about Catholic history and tradition. It also turned the light on for me; it helped me understand how I was a member of the body of Christ, how I belonged to the Kingdom of God and how I was one of the people of God. I began to see how, from the time of creation until the time of the "holy city, the new Jerusalem" described in Revelation 21:23, God has been gathering to Himself a people—holy as He is holy.

> . . . and the Lord has declared this day concerning you that you are a people for his own possession, as he has promised you, and that you are to keep all his commandments, that he will set you high above all nations that he has made, in praise and in fame and in honor, and that you shall be a people holy to the Lord your God, as he has spoken. (Deut. 26:18-19) [13]

The Lord is a Good Shepherd. We can look through history and see His care for us. This is so very obvious in the Old Testament: the manna in the desert, the prophets, all culminating in the coming of Jesus, as the Father prepares the way for the Son. In the New Testament the Son is obedient to the Father. In coming to save us, Jesus gives history its meaning. The old covenant gives way to the new. Jesus comes proclaiming the kingdom. He calls Himself the Good Shepherd, "I know my own and my own know me" (John 10:14).

Jesus gathered people to Himself when He was on earth. There was a caring aspect to His "gathering." "Come to me, all who labor . . ." (Matt. 11:28); "Let the children come to me . . ." (Mark 10:14); "Come and see" (John 1:39); "If any one thirst, let him come to me and drink" (John 7:37). After His resurrection, Jesus continues to gather a people by sending the Holy Spirit, the promise of the Father. Just as the Holy Spirit overshadowed Mary and formed the body of Jesus in her womb, the Holy Spirit broods over the people of God and forms them into the body of Christ, until all culminates in the coming again of Jesus, this time in glory.

Through Jesus, God promised He would not leave us orphans. Even though we may sin and we may be unfaithful, God is always faithful. As separated as the Lord's body on earth looks to us today, if we ask the Lord to give us eyes to see, we will be able to marvel at and testify to the many and varied ways God the Holy Spirit has provided for us through the almost two thousand years since the Incarnation.

In looking over the history of Roman Catholicism, I can see the Spirit caring for people through sacraments, through Church councils, through papal encyclicals and through a succession of dedicated and loving apostles and ministers. At times in the history of the Church when those exercising authority seemed more like hirelings than true shepherds, God provided in other ways, sometimes raising up Saints to minister to His people because He promised: "I will set shepherds over them who will care for them, and they shall fear no more, nor be dismayed, neither shall any be missing . . ." (Jer. 23:4). Whether the Saints were members of the hierarchy or laity and no matter what their mission, they were signs of God's caring love for His people.

Notes to Chapter 1

1. "Paul stood up to Peter; St. Jerome to Pope Damasus; St. Bernard of Clairvaux to Eugene III; St. Bridget of Sweden to Gregory XI; St. Catherine of Siena to Gregory XI; St. Philip Neri to Clement VIII." Elizabeth Hamilton, *Suenens: a Portrait,* Doubleday & Company, Inc., Garden City, New York, 1975, p. 163.
2. Karl Rahner, *Theological Investigations,* Vol. III, "The Church of the Saints," p. 97.
3. For an exploration of evangelization and initiation pertinent to what was just expressed, see Ralph Martin's *Unless the Lord Build the House . . .,* Ave Maria Press, Notre Dame, Indiana, 1971.
4. *National Catholic Reporter* (N.C.R.), May 14, 1976 reported on a "remedial Catholicism" course being taught at Gonzaga University, Spokane, Washington. The teacher, Jesuit Father Kenneth Baker was reported as having said that most students taking the course had "little or no knowledge of the Catholic religion although they graduated from Catholic high schools" (p. 5). George A. Lindbeck, a Lutheran theologian and Yale Divinity School faculty member, sharing his observations on the present state of the Catholic Church in *Commonweal* said: "Younger

Catholics even from devout traditional backgrounds know little or nothing of the novenas, benedictions, recitations of the rosary and cults of the saints which were the major affective components in their parents' religion." (February 13, 1976, p. 108.)

5. Baron Friedrich von Hugel seems a man who has yet to come into his own. More than fifty years after his death his influence is still felt and yet he is virtually unknown, except perhaps to some scholars. W.H. Auden began his "Introduction" to the book *The Protestant Mystics* (a Mentor Book, The New American Library of World Literature, Inc., 1965) with von Hugel's construct. Reverend J. Neville Ward uses the construct in his chapter "Coming to Church" in *Five for Sorrow, Ten for Joy.* Morton Kelsey in *Encounter with God* (Bethany Fellowship, Inc., Minneapolis, Minnesota, 1972, p. 27) comments upon the study of the religious thinking of our time, *Twentieth Century Religious Thought* by John Macquarrie. Out of the more than a hundred men considered in Macquarrie's work, there are only two "who clearly suggest that theological understanding requires a basis of some direct encounter with a more than human reality and purpose." One of these men was Carl G. Jung. The other, Friedrich von Hugel! Two recent books dealing with von Hugel, both by Jesuits, are: *The Spirituality of Friedrich von Hugel* by Joseph P. Whelan, S.J., Newman Press, New York, 1971 and *The Modernist Crisis: von Hugel* by John J. Heaney, S.J., Corpus Books, Washington-Cleveland, 1968. Another Jesuit, Harvey D. Egan, in his introduction to *The Spiritual Exercises and the Ignatian Mystical Horizon* (The Institute of Jesuit Sources, St. Louis, 1976) asks this question: "Is it totally unreasonable to ask if the Church of Ignatius' day was not yet ready for his Catholic and orthodox presentation of what was good in the Illuminati movement in much the same way that the Church early in this century was not yet ready to accept what was orthodox and Catholic in the modernist movement?" (pp. 5-6).

6. After I was baptized in the Spirit in 1966 the first book I read, other than Scripture, was the only "holy" book in the house, and that was *Mysticism* by Evelyn Underhill. It had been recommended to my husband by the Episcopal minister who was the best man at our Catholic wedding in 1958. Neither one of us had read it. Evelyn Underhill was an Anglican, whose spiritual director was Baron von Hugel, a Catholic layman. She mentions him many times in *Mysticism,* which was heavily influenced by his thought and was the book that led me to von Hugel's greatest work: *The Mystical Element of Religion as Studied in St. Catherine of Genoa and Her Friends.* "The Three Elements of Religion" is Chapter II of Vol. 1.

7. Douglas Steere is professor emeritus of philosophy at Haverford College in Pennsylvania, a participant in world ecumenical affairs and the author of several books on spiritual subjects. Dr. Steere was the Quaker observer at the Second Vatican Council. During the second session of the Council, in the fall of 1963, in the

"coffee bar" of St. Peter's Basilica, Dr. Steere broached the subject of holding an ecumenical Institute on the Spiritual Life to Reverend Godfrey Diekmann. Dr. Steere was convinced that "the deepest forces conducive to Christian unity [lay] in a renewed prayer and spirituality of all Christians, and in the mutual help they give to each other by sharing their spiritual traditions." The Institute was held in 1965 and subsequent meetings have continued to be held. Proceedings of the first Institute were published in *Worship* in December 1965 and a reprint in paperback was put out by The Liturgical Press, Collegeville, Minnesota in 1965, entitled *Protestants and Catholics on the Spiritual Life*. (The quote above is from the Editor, *Worship*, Vol. 39, No. 10, December 1965, p. 579.)

8. Douglas V. Steere, *Spiritual Counsel and Letters of Baron Friedrich von Hugel*, p. 7.

9. David J. du Plessis, *The Spirit Bade Me Go*, published by David J. du Plessis, 3742 Linwood Avenue, Oakland, California, p. 17. Du Plessis was the sole Pentecostal observer at Vatican II.

10. In "The Church of the Saints" in *Theological Investigations*, Vol. III, Karl Rahner writes:

> In his encyclical "Mystici Corporis," Pope Pius XII has shown that Christ is permanently the Head and ruler of the Church, not merely by the fact of having given the Church her ordinary magisterium and the pastors who govern the Church by his commission and his name. He also rules directly by Himself. He does this, in turn, not merely by enlightening and strengthening the ecclesiastical rulers, but "especially in difficult times, he raises up in the bosom of Mother Church men and women of outstanding sanctity to give example to other Christians and so promote the increase of his Mystical Body." There is, therefore, a driving force for the further development of life in the Church which does not originate from the official element but directly from Christ himself, a law of life which goes out from "Christ in a mysterious way in his own person" and embraces the saints who hold no office and through them affects the others and the official element. (p. 103)

11. O'Connor, *Pentecost in the Catholic Church*, Pecos, New Mexico, 1970; Logos, Watchung, N.J. 28f. as quoted in Hollenweger, *New Wine in Old Wineskins*, Fellowship Press, Gloucester, England, 1973, pp. 51-52.

12. Karl Rahner, *The Dynamic Element in the Church*, "The Charismatic Element in the Church," pp. 42-83.

13. All Scripture quotations are from the Revised Standard Version unless otherwise noted.

CHAPTER 2

Keep on Running

Fr. George Montague in *Riding the Wind* calls Saints, ". . . the Good News made visible." [1] St. Francis de Sales in 1604 wrote, ". . . the lives of the Saints: what are these save practical illustrations of the Gospel? The difference between the Word and the Saints' lives is like to that between music in score, and the same music sung by living voices." [2]

It has taken a number of years for me to see Saints as "treasures in the storehouse." Just as the person of Jesus had been somehow hidden from me, so too, Mary, His mother, and the Saints were obscured by exaggerated practices meant to honor them and by poorly written, overly-pious biographies of the kind which once prompted some wit to say with Milton "Avenge, O Lord, Thy slaughtered Saints." [3] In the same spirit, Ambrose Bierce in the *Devil's Dictionary* defines a Saint as a "dead sinner revised and edited."

Those of us who were educated in Catholic schools in the forties and fifties (and I would expect that this was so for earlier generations also), were introduced to lives of Saints in the first few grades. I can still remember vividly the story of St. Tarcisius from my third grade reader. Two pictures accompanied the text. As it was not uncommon in the early Church for Christians to carry the Eucharist home to the sick after the conclusion of the liturgy, the first picture showed Tarcisius, a young boy, walking by a ball field (it never occurred to me that baseball was unknown then) with his eyes piously cast down because he was sheltering the Blessed Sacrament under his cloak. The text described how the boys who were playing ball began to taunt and jeer at our hero for refusing to join in their game. Finally they set upon him and began to beat him up. Then there followed the second picture. It showed a bruised and battered Tarcisius lying dead but having successfully protected the Eucharist from being desecrated.

The truth is that an inscription of Pope Damasus is all we know of this third century saint. "St. Tarcisius went away bearing the mysteries of Christ, when a criminal had tried to profane them. He, for his part, preferred to allow himself to be murdered rather than to deliver the body of Christ to mad dogs." [4] Obviously the inscription had been embroidered by the time it reached my third grade book!

Such spiritual fare produced in me and in others [5] the idea that there were three kinds of Christians. The first kind became heroes or Saints. The second kind turned their back on God and were damned. The third kind were our kind, in between the two extremes.

All of us were pretty sure we would never commit a grave crime or turn our back on God, so we eliminated the possibility of being cast into eternal fire. The sister in parochial school, who taught us, would warn us not to bank on the Lord providing us with a deathbed conversion, but we somehow secretly felt secure that even if we fell into a sinful life as a grownup, God would provide us with a chance for a final confession or give us the grace of perfect contrition. After all, if the goal of the Christian life was saving our soul and getting into heaven, it didn't seem to matter too much what happened on earth as long as the desired result was obtained.

As for being a Saint, the motion picture we saw on the life of St. Therese, the "Little Flower," in fourth grade, killed that idea. As we left the darkened classroom and went blinking out into the sunshiny afternoon to jump rope or play baseball, some of us secretly hoped we would see a vision or have God write our name in the stars (Therese thought she had seen her name in the sky).[6] But it never happened and we were doomed to mediocrity.

As we grew older, we didn't feel so doomed or passed over by the Lord. Our "faith" made us feel comfortable and secure. On the one hand we were avoiding the pains of hell by doing most of the good things the Catholic Church told us to do. We went to Mass on Sundays and Holy Days and we abstained from meat on Fridays. We even fasted during Lent after we became twenty-one. (Those of us who went over the hill and became twenty-one before Lent during our last year in college, had deep ethical discussions as to whether a milkshake was food or drink!)

On the other hand we were avoiding mortification, except for Lent, and private prayer, except for perhaps a "Morning Offering," which some families I visited had glued to a corner of the bathroom mirror. (This was a good reminder because you couldn't miss it when you were brushing your teeth.) Some of us also had some bedtime prayers, like "Angel of God, my guardian dear . . ." which followed us into adulthood. Spending time in prayer, however, was for Saints, along with seeing visions and performing miracles. The movie "The Song of Bernadette" was another one which confirmed us in the belief that sanctity was for the few. Bernadette was a "chosen soul."

Fr. Francis MacNutt in his book on *Healing*[7] writes that he read lives of the Saints as a novice in the Dominican Order. The Saints appeared to be so extraordinary and so far removed that they seemed to him to be almost unreal.[8] Miracles such as healing the sick and other manifestations of God's power and love were seen in the lives of Saints but one was left with the feeling that one would be presumptuous to pray that a sick person be healed if one wasn't a "Saint." Instead, people took their sick relatives to shrines like Lourdes in France to seek cures, or they made novenas to St. Jude or some other Saint.[9]

Baptism in the Spirit has altered this way of thinking for many of us. Thousands of Catholics have been reevaluating their understanding of the gifts of the Holy Spirit, including healing. Thousands are also beginning to reevaluate their notion of sanctity. In other words, as Catholics and other Christians are beginning to exercise the charismatic gifts of the Spirit in order to minister to God's people, there is occurring, at the same time, a rediscovery of the universality of the call to holiness of life. Besides covering such areas as how to evangelize and how to exercise the spiritual gifts, teaching given in most prayer groups or communities for those newly baptized in the Spirit also stresses regular habits of prayer, how to recognize and avoid sin, and in general, how to grow in holiness.[10]

Through Baptism we are baptized into Jesus Christ who is called the "Holy One" (Rev. 3:7).

Do you not know that all of us who have been baptized into Christ Jesus were baptized into his death? We were buried therefore with him by baptism into death, so that as Christ was raised from the dead by the glory of the Father, we too might walk in newness of life. (Rom. 6:3-4)

Fr. Montague, in *Maturing in Christ* [11] speaks about God consecrating His people through Baptism, and he points out that in some texts St. Paul seems to suggest that there is a once-for-allness about this consecration that is, as it were, irreversible. "But you were washed, you were sanctified, you were justified in the name of the Lord Jesus Christ and in the Spirit of our God" (I Cor. 6:11). Through Baptism we are placed in a consecrated state. We are sanctified. We are set apart because we now belong to God. We are the Lord's. We are "saints."

St. Paul called the members of his communities "saints." To the Philippians he writes: "To all the saints in Christ Jesus. . . ." He used the word "saints" to mean brothers, disciples, or the faithful.

14

Although the usage of referring to all believers as "saints" was becoming less common, in Africa more than three hundred years after St. Paul, St. Augustine could address an audience as "your holiness."[12]

But if we are established in a holy state through baptism, how are we to interpret such Scripture texts as these? "Strive for peace with all men, and for the holiness without which no one will see the Lord" (Heb. 12:14). ". . . let us also lay aside every weight, and sin which clings so closely, and let us run with perseverance the race that is set before us, looking to Jesus the pioneer and perfecter of our faith . . ." (Heb. 12:1-2). St. John writes that Jesus said: "Every branch of mine that bears no fruit, he takes away, and every branch that does bear fruit he prunes, that it may bear more fruit" (John 15:2). The epilogue of the book of Revelation reads: "Let . . . the holy still be holy" or in the old Confraternity edition: "Let . . . him who is holy be hallowed still" (Rev. 22:11).

These passages and others certainly indicate that those who are "saints" because they have been baptized, are called to progress and grow in the holy state in which they find themselves. St. Paul's preoccupation with further sanctification shows up constantly in his first letter to the Thessalonians. [13]

God works further sanctification in us. It is His work. Man however has free will. We must will to cooperate with God in His work of hallowing us. We must keep on running!

The Ecumenical Council which met from 1962-1965, and for whose success Pope John XXIII wrote the now famous prayer to the Holy Spirit, produced sixteen documents. One of them, "Dogmatic Constitution on the Church," *Lumen Gentium* or *Light of All Nations*, has an entire chapter on the call to holiness. The following passage is from that Vatican Council document:

> . . . For Christ, the Son of God, who with the Father and the Spirit is praised as being "alone holy," loved the Church as His Bride, delivering Himself up for her. This He did that He

15

might sanctify her, He united her to Himself as His own body, and crowned her with the gift of the Holy Spirit, for God's glory. . . .

The followers of Christ are called by God, not according to their accomplishments, but according to His own purpose and grace. They are justified in the Lord Jesus, and through baptism sought in faith they truly become sons of God and sharers in the divine nature. In this way they are really made holy. Then, too, by God's gifts they must hold on to and complete in their lives this holiness which they have received. They are warned by the Apostle to live "as becomes saints" (Eph. 5:3) and to put on "as God's chosen ones, holy and beloved, a heart of mercy, kindness, humility, meekness, patience" (Col. 3:12) and to possess the fruits of the Spirit unto holiness.[14]

The fact that we are "saints" through Baptism and the fact that God calls all of us to be holy, as He is holy, is certainly not new; it may just *seem* new. Jesus counseled holiness of life for every one of His disciples. "You, therefore, must be perfect as your heavenly Father is perfect" (Matt. 5:48).

For many of us, before we were baptized in the Spirit, our notion of the Christian life was not only that of a medium between two extremes, it was a notion often characterized by individualism. It was "me and God." It was as though we thought we would present ourselves to the Lord at the end of our life with a bottle full of grace (one of the catechisms of my early years used drawings of milk bottles to represent the soul) [15] and a bag with some virtues in it, and depending on how much grace we had stored up and how many virtues we had, we would earn a certain amount of happiness in heaven. There was little personal experience of the joy of Christianity. We would not have understood then, as we do now, the great saying of St. Catherine of Siena: "All the way to heaven is heaven, because Jesus said, 'I am the Way.' " There was no realization of our being part of the body of Christ or of our needing other Christians to live the Christian life. What I am seeing emerge out of this tremendous outpouring of the Holy Spirit in our day is great numbers of people responding to the call to holiness, many responding together in community. The emphasis is not so much on being a holy person, as it is on being a holy people for the Lord.

Now, under the gentle influence of God's Spirit, Catholics who have been baptized in the Spirit are joining with other Spirit-filled Christians to praise, glorify and serve the Lord together. The sanctifying gifts of the Holy Spirit, those that many of us memorized in preparation for the sacrament of Confirmation and which derive from Isaiah 11:2 (wisdom, understanding, counsel, fortitude, knowledge, piety and fear of the Lord), are seen as pertaining to spiritual growth, personal holiness and union with God. The charismatic or ministry gifts of the Spirit (also called spiritual gifts) mentioned in I Corinthians: tongues, interpretation of tongues, prophecy, word of wisdom, word of knowledge, faith, healing, miracles and discernment of spirits, are being used as tools to build up the body of Christ.[16] That body may be a "Church community," a parish such as the Episcopal Church of the Redeemer, Houston, Texas, or a "community within the Church" as in the case of The Word of God, Ann Arbor, Michigan. A local prayer group, which perhaps cannot judge its fruit so concretely, could be said to somehow build up the mystical body of Christ.

Prior to the conversion of Constantine and the Edict of Milan (313), which was a charter of religious freedom, one couldn't imagine being a Christian without some roots in some community somewhere, be it in Rome, Ephesus or Corinth. After the Edict, however, "Christians could confess one God, one Lord, one faith, one baptism, one empire, and one emperor."[17] A result of this was a watering down of Christianity. A subsequent reaction to this development was the appearance of the ascetic movement, a movement characterized, among other things, by a desire to respond to God's call to "be hallowed still" and by community.[18]

The lives of most, if not all, Saints reveal a communal dimension to their spirituality. They were conscious that they went to God with others. Saints Benedict, Francis of Assisi, Dominic, Ignatius, Francis de Sales, Vincent de Paul, Julie Billiart, Teresa of Avila, Elizabeth Seton, Angela Merici, Norbert, Alberic, Stephen Harding, Robert of Molesmes, Anne-Marie Javouhey and Frances Xavier Cabrini,[19] to mention just a few, founded communities. Most other Saints were members of "established" communities: Anthony of Padua (Augustinian, then Franciscan*), Bonaventure (Franciscan), Thomas Aquinas (Dominican*), Margaret Mary Alacoque (Visitation), Dominic Savio (Salesian), Aloysius Gonzaga (Jesuit*) and Therese of Lisieux (Carmelite*). The Cure d'Ars, John Vianney, gathered his parish into a community. Mme. Acarie, before she was widowed and entered the Carmelites, and Anna Maria Taigi, who never entered any order, were married women who cared for their husbands and children. A sort of "unintentional" community of assorted persons gathered about them, including cardinals and other members of the hierarchy who came seeking spiritual direction. The same type of community gathered about Catherine of Siena.[20] Our God is a Triune God. Our God is a Community of Three Persons, Father, Son and Spirit. He is a Gathering of Three Persons. His overflowing love pours forth to men and He gathers His people to Himself to share in the very life of the Trinity. Saints eminently participated in the "gathering" activities of God. By the power of the Spirit, some of them intentionally gathered together in community, exhorting one another to holiness of life. They served as witnesses to their environment that "loving one another" was possible through the

---

* All words starred with an asterisk are found in the glossary.

reconciling, powerful love of Jesus Christ. Then in turn, unless the group was entirely contemplative (in which case it saw service in terms of intercessory prayer), the group reached out to all God's people in varying ways of depending on the needs of the times.[21]Some nursed plague victims, some ran schools, some offered themselves as ransom for hostages. Others gave missions in parishes to renew parish life and some were traveling evangelists. The very existence of these religious communities, orders, congregations, institutes and monasteries and their corporate witness, even when they were contemplative and enclosed, drew people to the Lord. For example, the little convent in Assisi, Italy, which had been gathered to praise the Lord by Clare, a friend of Francis, had a spiritual influence far beyond the walls of San Damiano. Her biographer wrote, "For forty-two years St. Clare of Assisi broke the alabaster vase of her body . . . so that the house of the Church is filled with the fragrance of her ointments."[22] Some Saints found themselves unintentionally the focus of community as has already been said. Still others in very different ways were instruments of God gathering to Himself a holy people. Many were drawn to Jesus by means of devotion to His "Sacred Heart" which derived from the "private revelations" of St. Margaret Mary Alacoque, a French nun who was a contemporary of Milton and Moliere. Another enclosed sister, St. Therese of Lisieux, through her autobiography, gathered a great number of people to the Lord although she never left her convent.

The Spirit of the Lord attracts people to Jesus through Saints. They are drawn by "the odor of His garments" (Ps. 45:8; Cant. 1:3) for the Saints are in an eminent way "the aroma of Christ to God" (2 Cor. 2:15).

1. George T. Montague, S.M., *Riding the Wind,* Word of Life, Ann Arbor, Michigan, 1974, p. 78.
2. Letter of St. Francis de Sales to the Archbishop of Bourges on preaching, October 5, 1604 from *A Selection from The Spiritual Letters of S. Francis de Sales,* Longmans, Green, & Company, London, 1909, p. 24.
3. Frank Sheed in "Assembler's Note" in *Saints Are Not Sad.*
4. Omar Englebert, *The Lives of the Saints,* p. 314.
5. Jacques Douillet, *What is a Saint?,* p. 18.
6. Fr. Etienne Robo in *Two Portraits of St. Therese of Lisieux* conjectures of this childhood incident which Therese recorded in her autobiography, that young Therese Martin probably thought she saw a "T" for Therese in Orion's belt because she was a self-centered and spoiled little girl. That she overcame all egocentricity in her later years, as her writings show, makes Therese for me a much more appealing heroine. There certainly seems to be a relationship between spiritual growth and personality development. An article on this subject with helpful footnotes which include bibliographical references is: "Saint Therese of Lisieux: A Case Study in Psychology of Religion" by Fr. Kevin Culligan, O.C.D. in *Spiritual Life,* Fall 1973.
7. Fr. Francis MacNutt, *Healing,* Ave Maria Press, Notre Dame, Indiana, 1974.
8. *Ibid,* p. 43.
9. Fr. MacNutt remarks that the healing ministry in the Catholic Church was preserved through shrines and devotions. When praying for healing was no longer done by priests or official representatives of the Church, people turned to the Mother of God and to the Saints (pp. 71-72). This is a good illustration of the von Hugel construct mentioned in Chapter 1. Here we have the charismatic/mystical element supplying something the institutional element was neglecting.
10. Many prayer groups and communities take seriously the obligation of providing sound teaching for those newly baptized in the Spirit. Some groups use a guide book entitled *Basic Christian Maturity,* which is a series of talks or seminars developed by The Word of God, a Christian community in Ann Arbor, Michigan.
11. George T. Montague, *Maturing in Christ,* The Bruce Publishing Company, Milwaukee, Wisconsin, 1964, pp. 21-24.
12. Emilien Lamirande, O.M.I., *The Communion of Saints,* p. 23.
13. Montague, *op. cit.,* p. 22.
14. Walter M. Abbott, S.J., *The Documents of Vatican II,* Herder and Herder, New York, 1966, *Lumen Gentium,* Chapter V. 39,40. See also Chapter VII, "The Eschatological Nature of the Pilgrim Church and Her Union with the Heavenly Church." All future citations from Council documents will refer to the Abbott edition.

15. Garry Wills relating his "Memories of a Catholic Boyhood" in *Bare Ruined Choirs* (Doubleday and Company, Inc., Garden City, New York, 1972, p. 29) speaks of religious life being presented as a "crude hydraulics of the soul." "Mortal sin emptied the reservoir, instantly, of all grace (grace being a quantifiable store of fuel not burned in any known activity, just collected for its own sake, like stamps). Confession pumped grace back into the reservoir. . . . Venial sins put leaks in the tank. Meritorious acts patched the leaks. . . . Manning the locks in this pipe system of the soul, one tabulated stores of grace, of merit, of indulgences, with prodigious feats of spiritual bookkeeping."

16. This not to say that there is not a communal dimension to the sanctifying gifts nor a personal dimension to the exercise of the ministry or charismatic gifts. St. Paul does not distinguish between the sanctifying gifts and the charismatic/ministry/spiritual gifts. St. Thomas Aquinas calls *gratia gratum faciens* a grace that makes its recipient holy, a sanctifying gift and *gratia gratis data* a grace given to someone for the benefit of others, i.e. a ministry gift. Karl Rahner considers St. Paul's way of looking at the gifts "very evangelical." *(The Dynamic Element in the Church*, "The Charismatic Element in the Church," p. 55.) "How else could one truly sanctify oneself except by unselfish service to others in the one Body of Christ by the power of the Spirit?" But Rahner makes note of the fact that Jesus did draw attention to men who worked miracles and yet displeased Him and he says that Aquinas' distinction is possible and in many cases appropriate.

17. Roland H. Bainton, *The Horizon History of Christianity*, Avon Books, New York, 1966, p. 97.

18. See *Unordained Elders and Renewal Communities* by Stephen B. Clark, Paulist Press, 1976, for an exposition of the ascetic movement of the fourth century.

19. The dates of any Saints mentioned in the text will be found in the Table of Saints located before Chapter 1.

20. In *New Blackfriars* in October 1973 there was an article suggesting that religious* should experiment with communities like the house St. Catherine ran in Siena. "The house in Siena brought priests and layfolk together primarily to pray with Catherine but also to form a pressure group for her various projects and to engage in a great variety of apostolic works. It no doubt took a charismatic figure to lead these extraordinary communities . . . it will surely only be when religious become adventurous enough in the power of the Holy Spirit to attempt such efforts at community-making that they will begin to offer the specific witness to Church and world that they have the call and the grace to bear." ("Priorities in Religious Life" by Fergus Kerr, O.P., p. 442. This article was based on an essay by Jerome Murphy O'Connor.)

21. Benjamin Zablocki, a sociologist, in *The Joyful Community*, an account of the

Bruderhof, a Christian community now in its third generation, discusses the tension in a community between the opposing needs for outreach and concern with internal matters. He says: "The Bruderhof does not outreach to fulfill its purpose as a movement. It can do this merely by existing as a community in brotherhood and peace—a goal which can reasonably be given first priority since there would be no purpose in reaching out if there was nothing to show people once they gathered in." (Benjamin Zablocki, *The Joyful Community*, Penguin Books Inc., Baltimore, Maryland, 1971, pp. 145-146.)

Avery Dulles, a theologian, writes: "While the Church promises communion, it does not always provide it in very evident form. Christians commonly experience the Church more as a companionship of fellow travelers on the same journey than as a union of lovers dwelling in the same home." Dulles cites the writings of Stephen Clark and Max Delespesse (basic reading for those in charismatic renewal and to be found in the Charismatic Renewal Services Catalogue) as proponents of the sociological concept of community as a principle for the renewal of the Church. Dulles speaks of modern day attempts at Christian community and writes these encouraging words: "Christians are obliged to strive unceasingly to build better and more Christlike communities on all levels, from the family circle to the United Nations. Some Christians—and not merely those who join religious orders—will be privileged and enriched by a common commitment to Christ and the gospel. Communities of this type are, in a very important sense, realizations of the Church." Avery Dulles, S.J., *Models of the Church*, Doubleday & Company, Inc., Garden City, 1974, pp. 52-57.

Joseph H. Fichter, S.J., a sociologist, discusses the tension between building community and outreach, action and contemplation with regard to the charismatic renewal in the Catholic Church in the chapter, "Personal Comfort and Social Challenge" in his book *The Catholic Cult of the Paraclete*, Sheed and Ward, Inc., New York, 1975, pp. 80-98.
22. Celano V, 10.

CHAPTER 3

Veneration and Canonization

Is veneration of the Saints and Mary, the mother of Jesus, a form of idolatry? How did it come about that the Catholic Church canonizes some people and prefixes the official title "Saint" to their names?

An underlying answer to the latter question rests in mankind's tendency to pay homage to leaders or exemplary figures. Certainly there is more to veneration of Saints than simply the honoring of outstanding Christian men and women, but it should be recognized at the outset that this very natural tendency is part and parcel of the custom and practice of veneration of Saints.

Veneration of Saints originated from the honor given to martyrs. Quite naturally the memory of men and women who suffered and died because they believed in Jesus Christ was held in great esteem.

As early as 155, Christians faced the question of whether veneration of martyrs would detract from worship due to Jesus. A significant document dating from that year is an account of the martyrdom of St. Polycarp, the eighty-six-year-old bishop of Smyrna. In it we read that, after the martyrdom, a certain Nicetas asked the governor not to give Polycarp's body to his friends lest they begin to worship him instead of the Man who was crucified. The document's author defines the honor paid to martyrs:

> They did not realize that we shall never bring ourselves either
> to abandon Christ, who suffered for the salvation of all those

that are saved in the whole world—*the Innocent for sinners!*—or to worship any other. Him we worship as being the Son of God, the martyrs we love as being disciples and imitators of the Lord; and deservedly so, because of their unsurpassable devotion to their King and Teacher. May it be our good fortune, too, to be their companions and fellow disciples! [1]

The document from which the above extract was taken is "The Martyrdom of Saint Polycarp" which has come down to us in five Greek manuscripts, of which, according to the Ancient Christian Writers series, the manuscript preserved in Moscow is regarded as the most trustworthy. The document is an eyewitness account of the death of the bishop of Smyrna which he suffered at the hands of Roman authorities in Asia for defending the Christian faith. It is obvious from this letter that the early Christians considered the question of whether or not honoring the Saints would detract from worship of Jesus, and they concluded that it did not.

As persecution fell on the early Christian communities, each locality began to keep a calendar which recorded the anniversary of its martyrs. Later, the local calendars began to include those honored elsewhere in the Church. In the fourth century the Church at Rome kept the anniversaries of Felicitas, Perpetua and Cyprian, all three of whom were martyred and buried in Africa. About this time the names of the apostles and St. Stephen were also added.

Throughout the centuries the Church has celebrated different feasts which commemorate events in the life of Jesus such as Easter and the Ascension. And just as we celebrate Christmas, Jesus' birthday, the Church designates a feast day to commemorate a Saint's life. The day the Church chooses is usually the day of the Saint's martyrdom or death. The day commemorates their entrance into eternal life. We then are celebrating on the day the Saint went to be with Jesus.

Church life, or the liturgical year, is family life. Throughout the year we relive events of Our Savior's life and we share fellowship with Him as well as with His friends, living and dead. The feasts of different Saints are so many birthday parties sprinkled throughout the year.

With the passage of time those who heroically "confessed" Christ but were not martyred were also honored. St. Antony of Egypt (251-356) was never martyred but was revered before and after his death as a holy hermit and confessor. In his *Life of St. Antony*, St. Athanasius tells us when Antony had returned from helping the faithful who were being persecuted in Alexandria, he had to battle with evil spirits in his hermitage in the wilderness more fiercely than with any judge in court.[2]

Publicly honoring martyrs and confessors is not the same thing as invoking them, that is, addressing prayers *to* them. However, it is known that the early Christians not only invoked the martyrs, but they also prayed to their relatives who had died in the Lord's peace. Hundreds of memorial inscriptions in the Roman catacombs bear the name of the person buried and ask for their prayers:

Pray for your parents, Matronata Matrona, who lived one year and fifty two days.

Mercury set up [this inscription] to his most worthy wife Justa, who lived with me for fourteen years and had seven children, of whom two survive. Pray, [Justa], pray for them.[3]

There is a passage in 2 Maccabees (considered canonical by Catholics and apocryphal by Protestants) [4] which suggests that those who died in the Lord, martyred or otherwise, may pray to God for those living. In this passage Judas tells his friends about a dream he had in which Jeremiah appears and is said to pray much for the people and the holy city (2 Macc. 15:11-16).

When St. Paula died, St. Jerome (342-420) said: "Goodbye,

Paula! This old man reveres you: sustain him by your prayers during his closing years. May your faith and your good works unite you with Christ; in his presence you will the more easily obtain what you ask." [5]

Regarding devotion to Mary, the most ancient prayer to the Blessed Mother is preserved in a papyrus of the fourth century, and before 431 Ephesus had a church called "The Church of Mary." [6]

Prayer to Mary and to the Saints, as Catholics understand it, does not contain any element of worship or adoration. The prayer is always in the context of the Saints' total dependence on God in Christ. In prayers such as the Litany of the Saints, the invocation to the Divine Persons is "have mercy on us" and that to Mary and the Saints is "pray for us."

As clear as this is in theory and as valiantly as the Church seems to have tried to keep a healthy balance in the lives of the faithful, one has to admit that some of the pious faithful have carried the custom of honoring the Saints to extremes. An enjoyable book on St. Augustine (354-430), *Augustine the Bishop*, devotes an entire chapter to "The Cult [7] of the Martyrs." Its author, Dr. Van der Meer, says St. Augustine's pastoral work concerning the veneration of Saints is confined to "moderating, pruning and forbidding." "Our altars are not erected to any martyr but to the God of the martyrs. . . ." said Augustine.[8] In his book, *The Work of Monks*, Augustine gives a warning against monks who peddle false relics.

But at the same time that Augustine was pruning and forbidding, he celebrated the feasts of the martyrs with joy. Dr. Van der Meer commends Augustine's wisdom and balance:

. . . it is to his [Augustine's] honor that instead of meandering off into panegyrics he should have preserved towards this, the first important manifestation of popular Christian devotion, an attitude that was sober and even critical. Nobody

26

showed greater deliberation or greater objectivity than Augustine when he performed the double function of both curbing and stimulating the veneration of the saints.[9]

Karl Rahner writing on this subject includes invocation in his use of the term veneration. He thinks it is not enough to say that veneration is not adoration and leave it at that. There is an underlying unity between the two. Love of neighbor is an act distinct from love of God, but love of neighbor can and should be an act of love of God Himself. So venerating a Saint is an act distinct from adoring God, but veneration of Saints can and should be an act of love of God. A unity exists between the two kinds of love.[10]

As I reflect on my own experience of praying to Mary and various Saints, it has always seemed very natural. Jesus "loved his own who were in the world, he loved them to the end" (John 13:1). Jesus wept over Lazarus. Even in His terrible agony on the cross He thought to give His mother to John and, I like to think, to all of us. Jesus not only gave His life for us, He gave us His Father: ". . . to all who received him, who believed in his name, he gave power to become children of God" (John 1:12). He gave us His Spirit: "I tell you the truth: it is to your advantage that I go away, for if I do not go away, the Counselor will not come to you; but if I go, I will send him to you" (John 16:7). Through Jesus we are drawn into the very life of the Trinity: "I do not pray for these only, but also for those who believe in me through their word, that they may all be one; even as thou, Father, art in me, and I in thee, that they also may be in us . . ." (John 17:20-21). Jesus shares His life and all that He is and has with us so it seems natural to expect that He shares His parents, Mary and Joseph, and His friends with us. These friends are not only His contemporaries like St. Peter and St. John and St. Mary Magdalen, but also all those who have ever been His friends from then until now. And just as I often ask brothers and sisters in my community (Mother of God, in Maryland) to pray for me for a particular intention or just in general, it seems natural to ask Jesus' other friends, His contemporaries or Saints of other centuries, to pray for me too. Over the years, the Saints I have prayed to and read about have become my brothers and sisters, just as much a gift from Jesus as are my brothers and sisters now living.

The Church allows and encourages veneration of Saints. They bear witness to the victory of God's grace. "God is glorious in His Saints," (Vulg. Ps. 67:36). In their holy lives the Saints attest to the fact that the Church is the fruit of salvation as well as the means to salvation, and remind us that from age to age God gathers to Himself a holy people.

A typical prayer I might pray to a Saint could sound like this: "Dear St. Monica, for years you prayed to God begging Him that your son Augustine would turn from sin and accept Jesus. I ask you now to intercede for me and ask God that my own son will experience the grace of conversion." At this juncture one might ask why I don't go straight to Jesus. Why do I feel I need to go through someone else? A lady present at a workshop I once gave on the subject of devotion to Mary, the Mother of Jesus, said she just couldn't see praying to Mary about anything. "When I'm sick," she said, "I go to the doctor, not the doctor's mother!"

Well, we can certainly go straight to Jesus and no one who invokes Mary or Saints would say any differently. But Jesus is not just a doctor. He is our brother. He is also our God and our Lord. There are times when we are very conscious of our sinfulness and the only prayer we can muster is "Forgive me. Have mercy on me." When we are in that state, and petitions spring to mind, how comforting to be able to turn to the communion of Saints, those dead as well as living, and say, "Pray to Jesus for me."

Veneration of Saints brings up the question as to who the Church will allow to be publicly venerated. The custom of canonization arose to resolve this problem. The word "canon" is derived from the cane or reed that was used as a measuring rod. So, in Church usage, "canon" came to refer to an official list or collection and the designation of Saints came to be known as "canonization."

There were no regulations governing the process of canonization in earlier ages of Church history. Veneration of martyrs extended to the honoring and invoking of people like St. Antony of Egypt. Between the sixth and tenth centuries there was a notable increase in the number of deceased who received the honor given to Saints. In early centuries the voice of the people or fame was enough to have names of deceased placed on Church calendars. The fame of sanctity resulted in pious visits to the tomb of the reputed Saint, prayers addressed to the Saint in the form of asking for intercession with the Lord, and the sharing of favorable results of those prayers. "I prayed to St. Peter and asked him to ask Jesus to heal my mother and, praise God, my mother was healed!"

After some passage of time it became the custom to present to the local bishop, in whose area the Saint lived, a biography of the deceased person and a history of his alleged miracles. If a favorable judgment was given, the body was exhumed and buried in a church. Then a day was assigned for celebration of the feast—the usual feast day of a Saint being the day of martyrdom or death as has already been mentioned.

Episcopal canonization or canonization by the local bishop gradually gave way to the custom of papal canonization, final formal approval of Sainthood being declared by the pope himself. The earliest known process of canonization was in 993 when a bishop of Augsburg asked permission to read an account of the life and miracles of his predecessor to a synod presided over by Pope John XV. Pope Alexander III (1159-1181) decreed that no one should give a public *cultus* [11] to any man, "however many miracles he may have done," without authority from the Church in Rome. [12] From that time onward the rules for public veneration of Saints became clearer until in 1634 Pope Urban VIII laid down the procedure that has more or less been followed to the present.

It was decreed that a spontaneous public cultus given to a deceased person was to be regarded more as an obstacle than as a first step towards canonization. It was forbidden to set up images of a person showing a halo or any other indication of sanctity. It was forbidden to publish anything about the miracles, holiness or revelations of a deceased until there was a judgment from Rome.

In miniature the wisdom of this procedure is evident to anyone who has had experience in a leadership capacity in a charismatic prayer group. It sometimes happens that an immature member will insist that he is getting direct revelations from God concerning the group. In most cases, but especially if this causes confusion and dissension in the group, the elders or leaders have to deal with the situation and in some way have to forbid the person from distributing the revelations and/or by teaching to instruct the other members how to discern what comes from the Lord and what does not.

Pope Benedict XIV (1740-1758) worked over the legislation of Urban VIII and the final form appeared in 1917 in the Code of Canon Law. The first step in the long process of canonization is called the "ordinary process." The bishop of a diocese is also called an "ordinary" and the first phase of the canonization process takes place in the diocese where the prospective Saint died. The "ordinary process" then takes its name from the fact that the process is instituted by the ordinary of the place. The bishop establishes a tribunal to hear witnesses and to gather evidence as to whether there is any real foundation for the fame of sanctity of a reputed Saint. The diocesan tribunal seeks to establish whether the servant of God (the usual "official" way of referring to a Saint or prospective Saint) exercised virtue in a heroic manner (manifested fruits of the Spirit in abundance) or whether he or she died for the faith. Besides interviewing witnesses, all that the prospective Saint wrote, including all personal correspondence, is scrutinized.

Upon completion of the ordinary process, the cause (term used as a synonym for the petition for canonization by those requesting it) is formally introduced in Rome and the cause passes from the local bishop's competency and comes under a branch of Church structure known as the Sacred Congregation for the Causes of Saints. What is known from then on as the "apostolic process" is thereby initiated.

The cause is brought before this Congregation by a priest called a "postulator." The postulator examines the claim in cooperation with the bishop in whose diocese the prospective Saint died. A promotor of the faith, popularly called the "devil's advocate," points out to the Congregation the weak points of the case. If the cause of the prospective Saint passes this phase of the process satisfactorily, another more lengthy and detailed inquiry is conducted into the life of the candidate. His virtues, the miracles performed through his intercession and the orthodoxy of his doctrine or teaching are reviewed. After the fulfillment of certain requirements (such as proof of martyrdom if that is the case) and many work sessions, at the last of which the pope is present, the candidate may be declared "Venerable" though no public cult is authorized. (The cause of venerable Francis Libermann (1802-1852), the son of a rabbi who became superior of the Holy Ghost Fathers, is one which has proceeded this far.) The next two steps are beatification and finally canonization.

For beatification, two posthumous miracles, specifically medical miracles, are required. This would mean, for example, that someone with a terminal cancer might invoke a prospective Saint, praying that he or she would ask Jesus for a healing. If the case had many witnesses and, in spite of the hopelessness of the situation, a complete cure followed after prayer, the Sacred Congregation for the Causes of Saints might accept the evidence as one of the medical miracles confirming Sainthood. After beatification the faithful may liturgically honor the candidate who is called "Blessed." After the completion of the beatification process two more miracles must occur before the candidate can be canonized. The emphasis in canonization is on evidence of heroic virtue in the life of the deceased prospective Saint, not on miracles. In some cases the pope has waived the rule on miracles in canonization or beatification. Principally this has been done in the case of those whose heroic life culminated in martyrdom. St. John Fisher and St. Thomas More were canonized in 1935 with dispensation from proof of miracles.

What does the Church look for when considering someone for canonization? Before answering this question it would be good to reiterate what was said in the preceding chapter. We are constituted "saints" through Baptism. We are sanctified, we are made holy. What the Church looks for in the canonization process is maturity of growth in holiness. Through Baptism we enter the race. What is looked for in prospective Saints is whether or not they have run the race and how well—which in the end is what will be considered at the time of Judgment.

Now to the original question. What constitutes the sanctity of a Saint with a capital "S"? "Sanctity properly consists in simple conformity to the Divine Will expressed in an exact fulfillment of the duties of one's proper state" declared Pope Benedict XV in 1916.[13] Thus defined, sanctity or maturity in spiritual growth is seen as doing the will of our Father in heaven and keeping His commandments. "Duties of one's proper state" refer to one's state in life and all the obligations that go with it. If one is a wife, sanctity consists in performing as well as possible all the duties that go along with being the kind of wife that is holy and pleasing in God's sight. When considering someone for canonization the Church looks for the manifestation of *all*, not just some, of the fruits of the Spirit: charity, joy, peace, patience, kindness, goodness, faithfulness, gentleness and self-control.

It has to be kept in mind that the Church doesn't canonize just for something to do. The canonization process developed as a response to initiative on the part of the faithful who wished to publicly honor and invoke certain exemplary Christians. In a sense the practice of canonization is a discernment process.

Two things might be said of Benedict XV's definition of sanctity. First, such a definition opens sanctity to all. All are called to grow in holiness and Saints come from all walks of life. Kings, peasants, doctors, lawyers, teachers, students, old and young are numbered among the Saints. Secondly, Benedict makes no mention of miracles. Sanctity does not consist in the working of miracles.[14]

St. Robert Bellarmine in the early seventeenth century listed seven honors due to Saints after canonization:

1. The name is inscribed in the catalogue of saints; i.e. public recognition of him is ordered.
2. His intercession is invoked in the public prayers of the Church.
3. Churches are dedicated to God in his memory.
4. The Eucharist and the Divine Office are celebrated in his honor.
5. His festival is observed.
6. Pictorial representations of him are made in which he is surrounded by a heavenly and glorious light.
7. His relics are enclosed in precious vessels and publicly honored.[15]

Canonization doesn't "make" a Saint. It is official recognition that the person was a Saint during his lifetime. Canonization also does not mean that the person was faultless and it is not blanket approval of everything the Saint said or did.

There is no single official register of Saints from earliest times. Saints' names are found in such places as ancient and modern Church calendars and Eastern and Western martyrologies. The Roman martyrology lists forty-five hundred names and is not exhaustive. One of the best collections in the opinion of most scholars is *Lives of the Saints* by Alban Butler. This was first published in 1786-9 but has been revised and updated through the years.

In the last few years, the process of canonization of Saints has been called into question, perhaps because interest in Saints (along with interest in God) has been in decline. Official statistics would seem to belie this. Writing in 1962, Paul Molinari, S.J., Postulator for the Causes of Jesuits, cited figures showing that 1,194 people were beatified between 1634 and 1962, of which number ninety-three percent were promulgated in the nineteenth century. He writes:

> The number of persons beatified between 1951 and 1960 so far exceeds the sum total of those enrolled among the Blessed between the years 1662 and 1852 that a single decade has witnessed more beatifications than did two centuries.[16]

However, Karl Rahner in 1971 could say this:

> The present situation . . . is that at least in the "Cisalpine" countries of Europe veneration of the Saints has suffered an extraordinary decline even among Catholics, so that the ability to practice such veneration seems to have undergone some kind of process of atrophy and decay. This assertion cannot, of course, be proved statistically, especially since the official cult of the Church has continued unchanged. But the fact itself should not be contested on this account. . . . The fact that modern churches are, to so large an extent, bereft of images and pictures is in itself a sign of this.[17]

During the years when a few bumper stickers on American cars protested God's death: "God isn't dead, He's bread" and "God isn't dead, I talked to Him this morning," the Saints died along with God and canonization was viewed as an outmoded custom. Another reason for the canonization of Saints falling into disfavor with some is the fact that anything the Church as an organization does these days costs money. The June 25, 1975 *Wall Street Journal* ran a front-page article on the then upcoming canonization of St. Elizabeth Seton. The headline read: "The Good Fight, American Saint's Cause Took Century of Work, Millions in Donations." The article focused mainly on the cost of the canonization procedure, and pointed out that Joel Wells of *Critic* said that canonization "belongs to the past, and there's a lot more the Church could do with the money spent on it." The article also called attention to the fact that the independent weekly *National Catholic Reporter* hadn't carried a single editorial on the Seton canonization because it felt it lacked importance. Interestingly enough, the July 4, 1975 issue of the *National Catholic Reporter* put a story on the *Wall Street Journal* article on its front page. A Philadelphia priest who worked on the beatification of Bishop Neumann, defended the money spent on the process to the *Journal*, "It cost six million dollars to inaugurate Richard Nixon, and who's more important?"

Some have criticized canonization for its seeming emphasis on priests, bishops and religious rather than laity, and in particular, on those who were celibate.[18] It must be admitted that the number of Saints who were married is small and there is no record of a case where both partners to a marriage were canonized. There are instances of mother and son (Monica and Augustine), of mother and daughter (Bridget of Sweden and Catherine), but none of husband and wife. Saints who were at some time in their life either a husband or wife include: Margaret of Scotland (1045-1083), Elizabeth of Hungary (1207-1231), Louis of France (1214-1270), Frances of Rome (1384-1440), Nicholas of Flue (1417-1487) who with his wife's permission left her and their ten children to become a hermit, Thomas More (1478-1535), Mme. Acarie (1566-1618), Louise de Marillac (1591-1660), Anna Maria Taigi (1769-1837) and Elizabeth Seton (1774-1821). Little is written about the few Saints who were married. Rosemary Haughton, herself married, has given us the book *Six Saints for Parents*, which includes only two Saints who were ever parents! We are indebted to a former Episcopal minister, Seldon Delany, who wrote *Married Saints* while he was studying for the priesthood in Rome.[19] This book appeared in 1935, and to my knowledge little has appeared on the subject in the forty or more years since then.

The canonization process has also been criticized for the preponderance of Italian Saints. In the January-February 1975 *Critic* Dan Herr reported, "Dutch Jesuit Rene Hols claims, in the *Catholic Herald* (London), that of 1,848 registered Saints, more than a third (626) are Italians and that more than half (1,044) were priests during their lifetime." Fr. Patrick Ryan writing in *America* in 1975 pondered the question of why the eight Frenchmen known as the North American Martyrs were canonized and "their fellow Catholics and heroes," the Hurons who were killed at Ossernenon in 1642 and 1646 were not. Fr. Ryan admits that Mohawk persecution of the Hurons was more ethnic than religious but he points out that both the French and the Hurons were captured and tortured primarily because they were allies of the Algonquins. Further, it seems that three of the Frenchmen, Rene Goupil, Jean de la Lande and the Jesuit priest Isaac Jogues were executed because the Mohawks feared witchcraft. For eample, Goupil's habit of teaching the sign of the cross to Mohawk children was not interpreted and quite naturally led the Mohawks to fear for the children and they killed him. Fr. Ryan reflects:

> For all the problematic elements in their understanding of the Mohawks, for all their limitations as Frenchmen of their generation, there is no denying the heroism of their witness. Not all their missionary techniques are imitable today, but the example of their steadfastness remains. They died, as we all must die, seeing only part of the total picture.[20]

Fr. Ryan then says that in view of the human limitations of the eight Frenchmen, to him it seems a pity that the Hurons were not canonized with them.

Donald Attwater, who revised *Butler's Lives of the Saints* in 1956, was aware of the criticisms leveled at canonization. In 1965, in his excellent introduction to *The Penguin Dictionary of Saints*, Attwater says that most new Saints who have been added to the calendar are indeed bishops and other clergy, nuns and monks. He lists as reasons the fact that people in public position attract attention more easily and in later times religious orders have pressed the claims of their members. The Church only canonizes those brought before her for examination and decision. Attwater makes the observation that the same numerical disproportion is not found among the martyrs in any age! [21]

As long as the Church continues to venerate Saints, a way will be needed to select and approve them. In time the procedure will most probably be revised, since the cost is prohibitive not only for religious orders but certainly for lay people as well. What wife has the wherewithal to see her husband through to canonization? Perhaps in the future the burden will shift. Instead of the Church waiting for causes to be brought to her for examination, she will actively go out and look for them.

The Vatican Council reaffirmed veneration and invocation of Saints in *Lumen Gentium*, VII, "The Eschatological Nature of the Pilgrim Church and Her Union with the Heavenly Church." However, the document on liturgy paved the way for needed reform.

The saints have been traditionally honored in the Church and their authentic relics and images held in veneration. For the feasts of the saints proclaim the wonderful works of Christ in His servants, and display to the faithful fitting examples for their imitation.

Lest the feasts of the saints, however, take precedence over the feasts which commemorate the very mysteries of salvation, many of them should be left to be celebrated by a particular church or nation or religious community; only those should be extended to the universal Church which commemorate saints who are truly of universal significance.[22]

In accordance with Council guidelines, the liturgical calendar was revised. In February 1969 Pope Paul VI issued an apostolic letter approving the general norms for the liturgical year and the new general Roman calendar. Part I dealt with the restoration of the liturgical year and the importance of sharing in "the whole mystery of Christ as it unfolds throughout the year." Part II said in part:

With the passage of centuries, the faithful have become accustomed to so many special religious devotions that the principal mysteries of the redemption have lost their proper place. . . .

As the council properly pointed out, over the course of the centuries more feasts of the saints were introduced than necessary. . . .

To put these decrees of the ecumenical council into effect, the names of some saints have been deleted from the general calendar. . . .[23]

Saints had not been news for quite a while but three months after the Holy Father's letter, Fr. McNaspy, an associate editor of *America*, wrote an article, "The Fracas About Saints."

How dare the Pope decanonize our St. Christopher? He'd understand better if he tried to walk through Roman traffic! And what of the cutback on sales of St. Christopher medals, when 15 per cent of purchasers are Protestants? And the Valentine card industry?

Osservatore Romano worriedly took the world press to task for "sensationalism" in reporting the "so-called demotion of saints." Actually, though the innocent reader would never suspect it from his daily papers, the Pope had done nothing more monstrous than approve a revised church calendar. . . . The new calendar, by limiting the number of saints' days in the Western Church at large to fifty-eight, shows the Church's intent to concentrate more on the seasons of the year (which focus on great redemptive mysteries) than on individual saints. . . .

For centuries now . . . scholars like the Bollandists have been engaged in the ongoing task of discerning between fact and fancy. Our new calendar rightly . . . stresses those saints whose lives are sharply discernable. . . . I, for one, am happy to have . . . St. Thomas More's feast day rather than, say, St. Vitus'.[24]

The documents of Vatican II and resulting pastoral action are reminiscent of St. Augustine's attitude and pastoral practice on veneration of Saints. There is the same encouragement with the same attempt to keep it in balance. We should not conclude that this issue of Saints is always one which causes problems. Attitudes towards sacraments have on occasion been exaggerated. Some Catholics can remember back to when devotion to the Real Presence in the Eucharist almost overshadowed the Mass with some people appreciating Benediction [25] more than the Mass. Placing something in proper perspective does not deny its excellence.

Notes to Chapter 3

1. James A. Kleist, S.J., translator and annotator, *Ancient Christian Writers*, No. 6, "The Didache, The Epistle of Barnabas, The Epistles and the Martyrdom of St. Polycarp, The Fragments of Papias, The Epistle to Diognetus," The Newman Press, Westminster, Md. 1948, pp. 98-99.
2. Douillet, *What is a Saint?*, p. 72.

3. *Ibid.*, p. 70.

4. 2 Maccabees is one of several such books included in the Old Testament canon by the Catholic Church: the full list is Tobit, Judith, Wisdom of Solomon, Ecclesiasticus, Baruch, three additions to Daniel, additions to Esther and 1 and 2 Maccabees. Their designation as apocrypha ("hidden") by the Protestants was not classifying them as spurious works but answering the question, "Are these authentic Jewish writings part of the inspired Word of God?"

The history of this dispute goes back to the earliest days of the Church and to the rabbinical debates of the first two centuries A.D. In general the Catholic Church has accepted (eventually by solemn definition at the Council of Trent in 1546) the Greek Canon of the Old Testament, known as the Septuagint, whereas the Protestant Churches have limited the Canon to the Hebrew version fixed by the Jewish rabbis in the first centuries A.D.

Christian attitudes towards these disputed books have become less polarized with the demise of Catholic-Protestant polemics and recently in *The Common Bible* the Churches have been able to agree on a format that is widely acceptable, viz., to insert such books between the Old Testament and the New Testament with a brief introduction indicating their status for different Churches.

A concise account of the history of the deuterocanonical or apocryphal books can be found in *The Common Bible*, Collins, New York, 1973, pp. viii-xi and a more detailed study is included in the chapters on "Canonicity" and "Apocrypha" in *The Jerome Biblical Commentary*, Prentice-Hall Inc., Englewood Cliffs, New Jersey, 1968, II, pp. 516-546.

5. Douillet, *op. cit.*, p. 71.

6. Lamirande, O.M.I., *The Communion of Saints*, p. 151.

7. I have tried to avoid the use of the word "cult" as much as possible because for many people the sole usage of the word is to designate religious groups which are unorthodox or heretical. However, the word has another meaning. It comes from the Latin *colere* meaning "to honor" and the honor given to Saints is called cult or cultus.

8. F. Van der Meer, *Augustine the Bishop*, p. 488.

9. *Ibid.*, p. 497.

10. Karl Rahner, *Theological Investigations*, Vol. VIII, Part One, "Why and How Can We Venerate the Saints?" pp. 3-24.

11. See footnote 7.

12. E.W. Kemp, *Canonization and Authority in the Western Church*, Oxford, 1948, p. 16.

13. Made in the allocution accompanying the promulgation in 1916 of the heroism of Jean Baptiste de Burgogne. From Pere Gabriele du Ste. Marie-Madeleine, *Present Norms of Holiness in Conflict and Light*, N.Y. Sheed & Ward, 1952, p. 158 as cited

in *Heroic Sanctity and Insanity*, by Thomas Verner Moore, Grune & Stratton, 1959, N.Y., p. 18.

14. The fact that sanctity does not consist in miracles must not be confused with the posthumous miracles usually required for canonization. As in the life of St. Therese of Lisieux, no miracles at all may be recorded in the life of a particular Saint.

15. Bellarmine, *Disputationes. Quarta controversia generalis, De Ecclesia triumphante*, lib. primus, cap VII, Cologne edition, 1628, as quoted in *Canonization and Authority in the Western Church*, by E.W. Kemp, p. 417.

16. Paul Molinari, S.J., *Saints, Their Place in the Church*, p. 4.

17. Karl Rahner, *Theological Investigations*, Vol. VIII, pp. 5-6.

18. Doris Donnelly, "Sanctity Without Sex," *National Catholic Reporter*, May 24, 1974.

19. Some interesting reminiscences on Seldon Delany and the mention of this book on married Saints can be found in *The Next Thing*, the autobiography of Katherine Burton, who for years was editor of the woman's page of *Sign* magazine. (Longmans, Green & Company, New York, 1949.)

20. Patrick J. Ryan, S.J., "Indians and Martyrs Reconsidered" *America*, October 18, 1975.

21. Donald Attwater, *The Penguin Dictionary of Saints*, p. 9.

22. *Constitution on the Sacred Liturgy*, Chapter V, 111.

23. Pope Paul VI Apostolic Letter: *Motu Proprio* "Approval of the General Norms for the Liturgical Year and the New General Roman Calendar." February 14, 1969.

24. C.J. McNaspy, "The Fracas About Saints," *America* May 24, 1969, p. 22.

25. Catholics believe that the symbols of bread and wine used in the Catholic service, the Mass, not only suggest a memory, they also present a reality: the body and blood of Jesus. "For my flesh is food indeed, and my blood is drink indeed. He who eats my flesh and drinks my blood abides in me, and I in him" (John 6:55-56). To onlookers, this belief in Jesus present in the Eucharist was so obvious and so strong, it led persecutors such as those who killed the martyrs of Lyons in 177 to accuse those Christians of "feeding on human flesh." (Recorded in Eusebius of Caesarea *The Ecclesiastical History* Book 5 as quoted in Butler's *Lives of the Saints.*)

Over the course of time, pre-Vatican II Catholic piety reached a point where, at the celebration of the Eucharist (the Mass), the attention of some was focused less on the entire service, which included listening to God's Word in Scripture and homily and praising Him, and was focused more on Jesus as really present in the communion host (wafer). This was best seen at a service called Benediction where a consecrated host (a communion wafer which had previously been consecrated at a Mass) was placed in a gold vessel with a round glass window (called a monstrance). The monstrance was placed on an altar and incensed while hymns were sung. On pages 118-119 of *The Riddle of Roman Catholicism*, Lutheran theologian Jaroslav Pelikan very well describes this piety at its worst. However, Pelikan was describing a pre-Vatican II situation and recent liturgical renewal has now shifted Catholic piety more in the direction of community rather than "me and Jesus" at the weekly Sunday Mass. There is also much more emphasis on God's Word in Scripture.

This does not mean that Catholics believe any less in the Real Presence of Jesus in the communion host they receive, just that it is seen more in perspective with other important truths comprising the whole celebration of the Eucharist. For a good discussion of this subject I would recommend the pages listed under Eucharist in *A New Catechism*, the "Dutch Catechism," published by Herder and Herder.

CHAPTER 4

Hagiography

The word "hagiography" comes from the Greek *hagios*, or "holy," and it names the area of learning concerned with the lives of Saints. For three centuries a small group of Jesuits in Belgium have devoted themselves to hagiography. This group, called Bollandists (after Fr. John Bolland who completed the work of Fr. Heribert Rosweyde, with whom the plans originated) have as their objective to sift fact from fiction in the lives of Saints, mainly in those who were "canonized" by public acclaim in the days before the canonization procedure was so rigorous. Their purpose has not been to attack the Saints, but rather to bring into sharper focus the kind of people the Saints really were.

Early in Christian history, when the accounts of Christian martyrs were being recorded, writers frequently embroidered the report to make it more "edifying." These "reporters" were not bothered by geographical detail or historical fact. The approach of the readers of these accounts was just as simple and naive as that of the writers, so, as many have observed, much writing of the age of persecution in the early Church makes monotonous reading. The emperor always exhibits terrible anger against the Christians and pagan justice is always unfair and cruel. The objects of this pagan fury are led through an appalling array of tortures which seemingly would have killed them ten times over, but they manage to limp through several more episodes before finally succumbing. Much of what was written after the age of persecution makes monotonous reading also. Confessors (already identified as those who were not martyred but who inspired many by their heroic "confessing" of the faith and by their holiness) are described in written testimony as possessing every imaginable virtue. An account of St. Fursey, an abbot, (d.c. 648) describes him for us:

> For he was comely to look upon, chaste of body, earnest of mind, affable of speech, gracious of presence, abounding in wisdom, a model of abstemiousness, steadfast in resolution, firm in right judgments, unwearied in longanimity, of sturdiest patience, gentle in humility, solicitous in charity, while wisdom in him so enhanced the radiance of all virtues that his conversation, according to the Apostle, was always seasoned with wit in the grace of God.[1]

St. Gregory the Great, who became pope in 590, wrote four books of *Dialogues* about the Saints in Italy, St. Benedict in particular. They are full of the miraculous. Fr. Jacques Douillet devotes two pages of his excellent book, *What Is A Saint?* to Gregory's writings. He makes the observation that Gregory's deacon, Peter, reveals the state of mind of the readers of those days when he says, "Miracles!—the more I hear, the more I want to hear!" Douillet concludes that when men wrote or listened to a Saint's life they were much less concerned to learn about what he had really done than to be enthralled by a good story.[2]

Writing as I do from the experience of charismatic renewal and Christian community where I see miracles frequently,[3]I would suggest that readers or hearers listening to Gregory's accounts were less interested in a good story than they were in rejoicing over the marvels of God's power and care for His people. Christianity is a religion of *power*. Jesus performed signs and wonders and told His disciples that they would do the same. The gospel was to be preached with "signs following" which would be done in and by the power of the Holy Spirit. The miraculous element has always been present in Christianity and it serves as a witness to

44

His people that God is alive and is in full control of the world He created. If early hagiographers can be faulted for being too credulous, naive and simple, perhaps modern hagiographers are sometimes lacking in their understanding and appreciation of signs and wonders.

A masterpiece of hagiography was produced by a thirteenth century Dominican,* Jacobus de Voragine.[4] He made a collection of legends about Saints which was called the *Legenda Aurea*, in English known as the *Golden Legend*. This was one of the most famous books of the Middle Ages and was a best seller. Over five hundred manuscripts of the book are in existence and within the first one hundred years of the invention of movable type the book appeared in more than a hundred and fifty editions. It is the opinion of modern scholars [5] that Voragine did not in his day equate the the word *Legenda* with legend; to him it meant lesson or reading. What Voragine envisioned and wrote was a layman's lectionary. But this does not mean that Voragine was unaware that some of his sources were dubious. He even says so in some places, but that didn't deter him from then going ahead and telling us the story anyway.

The *Golden Legend* fell into disfavor with the coming of the critical scholarship of the Renaissance but there has been in this century a revival of interest in the book, due in part to a more enlightened and sympathetic assessment of the Middle Ages.

In the days before printing, when the *Golden Legend* had to be copied by hand, an abridged version appeared known as the *Flos Sanctorum*. It was this book which found its way into the hands of a recuperating Ignatius Loyola. It was the right book at the right time, and it changed his life.

Fr. Hippolyte Delehaye (1859-1941), who was president of the Bollandist society from 1912-1941, has left us a classic book entitled *The Legends of the Saints*. In that book he tells us:

To declare that legend has flourished abundantly around the

45

sanctuaries is simply to state the importance of the cultus of saints in the life the people. The legend is the homage of the Christian people to its protectors. [6]

Later on Fr. Delehaye says of his book that although his study deals with the weak points of hagiographic literature, ". . . to give assistance in detecting materials of inferior workmanship is not to deny the excellence of what remains."[7] He explains that a "hagiographic document" is one that is of a religious character, written with the aim of edifying the reader or listener. He emphasizes the distinction between hagiography and history. The work of a particular hagiographer may be historical, but not necessarily, and any literary form may be employed.

Monika Hellwig, in an article on Saints in 1975, makes the excellent point that the passing on of recollections about Saints' lives from one generation to the next has always been interpretive, often employing a lavish style rich in hyperbole and metaphor. It is precisely in this lavish style, she says, that an important aspect of the message is contained. It is not enough, then, to aim merely for information retrieval when passing tradition along. [8]

While admiring the belief in the miraculous and the pious simplicity of early hagiographers, it must be admitted that some accounts of the miraculous were plainly ludicrous. Some tales abounded in flying crucifixes, dogs that preached the gospel and talking fish.

Talking fish reminds me of a fish story which has to do with how the Church developed the New Testament canon. I make this digression for anyone who thinks (as I did several years ago) that the New Testament must have been handed intact to St. Peter on Mount Tabor, or somewhere similar, rather like the way Moses received the ten commandments. Actually, for years there was no official "New Testament" and the Church early in her life had to make a decision as to which books to "canonize"— which books to put on her official list and which to reject.

Enthusiastic literature was widespread. There were written reports of miracle contests between Simon Peter and Simon Magus. In one episode Peter caused a dog to have a human voice and a dried sardine to swim. Simon Magus showed off by leaping about in the air was brought down by Peter's prayer.[9] Such literature was excluded from the New Testament and the canon was set in 367.

Good modern hagiography tries to take into account all the "ologies" that might be relevant to a particular Saint's life. More recent works pay particular attention to psychology, providing us with good insights into how Saints acted and reacted in their environment.[10] An understanding of psychology enables us to see a Saint's interior spiritual growth and the elements of his or her personality. We can appreciate "big" Teresa (Teresa of Avila) for her excellent knowledge of human nature and the perceptive psychological acumen that she manifests in dealing with people. We can appreciate "little" Therese (Therese of Lisieux) [11] of the same Carmelite order, as she overcomes excessive sensitivity and develops into a "living flame of love." Rosemary Haughton in a piece on St. Louise de Marillac[12] emphasizes Louise's growth into personal maturity.

Great care is also taken by modern writers to place the Saint and plunge the reader into the civilization, times, mores and century which influenced the Saint's life and thought. In the introduction to his book *Friar Thomas d'Aquino* (1974), James Weisheipl, O.P., says, ". . .it is wrong to read his works as though they were written in one sitting and devoid of all intellectual development. Thomas, like everyone else, developed intellectually and spiritually."[13] And in the first chapter Weisheipl counsels us:

As a general background to his life, thought and works, we should have an appreciation of the thirteenth century, especially of the many currents of thought, life-styles, and changes that took place. It is not easy to understand a century; we barely understand our own. [14]

Historical perspective is essential if one is to understand a Saint as well as possible. For example, history enables us to see how Sts. Norbert of Xanten and Robert of Arbrissel on the one hand, and Peter Waldo and the Poor Men of Lyons on the other, preceded and prepared the way for a Francis of Assisi to appear. In an address on "The Primary Needs of the Church" on October 12, 1974 Pope Paul VI said with reference to knowledge of the lives of the Saints:

> If in the past they offered a delightful pasture for popular culture . . . for us today, trained in historical studies and psychological criticism, they could offer a museum of incomparable human experiences and exciting examples for the possible progress of a real moral and spiritual improvement. Remember: "si isti et istae, cur non ego?" (If these men and women could do it, why can't I?) [15]

Revisionism is in vogue these days. Not only are such fictional heroes as Sherlock Holmes being analyzed, but such heroes as Winston Churchill are being cut to size by revisionist historians. The Saints can only benefit by such an approach. St. Anthony of Padua (1195-1231) can serve as an example in this regard for those who are familiar with this popular "Italian Franciscan"* who runs a heavenly lost and found department! Many over forty can remember as children searching for lost articles while praying: "Dear St. Anthony come around, something's lost and can't be found." Anthony also vied with St. Jude ("the Saint of the impossible") for the reputation of "the Saint of the miraculous" because so many people witnessed to having prayers answered through his intercession. (Actually, Anthony and his life, real or legendary, appealed to many people and so he was invoked more than other Saints, with the very natural result that he acquired a reputation which could not have been acquired by a Saint invoked less often!)

Popular statues of St. Anthony of Padua show him in a Franciscan habit holding a book upon which stands Jesus depicted as a young child. The image, then, that many Catholics have of St. Anthony is that of a miracle-working Italian Franciscan named Anthony, to whom Jesus appeared as a little child. The truth is that this Saint was a Portuguese Augustinian named Ferdinand to whom Jesus probably did not appear at all and of whom fewer miracles were recorded in his lifetime than many other Saints.

St. Anthony's baptismal name was Ferdinand and he was born in Lisbon, Portugal. He became a Canon Regular of St. Augustine at age fifteen and remained one for ten years, taking the name of Anthony only when he became a Franciscan in 1220. The first statue showing Anthony with the child Jesus dates from 1439,[16] two hundred years after his death. Although in keeping with the well-known legend that Jesus appeared as a child to Anthony, the original statues (some of them portraying Anthony as an Augustinian) probably meant to honor him under his title of "Herald of the Incarnate Word." Anthony was a great preacher and wrote many sermons: the Church declaring him a Doctor of the Church in 1946. There is a statue of Anthony at Santa Cruz in Coimbra, Portugal, showing Anthony garbed as an Augustine canon. In South America he is known under the title, "St. Anthony of Lisbon."

Revisionism or demythologizing, when done without faith, can amount to picking the petals off a flower. When you have finished there is nothing left. Subjecting the Saints to critical scholarship combined with faith in Christ Jesus, our Risen Lord, is like removing the tarnish from precious metal. The Saints emerge from the process as the treasures God made them.

Notes to Chapter 4

1. As quoted in Pere H. Delehaye, S.J., *The Legends of the Saints*, p. 25.
2. Douillet, *What Is A Saint?* p. 104.
3. In an article, "The Saints" in *Catechist*, October, 1975, Monika Hellwig says: "In a community of believers, of course, miracles should be happening constantly." (p. 14)
4. Jacobus de Voragine was Dominican provincial of Lombardy for almost twenty years and then was Archbishop of Genoa. He lived as a poor man and spent the revenues of his office on those in need. He was a real shepherd to his people. He died in 1298 and was beatified by Pius VII in 1816.
5. Granger Ryan and Helmut Ripparger, translators and adaptors, *The Golden Legend of Jacobus de Voragine*, pp. v-xvi.
6. Delehaye, *op. cit.*, p.v.
7. *Ibid.*, p.x.
8. Hellwig, *op. cit.*, p. 15.
9. Jacques Hervieus, *The New Testament Apocrypha*, Hawthorn Books, New York, 1960, p. 168.
10. For a delightful spoof of hagiography see *The Collected Writings of St. Hereticus* by Robert McAfee Brown, Westminster Press, Philadelphia, 1964. Here is a sentence or two from the final page: "Why has the Church seen fit to canonize this errant son of hers, [St. Hereticus] whose life appears to have been dedicated to confusing the faith, confounding the faithful, and comforting the faithless? The truth of the matter is very simple. Mother Church, in her infinite wisdom, would prefer heresy to flourish within her walls, where she can keep track of it, rather than to have it rampant in attack upon her from without." (p. 15)
11. See Note, 5 Chapter 2.
12. Rosemary Haughton, *Six Saints for Parents*, pp. 59-78. Mrs. Haughton takes Louise from her lack of success as a natural mother (she had one son "who grew up a dreary, feckless, young man") to her success as supernatural mother, foundress with St. Vincent de Paul of the Daughters of Charity.
13. Weisheipl, O.P., *Friar Thomas d'Aquino*, p.x.
14. *Ibid.*, p. 2.
15. Pope Paul's address, October 16, 1974, reprinted in part in the *Catholic Standard*, Washington, D.C.
16. Clasen, O.F.M., *St. Anthony*, p. 128.

CHAPTER 5

Relics

There is perhaps no subject connected with veneration of Saints that requires more sympathetic understanding, knowledge of human nature and a sense of humor than does discussion of relics. And no discussion of Saints, however brief, could exclude such a discussion. There is a delightful book entitled *Life on a Mediaeval Barony* which consists of a 400-page description of a typical but fictional thirteenth century feudal community. The *invented* seigneury is that of St. Aliquis in northern France. Five pages are devoted to "relics." Here is a sample:

> The monks at St. Aliquis are proud of their collection, although by no means the largest in the region. They have two teeth of the prophet Amos; hairs of St. Martin and St. Leonard . . . bits of the robe of St. Bernard . . . a chip of the stone on which Christ stood when He ascended to heaven . . . some of the hay from the manger of Bethlehem; and, last but not least, a fair-sized splinter of the true Cross. . . .
> It is advantageous to the whole region to save such a collection. If there is need of rain, the relics can be carried in procession around the thirsty country and relief is sure to follow.[1]

Lest we think that the subject is something that just belongs to the past, let us report without comment that a year ago a sacristan at the Basilica of St. Francis, in Assisi, Italy, gave the group that I was traveling with a special "extra" and exposed for veneration a large reliquary containing what he claimed was a piece of the Blessed Mother's veil! [2]

An interest in relics is not confined to Catholics and to "religious" people. In the spirit of the Bicentennial year, the Parker Pen Company offered for sale ($100.00) a pewter pen containing "an authentic relic of the signing of the Declaration of Independence." The "relic" was a bit of wood that was part of Independence Hall in 1776 and it had been embedded in the crown of a Parker pen.[3]

And the *Wall Street Journal* article which reported on the canonization of Elizabeth Seton said of her beatification:

> Shortly before the ceremony, Mother Seton's body was disinterred in Emmitsburg for positive identification of her remains which Rome requires whenever possible. In a traditional ceremony, redolent of the medieval origins of sainthood, one bone was removed and presented to the Pope. Others were divided into fragments, each of which was boxed and given to those who had worked hardest for the cause.[4]

From the time when the charred remains of St. Polycarp were reverently gathered up until the present, relics have been with us. A hundred years after the martyrdom of Polycarp when St. Cyprian was beheaded in Africa (258), his flock spread cloths on the ground to soak up and save his blood. Historian Henri Daniel-Rops calls this a "touching manifestation of loyalty, but it was not free from danger. . . ." [5] About two hundred years later, a Gallic priest, Vigilantius, denounced reverencing relics as a kind of transposed paganism. Here is how St. Augustine (and St. Jerome) responded:

> When Vigilantius attacked candles and relics, "unseemly" all-night vigils and monkish life-negation—whereupon Jerome hurled back even more angry abuse against Vigilantius, "or rather Dormitantius, who has opened his . . . stink-

ing trap against martyrs' relics once again" (but had also, unfortunately, dared to allude to Jerome's erstwhile sympathy for Origen)—Augustine calmly let all the candles go on burning, let any rich people who wanted to go on founding monasteries do so, and any religious people who felt like living in them do so too; let his successor build chapels to house new relics, and only kept an eye on the all-night vigils. He did not pull a face when he saw hordes of pilgrims; on the contrary he mixed with them and delivered a sermon for the occasion. No indulgent smiles at the stupidity of ordinary people; he had no higher form of piety which he kept to himself.[6]

For a long time the Church of Rome forbade interference with the burial places of Saints but the Churches in the East were less scrupulous. In the Orient the exhumation, dismemberment and transportation of "holy bodies" was occurring in the fourth century and by the fifth century it was an accepted practice.[7] Towards the close of the sixth century the empress at Constantinople asked the pope, St. Gregory the Great, to send her some of St. Paul's bones for the imperial chapel. The pope refused. However, the Church at Rome could not hold out forever and in the eighth century the moving about of relics, and false relics, was going on everywhere. Relics were even stolen! In about 1030 the monks of St. Augustine's abbey at Canterbury engineered the possession of the relics of St. Mildred, and in 1177 a canon regular of Bodmin in Cornwall stole St. Petroc's relics from his own monastery and presented them to an abbey in Brittany.[8]

A satire on a relic theft was written by Boccaccio. He tells of a friar who came to a village to beg for alms. He informed the faithful that he was going to show them a feather from the wings of the Angel Gabriel. Two wags go through the friar's possessions and steal a parrot feather from a little box wrapped in taffeta and substitute some coals for the feather. The friar all unsuspecting begins to eulogize the Angel Gabriel and opens his box only to find the coals. Without blinking he continues speaking and says that when he was in Jerusalem the patriarch there had shown him some rays of the star that appeared to the Magi, some other items and some of the coals that were used to roast the martyr St. Lawrence. He didn't want to soil Gabriel's feather by putting it in the box with the coals, so the feather and the coals were in two identical boxes. He has opened the box with the coals but God must have willed it so because it is just two days from the feast of St. Lawrence. The tale winds up with the friar marking crosses on the people with the coals, collecting a bigger offering than usual, and the wags splitting their sides with laughter.[9]

What happened in real life was sometimes almost as humorous. Thomas Merton, a famous Trappist monk who died in 1968, wrote the life of St. Lutgarde (1182-1246), a Cistercian nun, whose life was full of mystical phenomena (psychophysical accidents) such as levitation, ecstasy, visions, inedia,[10] and stigmata. Merton tells us that a Dominican friar, Thomas of Cantimpre, who was a theologian and studied under St. Albert the Great, knew Lutgarde well for sixteen years and wrote an account of her life. Lutgarde heard that, after her death, he was planning to cut off one of her hands for a relic. She confronted him. She laid her ring finger on the window sill and said: "You will have to be satisfied with this, after my death, that is all you are going to get." And she was right.[11]

Another finger story involves St. Teresa of Avila. One of the times that St. Teresa's tomb was opened, the Provincial, Father Gracian, mutilated the wonderfully preserved body by cutting off the left hand. Not only that, but in his own words: "When I cut off the hand I also cut off a little finger, which I carry with me. . . . When I was captured by the Turks they took it from me, and I redeemed it for about twenty reals and some gold rings." [12] Of this incident Fr. Jacques Doiullet remarks: "Mother Teresa of Jesus was very fond of Father Gracian, but she always distrusted his naivety." [13]

While we are mentioning Teresa's body, it is interesting but sad to learn what happened to the rest of it. We might well say again, this time in a context other than that of poor hagiography, "Avenge, O Lord, Thy slaughtered Saints!" Teresa died on the feast of St. Francis in October of 1582. The day after her death she was buried in the town of Alba in a coffin with so many bricks and stones piled on top of it that the top gave way and some of the rubble fell in. Such a delightful fragrance [14] issued from the tomb that the nuns began to yearn to see the body of their "Mother" once more. Nine months after burial, during one of Gracian's visits, they exhumed the body. ". . . they found the coffin lid smashed, half rotten and full of mildew. . . . The cloths had also fallen to pieces. . . . The holy body was covered with the earth . . . but as fresh and whole as if it had only been buried the day before." [15] It was at this time that Gracian cut off Teresa's left hand. The house was filled with a wonderful fragrance. The nuns washed the body and dressed it in a new habit and buried it again.

At a chapter meeting of discalced friars [16] it was decided that Teresa should be moved to the town of Avila. This had to be done secretly or the Duke of Alba would have prevented it. Some friars went to get the body. They severed the left arm, (the one from which the hand had already been removed) left it in Alba, and took the body to Avila. This was three years after Teresa's death.

The nuns in Avila were overjoyed. They displayed Teresa in a decorated casket and the bishop came to visit.

> The doctors examined the body and decided that it was impossible that its condition could have a natural explanation, but that it was truly miraculous . . . for after three years, without having been opened or embalmed, it was in such a perfect state of preservation that nothing was wanting to it in any way, and a wonderful odor issued from it. [17]

The Duke of Alba heard about the secret removal of the body, petitioned the pope, and the body was ordered back to Alba and back it went. The body was exhibited thereafter many times. In 1588 (six years after Teresa's death) one friar wrote, after viewing the body, that it had been a great consolation and his only regret was to think that the body would one day "be dismembered, at the entreaty of important personages or at the request of her convents."[18] And that is just what happened, as Marcelle Auclair tells us:

> The body of Mother Teresa of Jesus was dismembered and the parts sent to different places. The right foot and a piece of the upper jaw are in Rome, the left hand in Lisbon, the right hand, the left eye, fingers, fragments of flesh, scattered all over Spain, and indeed over all Christendom. Her right arm and heart are in reliquaries at Alba de Tormes, with what remains of this perfect and incorruptible body.[19]

Had I the opportunity and authority, I would gather the fragments and bury them all in one place, and that goes for all the rest of the Saints.

Before we too easily condemn activities such as the struggle of two towns, Alba and Avila, for possession of the remains of St. Teresa, we must remind ourselves that this event took place in an age far different from our own. We live in a post-Christian era and it is perhaps hard for us to comprehend that exemplary Christians, in prior centuries, were considered real heroes and were honored as such. It was only natural that cities or towns would vie for the honor of being the final resting place of the hero.

This tendency in man is not confined to prior centuries. Marshal Petain was exiled to the island of Yew as punishment for collaborating with the Nazis during World War II. He died there in 1951. In 1973 his body was secretly dug up by sympathizers and transported to the mainland for burial outside Verdun. Almost immediately the transfer became known and within four days the government saw to it that Petain was en route back to the island.[20]

It must be noticed that not just simple, pious people, but bishops and doctors witnessed the fragrance and the incorruptibility. Teresa is not the only Saint whose body has exhibited such phenomena. This is one of the reasons why people valued relics. According to a 1962 book by two Dominican priests on *The Theology of Christian Perfection*, incorruptibility of the body is a relatively common phenomenon in the lives of Saints and they mention a few examples: St. Francis de Sales, St. John of God, St. Frances of Rome, St. John Capistrano, St. Francis of Paula, St. Paul of the Cross, St. Pius V, St. Philip Neri, St. Ignatius Loyola, St. Rose of Lima, St. Joseph of Cupertino and St. Teresa of Avila. They state that the bodies of those persons were found to be temporarily or permanently incorrupt.[21]

Absence of rigor mortis is another curious phenomenon seen in numerous cases of deaths of Saints. Besides being immune from decay, some Saints' bodies emitted a delicate fragrance from whence comes the phrase "the odor of sanctity." Regarding conclusions to be drawn from these phenomena, the authors of the work just cited remark:

What is to be said about these various prodigies relating to corpses? The truth of the matter is that very little can be said definitely. Granted that any one of them could possibly be supernatural in origin because of a divine intervention, or that any of them could, with God's permission, be the work of the devil, it is much more scientific and prudent to withhold judgment in most instances. Possibly in some future day the scientists will be able to give a natural explanation for many of these strange occurrences which in many cases seem to have no purpose from a spiritual point of view.[22]

The phenomena surrounding the bodies of Saints such as fragrance, lack of rigor mortis and incorruptibility gave the bodies even more significance than they already had—if that were possible. As we have seen, the origin of veneration of relics (bodily remains of Saints, objects used by them in their lifetime or used in their martyrdom) lay in the anxiety for preservation of the bodies of martyrs. It certainly was a most natural thing for members of the primitive Church to have a solicitude for the bodies of those who were put to death for their belief that Jesus is Lord. It became a favorite custom for people to be buried near the graves of martyrs.

Another factor in the value given to relics, besides their being keepsakes of those who died for the faith, or being seen as pertaining somehow to the marvelous phenomena surrounding Saints' bodies, was the fact that most Saints had some miracles attributed to them while they were living, and miracles were seen to happen through their intercession after their death. These miracles sometimes were associated with a relic. For example, when a person became ill, relatives would not only ask the Lord to heal the person, they would also ask one or more of the Lord's friends like St. Peter or St. Paul to pray also. If the relatives happened to have a relic of the Saint that they were invoking, they might apply it to the affected area of the ill person while they were praying. When a healing took place, people thanked God for the miracle and they also thanked the particular Saint they might have been invoking. It is easy to see how, for some, the distinction could blur between the healing taking place through the action of God and it taking place because of some innate power in the relic itself. However, the same danger exists with faith healing. It is easy for people to eulogize those who manifest the charism of healing and to forget that the power derives from God and does not reside in the healer. Abuses in the use of relics included attributing to them as objects power which they did not possess, forging of relics and sale of relics, all of which were forbidden by the Church.

There are three classes of relics. First-class are bodies or portions of bodies of Saints. Second-class relics are articles used by a Saint during his or her lifetime such as clothing, books, or a rosary. Third-class relics are articles, such as a piece of cloth, which have touched a first- or second-class relic. The only certainty one has as to the genuineness of a relic is that true relics should have with them a document from Rome attesting to their authenticity. In other ages such documents were sometimes forged.

The desire to have a memento of a loved one or a souvenir of a celebrity is somewhat natural. People hound movie stars or celebrities and long for some keepsake used by them or in some way connected with them. People value belongings of a beloved relative. This very natural bent is part of the whole mentality surrounding relics. Also, Christians are temples of the Holy Spirit and their bodies should be treated with reverence. With regard to first-class relics, I feel, as do many Catholics today, that bodies of Saints should remain intact.

Sometimes individuals or religious orders went to great lengths to keep the body of a Saint or "their" Saint in their midst. A recent book on Thomas Aquinas (1225-1274), *Friar Thomas d'Aquino* by James P. Weisheipl, O.P., reveals the gruesome details surrounding the treatment of Thomas Aquinas' body. Aquinas, a Dominican, had the misfortune (only from the point of view of what later happened to his body) to die in a Cistercian monastery. He was on his way to the Second Council of Lyons, became quite ill, and stopped to stay with his niece who lived in the castle of Maenza. When Aquinas felt himself near death he asked to be taken to the Cistercian Abbey of Fossanova nearby. Thomas died a week or so after being moved and it was almost a hundred years before the Dominicans succeeded in having what was left of him removed from the Cistercians. The monks had first decapitated the body, apparently figuring if they had to give up the body they would keep the head. Then they seem to have boiled the body in order to remove the flesh from the bones. In this way the bones could be kept in a very small casket, which was easy to hide.[23]

If a Saint was lost to the Dominicans for a hundred years through no fault of theirs, the Franciscans themselves succeeded in losing their most important Saint for six hundred years. Quite simply, Elias of Cortona, who succeeded Francis of Assisi (Peter Catani governed for a brief period) put Francis' body in a nice safe place, so safe that it was not found until 1818.

The pope desired that a new church be built in Assisi over the tomb of Francis. While the church was being built, Francis' body rested in the church of San Giorgio. The lower church and friary of the Basilica of St. Francis were completed in 1230 in time for the general chapter meeting. Everyone, including papal legates, expected that there would be a grand procession on the occasion of transferring the body of Francis from San Giorgio to the new church. It turned out that Elias had already placed the relics of Francis in a stone coffin "somewhere" under the lower church. He said he did this to protect the relics against theft. This act provoked many friars to exasperation and frustration. Fr. Sophronius Clasen says that St. Anthony of Padua acted as peacemaker on this occasion.[24] In 1818 the Franciscans excavated under the lower church and found the coffin.

Some Catholics may be somewhat chagrined to learn of the dismemberment of St. Teresa's body, the boiling of the Angelic Doctor or "the Blessed Mother's veil" in Assisi. But unless we have even some small idea of the abuses and excuses connected with relics, we will never understand why Protestant reformers inveighed against them. Perhaps we need a jolt in order to have a fresh view of the subject. Protestants, however, were not the only ones to criticize relics and the customs surrounding them. Catholic Saints like St. Bernard of Clairvaux were quite vocal. He denounced the monks of Cluny for their pride in relics.[25]

On the other hand, Catholics and Protestants highly critical of the custom of preserving and venerating relics should guard against pride in supposedly possessing a superior form of piety. The uneducated will by nature possess a more simple faith and will be more credulous. The educated will have to work at becoming more simple. ("Unless you become as little children. . . .") It is the responsibility of shepherds to guard the sheep from such dangers as superstition but it must be done with sympathy and understanding and a real sense of how to preserve what is true and good while pruning unhealthy tendencies. Perhaps St. Augustine and his wise pastoral strategy with regard to popular forms of piety could serve as our example.

Two incidents in Saints' lives speak to me about different aspects of the subject of relics. The first one comes out of the life of St. John Vianney, the French Cure d'Ars (1786-1859). John founded a combination girls' school and orphanage called the "Providence." One time the supply of wheat ran low, there was none in the village owing to a poor harvest and he was faced with having to send away some orphans. He went to the granary, made a pile of what little wheat was left, prayed and put a relic of St. John Francis Regis (1597-1640) under the pile, and then went and told the students in the school to pray. The grain was multiplied and filled the granary. As Lancelot Sheppard points out in his biography in 1958:

> The evidence for this remarkable story is better than is usually the case on occasions of this nature. It happened, it should be remembered, not five or six hundred years ago, but less than one hundred and forty. We have the evidence, given under oath, of contemporaries.[26]

The curate (assistant priest) at Ars testified that of this incident John Vianney told him:

> I had a great number of orphans to feed and in the granary there remained only a handful of wheat. It occurred to me that

61

St. Francis Regis, who had fed the poor miraculously in his lifetime, might well do it again after his death. I possessed a relic of this saint; I placed it among the wheat which remained, the children prayed and the granary was full.[27]

I tend to think that this prayer would have been answered even had he not applied the relic to the wheat. John's work with orphans (although that was not his primary work) and his trust in God to provide for them is very like that of George Mueller in England.[28] On another occasion food was multiplied at the Providence. This time the women in charge of the kitchen asked the Cure to pray, which he did. This time there was no reference to a relic.

What strikes me about the episode of the wheat and the relic is first that John Vianney was humble and self-effacing. Knowing that God is using one is no sign of sanctity, but knowing also the inability of most people to remember that, when possible, he seems to have asked God to channel the gift of the Spirit of miracles himself in some way so that no attention would be drawn to himself. If any attention were to be focused on God's instrument (like that which was given Kathryn Kuhlman as God's instrument) John wanted it focused on a relic or on the prayers of his school children, anywhere other than on himself. I wonder how many other users of relics in the past have had the same motive? I think also that the custom of applying a relic to an ill person and praying for them was a way the laying on of hands and praying for healing was retained in the Church. Another way of course was the sacrament of the anointing of the sick or Extreme Unction. However, Extreme Unction could only be administered by a priest (whereas anyone could place a relic on the affected part of a sick person) and although one could be seriously ill but not necessarily in proximate danger of death for reception of this sacrament, in many peoples' minds, it was reserved for illness in its last extremity and was a sign that death was on its way.

The second incident illustrates the last, and perhaps the most important point I want to make. In Paris, one night in July 1830, a young nun (novice), while praying to the founder of her order, St. Vincent de Paul, took a tiny piece of a surplice he had worn (a relic), and swallowed it! The novice was later canonized as St. Catherine Laboure, not for the visions or revelations she experienced, which are so famous (Miraculous Medal) but for her years of service to the poor in Paris and the heroic practice of the virtues of her state in life.

What I love about this incident is that it symbolizes for me the broadness and variety in Catholicism. The Church embraces a Thomas Aquinas and a Baron von Hugel as well as a Catherine Laboure. Of the above incident of relic-swallowing, Fr. Dirvin, an authority on Catherine's life writes:

> It was a simple act of devotion, growing out of a simple faith. Sophisticated rationalists might sniff at it as ludicrous superstition, but those whose believing mothers have signed their brows with the sacred wedding ring and given them holy water to drink will understand.[29]

In *Charismatic Bridges,* Dr. Synan shares with us the humorous story of how he once let the air out of a Catholic priest's tire and thought he was doing the Lord a favor, says how amazed he was to find the Catholic Church embracing Pentecostalism. He says: "Before 1967 it was generally accepted that pentecostalism could never flourish within the doctrinal and ecclesiastical framework of Roman Catholicism." However, the framework Dr. Synan speaks about refers to the intellectual and institutional elements in the Church. Catholicism has always had a mystical element. It has always been a religion of visions, revelations, relics, incense, pictures and statues. And so tongues, clapping, singing in the Spirit and such are right at home in a Catholic framework. The Church is big enough to include those who do not care for relics, and those who swallow them!

Notes to Chapter 5

1. William Stearns Davis, *Life On A Mediaeval Barony*, Harper & Row Publishers, New York, 1951, p. 308.
2. Author Joan Barthel, in an article on Mother Seton in the *New York Times Magazine*, wrote: "At Vatican II, a Spanish bishop complained about such 'relics' as St. Joseph's sandals and Our Lady's milk and veil, demanding to know how long such nonsense would be allowed. The Church says it isn't allowed, really. . . ." September 14, 1975, p. 85.
3. See advertisement p. 727 in *National Geographic*, November, 1975. Also mentioned in *Consumer Reports*, July 1976, p. 393, as an example of commercialization of the Bicentennial.
4. "The Good Fight," *Wall Street Journal*, June 25, 1975, p. 1.
5. Henri Daniel-Rops, *The Church of Apostles and Martyrs*, Vol. II, Image Books, Doubleday & Company, New York, 1962, p. 269.
6. Van der Meer, *op. cit.*, pp. 574-575.
7. *New Catholic Encyclopedia*, Vol. 12, McGraw-Hill Book Company, New York, 1967.
8. Douillet, *op. cit.*, p. 91.
9. "Boccaccio" on relics, Novelle IV, 10, as quoted in Roland Bainton, *The Medieval Church*, D. Van Nostrand Company, Inc., Princeton, New Jersey, 1962, pp. 184-185.
10. The meaning of this and other terms may be found in the glossary.
11. Thomas Merton, *What Are These Wounds?*, p. 180.
12. Douillet, *op. cit.*, p. 92.
13. *Ibid.*
14. Marcelle Auclair, *Saint Teresa of Avila*, p. 430.
15. *Ibid.*
16. St. Teresa of Avila led a reform of a religious order of men and women dedicated to Our Lady of Mount Carmel. The Carmelites of the reform were known as the "discalced" Carmelites, those who did not wear shoes.
17. Auclair, *op. cit.*, p. 434.
18. *Ibid.*
19. *Ibid.*, p. 435.
20. *Washington Post*, February 20, 1973, p. 1.
21. Antonio Royo, O.P., and Jordan Aumann, O.P., *The Theology of Christian Perfection*, p. 674.
22. *Ibid.*, pp. 674-675.

23. James A. Weisheipl, O.P., *Friar Thomas d'Aquino*, pp. 320-331.

24. Sophronius Clasen, O.F.M., *St. Anthony*, p. 99.

25. *New Catholic Encyclopedia*, Vol. 12, p. 237.

26. Lancelot C. Sheppard, *Portrait of a Parish Priest*, p. 83.

27. *Ibid.*

28. George Mueller, born in 1805, is a famous Christian who is best remembered for his work with orphans in England. His life is in print. *George Mueller*, by Basil Miller, Dimension Books, Bethany Fellowship, Inc., Minneapolis, Minnesota.

29. Joseph Dirvin, *Saint Catherine Laboure*, p. 81.

CHAPTER 6

Obedience

One of the things the Lord has been showing Catholics baptized in the Spirit is the need for order in prayer meetings and a reappreciation of the order in the Church. Many people seem to have a new feeling of freedom soon after receiving the baptism in the Spirit and some begin to think that they will never need any rules or structure in their lives again, even though their lives are relatively free of rules or structure to begin with. But an experience of charismatic chaos at a leaderless prayer meeting or in a poorly-structured household or prayer community or in one's own personal life is usually enough to lead one to suspect that God might just have a plan for the situation and to seek out His will.

A good illustration of the above appeared in 1972 in an article by a Scottish evangelist, Simon Cameron. Mr. Cameron shared with us that he was so sick and tired of control he wanted no control and even gave teachings along these lines about independence and freedom. Then he began to reap the fruit of such teaching. He found that people could not be disciplined or corrected and that they began to lose their reverence for one another and for God.

We were so free that nothing was sacred any more and we began to lose the blessing of God. You can go that way in five minutes—it does not take long at all. You can come to the place where you hate the word "obedience" and you cannot stand any form of authority. You say, "No one is going to tell me what to do. I am free!" You will end up ten times more bound than you were at the start![1]

Many people today resent authority in any form. Our age has all the marks of a "lawless generation." Children disobey parents, parents cheat on their income tax and ignore traffic laws, parishioners defy pastors, students rebel against teachers and so it goes. Baptism in the Spirit and growth in the Spirit are marked by a rediscovery of the commandments and a new respect for authority as coming from God. One of the many things we can indeed rejoice about in this outpouring of the Spirit in our time is the new striving of so many of the children of God for order, God's order, in their lives. But a good question we might ask ourselves is: how will we even begin to know how to be obedient to the Father if we have not experienced obedience in our youth in the home as Jesus did, or if, as adults, we are having no experience of being obedient to those in authority over us?

Many people in our world today follow the dictum "if it feels right, do it." Yet this is completely at variance with the kind of life Jesus calls us to lead. The life He calls us to is one of submission to the Father and to His will as expressed in the commandments of God, the laws of His Church and all other manifestations of His will.

Many people today rebel at any semblance of authority as they feel it conflicts with the "equality" that is supposed to characterize all relationships. It is true that we are all equal in the sight of God. All of us are His children. But there is a hierarchy of relationships in the body of Christ. Not all are called to be hands. Not all are called to be feet. Not all are called to be heads. The rest of the body needs to be submissive to headship or the body won't function well.

People attending prayer meetings and getting baptized in the Spirit are grateful to know God loves them. But this isn't much of a foundation for building a Christian life and many people today are missing very basic formation in their lives. Young people don't reverence their parents. They think nothing of cheating on exams. "Everyone else does." Adults cheat on their income tax and pad their expense accounts. Many people's lives are just basically out of order, and baptism in the Spirit isn't enough. People desperately need teaching to be able to grow and mature as Christians. People need teaching on basic fundamentals of Christian living. People who do not get the teaching and formation they need after the baptism in the Spirit will soon revert to old habit patterns once the glow wears off.

The lives of the Saints provide teaching much needed in the areas of order, authority and obedience. The Saints were models of obedience. They excelled in obedience. And because they did, they experienced freedom—the freedom of the children of God.

All Saints patterned their lives on the life of Jesus and the entire life of Jesus could be summarized by saying that He did His Father's will. Jesus was obedient to the Father. "My food is to do the will of him who sent me, and to accomplish his work" (John 4:34). For years Jesus was obedient to his parents. "And he went down with them and came to Nazareth, and was obedient to them . . ." (Luke 2:51). Before His death, Jesus said to His Father ". . . not my will, but thine, be done" (Luke 22:42). Jesus also said ". . . whoever does the will of my Father in heaven is my brother, and sister, and mother" (Matt. 12:50). "Not everyone who says to me, 'Lord, Lord,' shall enter the kingdom of heaven, but he who does the will of my Father who is in heaven" (Matt. 7:21).

God provides for all our needs. The more the children of God begin to hunger to live under the rule and reign of God, the more will God honor that need and raise up men and women to whom He delegates and entrusts His authority. Sheep need shepherds and those desiring to live in submission in every area of their lives need people in headship to whom they may be submissive. Charles de Foucauld, who will probably be canonized one day and who was the inspiration for the foundation of the Little Brothers and Little

Sisters of Jesus, lived as a hermit in North Africa. Since he did not have a community of people to whom he could be submissive, he promised obedience to a French parish priest of exceptional holiness, Abbe Huvelin.[2] Foucauld expresses it this way:

> In Jesus, through obedience—for the more ardent my longing to do his will, the more I feel that the only security for me, uncertain and fearful as I am, is in obedience. So I bless Jesus in his manger, at the foot of which I stay as long as I can at this holy season, from where he has put me into your hands, my dear father, and I beseech you to guide me ever more clearly in all things, so that I do whatever is pleasing to God, and am prevented from doing anything displeasing to him. Everything you tell me to do, I will do—everything.[3]

For those who might not know Foucauld, who was murdered in the desert at Tamanrasset in 1916, the above passage might just reflect someone possessed of an insecure and fearful personality who needed healing. Foucauld was anything but insecure. Before he met the Lord, Foucauld was a French nobleman of whom a friend once wrote:

> The man who has never seen Foucauld in his room, wearing frog-fastened white flannel pajamas, comfortably resting on a chaise lounge or in a fine armchair, enjoying a delicious pate de foie gras and washing it down with choice champagne, doesn't know how much a man can enjoy his life.[4]

After his conversion and after he began to grow in docility to the Holy Spirit and love of the Lord, Foucauld wished never to transgress God's will.

Two examples of obedience come from the life of a Saint who was also a desert-dweller. One who was not a run-of-the-mill type was St. Simeon the Stylite. Simeon, born around 390 in Syria, lived much of his life on the top of a pillar, the last twenty being spent on

70

one raised more than sixty feet in the air. (Simeon's style is more than a little reminiscent of flagpole sitting which goes to show that this tendency was not just an oddity of the fourth century!) There were many pillar dwellers in Simeon's day, this phenomenon being confined to the Eastern Church. From his pillar Simeon became an evangelist with far-reaching influence. Thousands of people, Persians, Armenians, Iberians, thronged to see him and he exhorted the crowds twice a day. Emperors consulted him and asked his prayers. A monastery was organized around him as well as many charitable works.

Simeon lived this unusual life, which seemed to suit the mentality and environment of that age and which included much penance, prayer and fasting, until the age of sixty-nine. He was acclaimed a Saint, not for the many miracles he worked or the wisdom of his discourses, but due to the extraordinary manner in which he manifested the virtues of charity, patience and humility.

Two incidents in St. Simeon's life reflect a spirit of obedience, a spirit of submission, a willingness to be ordered under those in his life who were representatives of God's authority. Before ascending his first pillar [5] Simeon lived at the foot and then the top of Mount Telanissae. At the summit he made a little enclosure, which was roofless and gave no protection from the weather, and he chained his right leg to a rock. The vicar of the Patriarch of Antioch, Meletius, told Simeon that God's grace was sufficient to enable him to remain in his manner of life and that the bodily restraint was unnecessary. Simeon obediently sent for a smith and had the chains knocked off. A proud man would have argued with the vicar and claimed the certainty of some private inner revelation as a pretext for remaining in chains.

It was to remove himself from the multitudes seeking not only his prayers and advice, but to touch him, that led Simeon to construct the first pillar. Naturally this singular way of life was condemned by many and looked upon askance. To test Simeon's humility, an order was sent him in the name of the neighboring bishops and abbots to leave his pillar and give up his unusual way of life. At once Simeon prepared to descend. At this prompt expression of obedience Simeon was allowed to remain on his pillar with the permission and blessing of all.

At least twice in his life Simeon was called upon to obey ecclesiastical authority and give up *his way* of following the Lord. Very simply and humbly he obeyed. In 1 Samuel 15:22 we read, "To obey is better than sacrifice." "[Jesus] became obedient unto death, even death on a cross" (Phil. 2:8).

Most Christians are in situations every day that call for obedience: children to parents, students to teachers, parishioners to pastors, citizens to representatives of governmental authority, motorists to traffic laws, workers to supervisors, community members to the order of the community, priests to bishops, and so on. Pride inclines us to do our own will and not to wish to be directed by others. Obedience is opposed to pride.

Chapter five of St. Benedict's [6] famous rule for monasteries begins: "The first degree of humility is obedience without delay." Catherine of Siena wrote an entire treatise on obedience which forms part of her well-known *Dialogue*. St. Francis de Sales, famous Bishop of Geneva, in his treatise, *The Love of God*, gives three proofs or tests to discern whether inspiration comes from God or from Satan. The first is that in pursuing the proposed course we persevere in our vocation. This would mean that an inspiration to leave all and go to preach God's word in Iceland would be suspect if it was the inspiration of a married woman with twelve children and many obligations. The second test that a leading is from God is peace of soul in the recipient:

> The Holy Spirit is indeed violent, but there is a gentle charm, a peace about his violence. He came like a strong wind blowing at Pentecost, like thunder from heaven, yet he did not utterly disconcert the apostles; he scarcely disturbed them at all. The

fear they felt at the sound of his coming was but momentary; it was instantly followed by a calm assurance. That is why tongues of fire came to rest on each of them—as though finding and giving a sacred peace.[7]

The third test St. Francis de Sales lists is obedience to the Church and to superiors. St. Francis de Sales cites St. Simeon the Stylite as an example of obedience, and also St. Paul. In Acts 9:6 is recorded the instruction to St. Paul, ". . . rise and enter the city, and you will be told what you are to do." St. Paul was to obey Ananias.

Jesus blesses obedience. In 1673, St. Margaret Mary Alacoque, a Visitation sister, received revelations about the immense love of Jesus for mankind which resulted in devotion to the Sacred Heart of Jesus. To preserve Margaret Mary's spirit of littleness and to test her, her superior sometimes sent Margaret Mary, during the time of community meditation, to keep watch over a donkey in a meadow. Fr. Garrigou-Lagrange suggests that Margaret Mary in obeying made a better meditation in the meadow than she would have made in choir had she wished to go there contrary to her Superior's will.[8]

The new American Saint, Elizabeth Seton, was able to establish St. Vincent de Paul's Daughters of Charity in this country because God blessed her obedience. One day in 1808 she heard Jesus saying to her in a clear voice: "Go, address yourself to Mr. Cooper [a wealthy seminarian]; he will give you what is necessary to commence the establishment." The only obstacle that had been standing in the way of making such a foundation was lack of necessary funds.

Elizabeth consulted the priest who was her spiritual director. Her director said that the voice she heard might be her imagination and he forbade her to approach Mr. Cooper. The priest reasoned that if it was really God's will that Mr. Cooper provide the needed money, then God would make His will known to Mr. Cooper. Elizabeth could have argued and could have insisted that she knew the voice of the Lord. She could have approached Mr. Cooper anyway. But she obeyed. On the evening of the same day Mr. Cooper came to see the priest. God had put the desire in his heart to support the very kind of work that Elizabeth was envisioning. The priest confirmed that indeed God had spoken, the funds were forthcoming and Elizabeth began her life's work serving God as a Daughter of Charity.[9]

God blesses obedience. He blesses submission to authority, wives to husbands, children to parents, and so on. All Catholic religious orders have functioned with some pattern of authority and submission. Those who felt called by God into a fuller relationship with Him and yet did not feel drawn to—or (because of their obligations) could not enter—religious life, looked for a way or ways to practice obedience. A common way was to have a spiritual director. Sometimes, but not always, a person would make a promise to obey the director. Charles de Foucauld felt God was calling him to obey Abbe Huvelin. St. Elizabeth Seton obeyed her director.

Certainly the director-directed relationship can be abused, as can all headship-submission relationships. And the history of the Church knows of such examples. But God is a good God and if a person in good faith, gets into a headship-submission relationship with an unscrupulous head, God provides for or blesses the situation somehow.

Two examples of this readily spring to my mind. First, the sister in the convent in headship over St. Bernadette caused Bernadette much suffering but it also helped Bernadette to become holy. One might say Bernadette could have become holy without it, but who is really sure of that? God allowed the situation and Bernadette drew good from it. The other example comes from the life of St. Jane de Chantal. St. Jane made a vow of obedience to a spiritual director. This priest's direction, which encouraged St. Jane in making long vigils and doing penance, caused St. Jane much interior suffering. She had a nature which did nothing by halves and her urges to pray for long periods and multiply austerities should have been tempered and modified. Instead, this director increased the devotional practices. This priest also exacted four promises or vows from her. St. Jane was to obey him, not leave his direction, not divulge anything he told her, and not seek advice from anyone else. God brought St. Francis de Sales into St. Jane's life. Through a fortunate series of circumstances, St. Francis de Sales became St. Jane's director. Her peace of mind was restored under this bishop's wise guidance and St. Jane went on to found, with the bishop, a religious order.

Obedience or submission to authority pertains to the institutional element of the Church (one of the three ingredients in von Hugel's construct). Certainly in the minds of those not Catholic, the institutional element of Catholicism looms large while the intellectual and mystical/charismatic elements are less well-known or have been considered nonexistent by some critics. That Catholics could be baptized in the Spirit has come as a shock to some classical Pentecostals. "They were singing 'our' songs and exercising 'our' gifts. It was more than I could take," wrote Dr. Vinson Synan [10] about his visit to the 1972 International Conference on the Charismatic Renewal in the Catholic Church. Dr. Steve Durasoff, a professor at Oral Roberts University, commenting on Pentecostalism today wrote:

> They [Catholic Pentecostals] have found no credibility gap between the charismatic revival and structural forms which for Catholic Pentecostals, go hand in hand. Classic Pentecostals accept the validity of the Catholic's reception of the supernatural gifts of the Holy Spirit, although they still tend to be amazed at the very existence of such a thing as a Catholic Pentecostal. [11]

Dr. Durasoff cites examples from the early days of the charismatic renewal in the Catholic Church where bishops in a few localities laid restrictions on prayer groups. One group was given orders that all speaking in tongues was to cease along with any laying on of hands. The group was obedient and their numbers increased noticeably. The bishop lifted the ban in a few months. Another group was similarly restricted by a bishop and during the time of trial received this prophecy which Dr. Durasoff noted: "Bear in all patience what has happened to you. Obey those I have put over you. See the care I have for my flock." Here too the bishop eventually allowed free exercise of the spiritual gifts.[12]

It is precisely in this area of order and submission to authority that some see the chief contribution of Catholicism to those of other traditions in the charismatic renewal. Michael Harper, a priest of the Church of England and widely known teacher and writer, wrote in 1972:

> If I were to name the specifically Roman Catholic contribution to the charismatic renewal I would call it a concern for theological wholeness. There is a real effort to see the experience of being baptized in the Holy Spirit within the context of the whole experience of life as a Christian. . . . Catholics more than Protestants are concerned with the whole Church. A deep loyalty to the body which nurtured them not only preserves them from the vice of mudslinging but also makes them concerned about their bishops, their parishes, their fellow laymen. . . . The Protestant temptation is to hope that the official church structures do not interfere; the Catholic expectation is that the official church structures themselves become renewed. Already the fruit borne of this Roman loyalty has had its impact on Protestant brethren.[13]

Many in the charismatic renewal are experiencing a hunger to understand how to be obedient to the Father's will and many are seeing the necessity of there being some people who exercise spiritual authority while others are submissive to that authority. Many are seeing that a Church of all chiefs and no Indians won't work. At the 1975 Lutheran Charismatic Renewal Leaders Conference, Pastor Don Pfotenhauer of Minneapolis noted that the Church included many believers but few submitters. [14] Larry Christenson, head of the Lutheran Charismatic Renewal Service Committee, devoted a whole chapter to "Authority in the Body of Christ" in his book *A Message to the Charismatic Movement.* Christenson wrote:

> Perhaps the time has come for someone to say a good word for "authority," and even for "authoritarianism," rightly understood. Our culture has developed an almost Pavlovian response; we come up frothing at the mere mention of the words. And not altogether without cause. Our age has suffered through some frightening abuses of authoritarian power. Yet we need to ask ourselves whether reaction against bad authoritarianism validates a rejection of the authoritarian in our culture. . . . To this day, the authoritarian figure of Moses towers over the Judeo-Christian heritage. In the New Testament, the Apostle Paul did not shy away from speaking to the Corinthians in strong authoritarian tones threatening to come to them "with a rod." [15]

The investigation into the life of a prospective Saint which is part of the canonization process, examines submissiveness to authority in every area of the candidate's life. The investigation goes beyond merely establishing that the candidate was truly submissive to the Holy Father, local bishop, local pastor and in the case of a religious, the religious superior, in the event that the candidate was a religious. The process seeks to uncover underlying attitudes. How did the candidate evidence docility to the Holy Spirit and submissiveness; with servility, or with obstinacy—or with meekness and humility? Blessed Anne-Marie Javouhey, foundress of the Sisters of St. Joseph of Cluny, was unjustly and wrongfully censured by a bishop and for about two years she was not allowed to receive Communion. She patiently and heroically endured this trial which was a public rebuke as well as a private deprivation. When others made condemning remarks about the bishop, Blessed Anne-Marie did not allow one word of criticism to escape her lips.

The documents produced by Vatican Council II mention obedience in various places. Perhaps a section that might speak to the concern expressed by Larry Christenson is one which is included in the most controversial document of the council, the "Declaration on Religious Freedom." Christenson speaks of the need for authority in the Church [16] while at the same time pointing out that we have seen in our time awful abuses of authority. The "Declaration on Religious Freedom" states:

> Many pressures are brought to bear upon men of our day, to the point where the danger arises lest they lose the possibility of acting on their own judgment. On the other hand, not a few can be found who seem inclined to use the name of freedom as the pretext for refusing to submit to authority and for making light of the duty of obedience.
>
> Therefore, this Vatican Synod urges everyone, especially those who are charged with the task of educating others, to do their utmost to form men who will respect the moral order and be obedient to lawful authority. Let them form men too who will be lovers of true freedom—men, in other words, who will come to decisions on their own judgment and in the light of truth, govern their activities with a sense of responsibility, and strive after what is true and right, willing always to join with others in cooperative effort.[17]

Although the subtitle of this document is "On the Right of the

Person and of Communities to Social and Civil Freedom in Matters Religious," what is said reflects the traditional Catholic understanding of the need for submission to authority joined with the modern awareness of responsible freedom. The section on obedience and freedom in this document manifests the wisdom of the Spirit which is so often characterized by paradox. We must lose our life in order to keep it we are told in Matthew 10:39; 16:25, Mark 8:35 and Luke 9:24. When we are weak, we are strong says St. Paul (2 Corinthians 12:10). The footnote to the above quoted passage in the Abbott edition of the "Declaration on Religious Freedom" reads:

> The Council calls attention to the paradox of the moment. Freedom today is threatened; freedom today is itself a threat. Hence the Council calls for education both in the uses of freedom and in the ways of obedience. When freedom is truly responsible, it implies a rightful response to legitimate authority.[18]

The hunger people in the charismatic renewal are experiencing to know the will of the Father and to do it pertains to the *mystical/charismatic element* of the Church. The *intellectual element* of the Church in recent years has written reams on the relation of responsible decision-making to obedience, particularly in relation to the updating and renewal of the life of monks and nuns and of the vow of obedience. It remains, however, for authority to be recognized as legitimate and the *institutional element* of the Church to be appreciated. Not only that, those already in positions of authority in the Church and those the Lord is now raising up, need to properly exercise that authority. Otherwise there will be no active, effective headship for people to respond to and be submissive to.

Not only did Saints submit to the various manifestations of authority in the Church, those Saints who founded religious communities or who became heads of monasteries or orders, truly exercised their God-given authority and taught others in similar positions to do so by example, or by written word. How many of us know that gentle Francis of Assisi, encountering a brother who had come to see him without permission, had the brother's capuche (hood) thrown into a fire?[19] Francis taught that money and dung were of equal value and that money was to be shunned like the devil himself. How the Francis of the birds and flowers, too often seen only as a patron Saint of ecology, exercised headship when correcting someone, is illustrated by the following incident recorded in the same primary source material as the first related incident, in Celano's *Second Life of St. Francis.*

> It happened . . . one day that a certain secular person entered the church of St. Mary of the Portiuncula to pray, and he left some money near the cross as an offering. When he had gone, one of the brothers simply touched it with his hand and threw it on the window sill. The saint heard what the brother had done, and the brother, seeing that he was found out, hurried to ask pardon, and casting himself upon the ground he offered himself to stripes. The saint rebuked him and upbraided him most severely because he had touched the money. He commanded him to lift the money from the window sill with his mouth and to place it with his mouth on the asses' dung outside the walls of the place.[20]

Many people today in positions of authority are not exercising authority or do not know how to exercise it. One Catholic school in which I taught a few years ago had a rule which stated that students could not smoke in school or on campus. At a faculty meeting there was recognition of the fact that some students were smoking and only some teachers were enforcing the rule and punishing students who were found to be in violation. Teachers who were known not to enforce the rule were very popular with students who were smokers. At this particular faculty meeting, teachers who enforced the rule said that either the rule should be changed, or all the faculty should enforce it whether they agreed with it or not. At that juncture one of the teachers stood up and said emphatically, "I just want you to know that I am a teacher, not a policeman, and I will not be a policeman!" Her remark poignantly illustrated for me the distaste so many parents, pastors and teachers have for the exercise of the authority their position demands.

It could be that one of the reasons why members of some Catholic religious orders have been restlessly seeking "new" interpretations of obedience is that provincials and superiors general have abdicated responsibility and are not exercising authority. And the reason why some pastors, provincials, teachers, parents and religious superiors are not exercising authority may lie in the fact that they don't know where they are going. They have lost a sense of directedness and so can't lead anyone anywhere.

A spiritual writer much read in the charismatic renewal is the late Watchman Nee.[21] Addressing himself to this subject in a book called *Spiritual Authority,* Nee wrote: "For one to be in authority does not depend on his having ideas and thoughts: rather does it hinge on knowing the will of God. The measure of one's knowledge of God's will is the measure of his delegated authority."[22]

Successful and fruitful exercising of authority will depend on how well the one in authority knows God's will, which in turn depends on the depth of a person's communion with Him. Perhaps some in positions of authority in the Church today who are failing in their responsibility to exercise headship either do not have a personal relationship with God in Jesus, or they do not consider God as having a plan or vision for their order, institute, parish, family or diocese. They do not spend enough time with the Lord seeking His face, asking for His direction, getting a vision of how

He is working in His people today, and receiving knowledge of His will for general and specific situations. This is surely why all the Saints have stressed knowledge of God's will and the importance of subsequent discernment. He was training men for responsible positions in the Church and the key to exercising authority in the Lord is being able to discern His will. It is interesting to see many of Nee's ideas echoing centuries-old Catholic tradition. For example, there are many parallels between Watchman Nee's book on *Spiritual Authority* and *The Counsels to Religious (The Six Wings of the Seraph)* [23] by the Franciscan St. Bonaventure (1221-1274).

BONAVENTURE	NEE
. . . a superior must be prudent in his behavior and speech. . . . One who is expected to live as an example to many . . . needs great wisdom if he is to remain on the middle road, between being immoderately sad or merry, severe or lenient, friendly or distant, silent or garrulous. . . . (pp. 182-183)	Many legitimate things we [those in authority] cannot do and many lawful words we cannot speak. . . . Even our fellowship with brothers and sisters must have a limit beyond which we will neither be casual nor frivolous . . . an example to all. (p. 180)
A superior should also BE HUMBLE. His way of life must prove that he does not think highly of himself, and that he is not elated by his superiorship. Rather, he should be afraid of it, and bear it with a sense of duty, while much preferring to obey. (p. 166)	The condition for authority is a sense of incompetency and unworthiness. From the Bible we can conclude that God has never used a proud soul. (p. 176)
. . . the guide of souls must be principally intent upon acquiring this grace [the grace of devotion] which will always suggest to him that right course of action, help him to follow it, and keep him from straying. (p. 189)	Those who are God's delegated authority need to maintain close fellowship with God. There must be not only communication but also communion. . . . I must live in His presence, commune with Him continuously, and seek to know His mind. (pp. 119, 121)

All of the Saints in the body of Christ down through the ages have sought to be obedient to the Father, as Jesus was, because the Holy Spirit conforms us to His image. All Saints can say with St. Catherine of Siena in her *Dialogue:* "The truly obedient man always retains the desire of submission, and this desire is like an inward refrain of music."

Notes to Chapter 6

1. "After Tongues What?" by Simon Cameron, *New Wine*, June 1972.
2. Abbe Huvelin (d. 1910) was not only the spiritual father of de Foucauld, he was also a crucial figure in the life of von Hugel, who describes Huvelin in this way:

> There is before my mind with all the vividness resulting from direct personal intercourse and deep spiritual obligations, the figure of the Abbe Huvelin. . . . A distinguished Hellenist, a man of exquisitely piercing, humorous mind, he could readily have become a great editor or interpreter of Greek philosophical or patristic texts, or a remarkable Church historian. But this deep and heroic personality deliberately preferred "to write in souls," whilst occupying, during thirty-five years, a supernumerary, unpaid post in a large Parisian parish. There, suffering from gout in the eyes and brain, and usually lying prone in a darkened room, he served souls with the supreme authority of self-oblivious love. . . . (von Hugel, *Eternal Life*, T. & T. Clark, 1912, pp. 374-376).

There is a life of Huvelin by M. Th. Louis Lefever, *Abbe Huvelin: Apostle of Paris*, Burns & Oates, London, 1967.

3. Jean-Francois Six, Editor, *Spiritual Autobiography of Charles de Foucauld*, p. 104.
4. Jean-Francois Six, *Witness in the Desert*, quoted from front flap.
5. The first pillar was six cubits high (a cubit was a measure of between eighteen and twenty-two inches) and on it Simeon remained four years. The second pillar was twelve cubits high and was used for three years. The third was twenty-two cubits high and was in use for ten years. The last, used for twenty years, was forty cubits high.
6. St. Benedict was born about the year 480 and died about 547. He is known as the father of western monasticism. His *Rule* dominated western religious life for hundreds of years.
7. St. Francis de Sales, *The Love of God*, Book 8, Chapter 12.
8. *The Three Ages of the Interior Life* by R. Garrigou-Lagrange, O.P., Vol. II, p. 153.

9. William V. Dubourg, S.S., "Mystical Experience for Mother Seton, Rich Seminarian" in *The Tablet*, (Brooklyn) Sept. 11, 1975, p. 12.

10. Synan, *Charismatic Bridges*, p. 25. Of this experience Synan wrote: "The Lord did a mighty work in my heart that week that has continued to this day. For the first time in my life, I found myself praying and worshiping with people against whom I had harbored much prejudice and suspicion." (p. 26).

11. Steve Durasoff, *Bright Wind of the Spirit*, Prentice-Hall, Inc., Englewood Cliffs, New Jersey, 1972, p. 214.

12. *Ibid.*

13. Michael Harper, "Anglican Renewal," in *New Covenant*, May 1972, p. 5.

14. Mary Ann Jahr, "Lutheran Charismatic Renewal Leaders Conference, Following God's Plan for Renewal" in *New Covenant*, April 1975, p. 28.

15. Larry Christenson, *A Message to the Charismatic Movement*, Dimension Books, Bethany Fellowship, Minneapolis, 1972, pp. 100-101.

16. *Ibid.*, pp. 93-107. Christenson writes:

> Arising in protest against spiritual lethargy in the Church, revivals often look warily at anything that smacks of "order" or "office" as the sure corollary to spiritual death. . . . Without the gifts of the Holy Spirit freely manifested through a many-membered Body, the Church can all too easily become a museum piece. But without the Christ ordained ministers of authority, without Spirit-given structures to direct and shepherd the life, the fire of the Spirit can too easily become wild fire, and burn itself out in a short display of spiritual pyrotechnics. (p. 106)

17. Para. 8.

18. *Ibid.*

19. Thomas of Celano, "Second Life of St. Francis" in Marion A. Habig, Editor, *St. Francis of Assisi Omnibus of Sources*, p. 486. Celano describes the conclusion of the incident this way:

> . . . when no one withdrew the capuche, for they were frightened whenever the face of their father was even somewhat disturbed, the saint commanded it to be withdrawn from the flames; and it had not been harmed. Although the merits of the saint could bring this about, perhaps merit was not entirely lacking on the part of that brother. For the desire to see the most holy father had spurred him on, though discretion, the charioteer of virtues, was not in him.

20. *Ibid.*, pp. 417-418.

21. Watchman Nee was a Chinese Christian of Methodist Christian background who had a personal salvation experience in the early 1920s. He was part of a

movement in the 1930s that saw thousands of Chinese Christians receive the baptism in the Spirit and come together in hundreds of local Spirit-filled assemblies. Nee's insights into Scripture and his experiential knowledge of life in the Spirit are contained in many books. Some, such as *The Normal Christian Church Life* were intended to be books. Others are collections of talks he gave. Those who appreciate the *Spiritual Canticle*, inspired by the Song of Songs, of St. John of the Cross, will want to read Nee's devotional exposition of the Song of Solomon (*Song of Songs*, Christian Literature Crusade, Fort Washington, Penna., 1966). Nee was imprisoned by the Red Chinese in the late 1940s or early 1950s and was kept in solitary confinement. The only visitor permitted him through the years was his wife, Charity, who visited him once a month until she died in 1971. Nee died a year later.

22. Watchman Nee, *Spiritual Authority*, Christian Fellowship Publishers, Inc., New York, 1972.

23. *The Works of Bonaventure*, III, "The Six Wings of the Seraph," St. Anthony Guild Press, Paterson, N.J.

CHAPTER 7

Letters from Saints

Reading the letters of Saints is a wonderful way to get to know them. Letters reveal more than books and sermons written for public consumption. They often display a Saint's deep capacity for friendship, sense of humor and intellectual development. Letters also sometimes contain some of a Saint's best teaching, which is one of the reasons why, during the canonization process, the Church examines all extant correspondence of a prospective Saint, along with everything else he or she wrote.

One of the most well-known of Saints' letters is one St. Jerome [1] wrote which deals with a plan for the education of a little girl, Paula. It sounds like the Montessori method years before Maria Montessori ever lived. What is also unique is that Jerome was suggesting this for a girl. The beginning of the letter which does not deal with educational method is usually passed over. That section offers encouragement to those who might find themselves married to an unbeliever. It should be of interest to all in similar situations who are praying for their marriages to be transformed in the Lord. In the year 403 Jerome wrote to Paula's mother:

> You are the daughter of a mixed marriage, but as for Paula—why, her parents are none other than yourself and my dear Toxentius. Who would have credited the fact that in answer to a mother's promise, a Christian granddaughter should have been granted to Albinus, a pagan high-priest, that her grandfather should listen with delight to the little one

babbling Christ's Alleluia, and in his old age pillow on his breast a child vowed to God? The man who is surrounded by a crowd of Christian children and grandchildren is pretty well already a candidate for the faith. Yes, he may spit on this letter of mine and hold it up to ridicule, call me a blockhead and a fool, but his son-in-law did precisely the same thing before he too received the faith. Christians are made, not born. I tell you this, Laeta, most devoted daughter in Christ, to teach you not to despair of your father's salvation. The same faith that has earned you a child may win over your father also, and you may one day rejoice over the blessedness of your entire household. Remember God's assurance; "Things that are impossible with men are possible with God." (Luke 18:27) [2]

St. Therese of Lisieux (1873-1897) wrote many letters in haste while standing, with no eye to their ever being published. Venerable Francis Libermann (1802-1852), a renowned spiritual director, whose letters fill several volumes, wrote in the midst of much activity, often while suffering from a migraine headache. St. Peter of Alcantara (1499-1562) loved the Lord so much that in imitation of Christ's poverty Peter would write a letter on a small sheet leaving no room for another word even though rules of etiquette prescribed leaving a margin blank. St. Francis Xavier (1506-1552) was a missionary who traveled miles away from homeland and friends. His brother Jesuits corresponded with him and Francis cut the signatures from their letters and pinned them under his habit near his heart. St. Teresa of Avila (1515-1582), seldom reread the letters she wrote. She told her brother, Lorenzo, "You must not give yourself the trouble of rereading the letters you write me. I never reread mine. If a word here or there should have a letter missing, just put it in, and I will do the same for you, for your meaning is quite clear." [3] On the other hand, Mother Seton (1774-1821), American foundress of the Sisters of Charity, wrote to her friend Julianna Scott in 1799, "Very often when I read my letters over, I resolve not to send them for I find so many inaccuracies of expression. But Julia, there are no mistakes of meaning when they express how much I love you and how much I am your own." [4]

Besides the letters that Saints wrote to friends, relatives and people they were guiding, there exists correspondence between Saints—that of Saint to Saint. The old saying goes, "Water seeks its own level." Saints seem to recognize Saints and through their correspondence it is sometimes possible to see how they influence each other. St. Francis de Sales' letters to St. Jane de Chantal and to others are classics.

St. John of the Cross, Teresa of Avila's co-worker in the reform of their religious order, the Carmelites, wrote in one of his books, *Ascent of Mount Carmel*, that when God communicates something to a person, if the message is to be shared, He reveals with whom to share it. [5] A good example of this is a letter Teresa received from St. Peter of Alcantara. Teresa had written to him because the Lord inspired her to ask Peter's advice about founding the houses of the Carmelite reform in poverty. Here is an excerpt from Peter's letter to Teresa dated April 14, 1562:

Madam, may your soul be dilated by the Holy Spirit!
I received your letter, which was delivered to me by Senor Gonsalvo de Aranda. I definitely think that you are seeking advice from learned men about a question which it is quite out of their province to answer. If the matter concerned the law, or cases of conscience, it would be well to take the opinion of lawyers, or theologians, but no one should decide about a life of perfection except those who themselves live it, for as a rule people's conscience and opinions are no higher than their actions. As regards the evangelical counsels [6] we must not question whether it would be well to follow them or not, or

whether they are practicable or not; such a doubt contains the germ of infidelity. A counsel given by God cannot but be good nor can it be difficult to practise, save by the faithless and by those who . . . have little trust in Him.

If, then, you wish to practise Christ's counsel of greater perfection, do so, for He gave it not only to men but also to women, and He will see that all prospers with you.. . . If you see a want of necessities in communities of nuns who practise poverty, it is because they are poor against their will and because they cannot help it, and not because they wish to follow the counsel of our Lord.[7]

A few days after writing the letter Peter died. Some time later, when people were attempting to persuade Teresa to have an income for her foundation, she writes in her autobiography that Peter of Alcantara appeared to her to warn her against doing so.[8]

Peter's letter is somewhat reminiscent of something the Jesuit priest and theologian Bernard Lonergan said in 1968: ". . . religion is one thing, and theology is another. Most saints were not theologians, and most theologians were not saints. Theology stands to religion as economics does to business, as biology does to health, as chemistry to DuPont industries." [9]

Teresa of Avila persuaded John of the Cross (1542-1591) to introduce reform among the men of the Carmelite order. This he did despite great opposition. Twice John was kidnapped and locked up by unreformed Carmelite friars. Like Teresa, John left behind many writings on the spiritual life which earned for him title of Doctor of the Church.

Of the vast number of letters extant of St. Teresa, none remain of her correspondence with St. John of the Cross. Once when John was kidnapped, according to a contemporary biographer, he destroyed her letters so they would not fall into the wrong hands and be used in the dissension between reform and mitigated Carmelites. Another friar says that John used to carry Teresa's letters about with him in a pouch containing the Bible. He found comfort in them but one day, in an act of detachment, he burnt them.

We know Teresa had a delightful sense of humor. Not even austere John of the Cross was exempt from Teresa's teasing. This is evident in a judgment [10] given by St. Teresa upon various writings, including his. Towards the end of 1576 St. Teresa heard interiorly these words of Our Lord: "Seek thyself in Me." She asked for an explanation of these words from several people, including St. John of the Cross. The Bishop of Avila sent the written opinions to Teresa who was in Toledo. She responded by writing commentaries on the opinions. Julian de Avila, she said, "began well but finishes badly." She winds up her judgment of him by this final sentence, "However, I forgive him his errors, for he was not as lengthy as my Father Fray John of the Cross."

Then Teresa lets us know how she feels about St. John's answer:

This Father in his reply gives some remarkably sound doctrine for those who are thinking of following the Exercises practised in the Company of Jesus, but it is not our purpose. . . . God deliver me from people who are so spiritual that they want to turn everything into perfect contemplation, come what may. At the same time we are grateful for having been given so good an explanation of what we had not asked about. For this reason it is well to speak ever of God; we shall derive benefit from a place where we are least expecting to find it. [11]

Teresa's writings include *Interior Castle, The Way of Perfection, The Book of the Foundations*, and her *Life.* Her *Letters*, which fill several volumes, reveal thoughts on many matters including community structure which should be interesting to those involved in building Christian community. For example, Watchman Nee in *The Normal Christian Church Life* [12] discusses what questions should be decided by the entire Church or the total community and which matters should be taken care of by only part of the community or Church, that is, by the ministering members. He suggests that matters relating to the life of a community be decided by the total membership but those having to do with ministry be the concern of the ministering members.

Long before Watchman Nee, Teresa of Avila followed this same course. In her business of founding convents and writing books she ran into problems created by unreformed Carmelites, the Inquisition, and other factors. She pursued her ministry and carried on these many affairs without disturbing the peace of the sisters in her communities. In a letter [13] to her brother, Lorenzo De Cepeda, in January 1577, she tells him that the papal nuncio wants some statistics about her foundations. He wanted to know the location of her convents, number of nuns, where they were from, their ages, and so on. She asks her brother in Avila to tell this to the subprioress so that she can send Teresa all the details. Then Teresa adds, "The sisters need know nothing about it."

In the same letter Teresa shows how she felt about conserving resources. Her wisdom could be well applied to what is happening in some places where the Lord is raising up new Christian communities. [14] For example, today, a young person may receive the baptism in the Spirit, return to the sacraments, begin to spend time daily in prayer, make an act of commitment and join the prayer group or Christian community where he received the baptism in the Spirit and where his faith is strengthened. Perhaps he takes on some service such as setting up chairs for prayer meeting. At the same time he may be approached by his parish to teach CCD, or the choir director may ask him to sing at Sunday Mass. He may be asked to assist with the teen club or third order group. The Newman Club on his college campus may try to enlist his help. If the young person, who is immature in the Spirit and still weak in faith, gives in to any or some of these demands he may well wind up drained. If this is multiplied by very many of the members of that charismatic community or prayer group the life of the group will diminish along with its capacity to nourish and keep alive the faith of the participants or members.

In conserving the energy of a community and wisely using resources to have a healthy, powerful body for the Lord,[15] one runs the risk of being tagged "elite." Apparently this didn't bother Teresa. In this same letter to her brother she says: "People say that the nuncio requires this [the statistics on her convents] in order that he may constitute us as a separate province, but I fear that he wishes our sisters to go to other communities to reform them. This would not be well for us; it is enough that we should help those of our own Order."

While we're on the subject of St. Teresa, it might be fun to mention here that in a letter to St. Margaret Mary Alacoque, Blessed Claude de la Colombiere relieves her mind with the assurance that, even though she has been advised to read St. Teresa's life, she shouldn't worry about reading it if she doesn't feel attracted to it.[17]

From St. Teresa of Avila, Spain, the "big" Teresa, let's shift to the "little" Teresa, St. Therese of Lisieux, France (1873-1897), also a Carmelite. Most people, commenting on her life, wind up saying that the only thing extraordinary about Therese was the way she did very ordinary things. Under obedience she wrote her autobiography, *The Story of A Soul*. This account of her life has influenced thousands although she lived only twenty-four years, nine of them in a Carmelite convent. Her letters, together with other fragments of writing, number 247. We have already noted that Therese often wrote standing up, in haste. One of her letters to her sister Celine ends this way, "I have no more ink, I have been obliged to spit into the inkwell to make some; that makes you laugh, doesn't it?"

In her last letter [19] to Pere Roulland, a missionary in China, she wrote:

> . . . When you get this letter, I shall pretty surely have left the earth. The Lord, in His infinite mercy will have opened His Kingdom to me, and I shall be able to draw upon infinite treasures and shower them on souls dear to me. . . . Brother, I feel I shall be much more useful to you in Heaven than on earth.
>
> I am perfectly sure I shall not stay inactive in Heaven, my desire is to go on working for the Church and for souls, that is what I keep asking God. . . .
>
> What attracts me to the Homeland of Heaven is the call of Jesus, the hope that I may at last love Him as I have so longed to love Him, and the thought that I shall bring a multitude of souls to love Him, who will bless Him for all eternity.
>
> Brother, you will not have to send me the list of things I can do for you in Heaven, but I guess them; and in any event you will have but to whisper them and I shall hear you and faithfully bear your messages to Our Lord, to our Immaculate Mother, to the Angels and the Saints you love. . . .[20]

This excerpt from one of Therese's letters shows her great faith, hope, and love and belief in intercessory prayer and the communion of Saints.

Letters of an entirely different kind but reflecting the same virtues are those of Venerable Francis Libermann. His letters of spiritual direction have been published recently by Duquesne University Press and are a wonderful source of teaching on guidance. Venerable Francis was born Jacob, son of Lazarus Libermann, rabbi of Saverne, Alsace, in 1802. He was converted to Catholicism and was baptized in 1826 taking the name of Francis Mary Paul. He then sought to become a priest and entered a seminary but he suffered from epilepsy, and so was barred from major orders. He founded the Congregation of the Holy Heart of

Mary and was finally admitted to ordination and became a priest in 1841. In 1848 his congregation merged with that of the Holy Ghost and Francis became Superior General of the Holy Ghost Fathers. He died in Paris in 1852 and his cause of beatification was introduced in 1876. On June 19, 1910, the Holy See issued the decree declaring that Venerable Francis Libermann had practiced the Christian virtues in an heroic fashion.

In his letters, Francis is very direct. One priest with whom he corresponded was the Bursar of the Sulpician Seminary of Issy. In 1838 Francis wrote to Fr. Francis Telles to tell him that he thought that he was neglecting the people who came to him for guidance, often getting rid of them in a hurry. He also commented on the way Fr. Telles formed his opinions regarding the seminarians:

> I believe that in evaluating the seminarians of your community, you take too much into consideration: their talents, their science, their birth, their connections and the exquisite politeness that results from a polished secular education. It happens even sometimes that you manifest these partialities outwardly. . . . If we would judge in a holy manner and in God, we should be guided by the principles of Our Lord, and measure everybody with the yardstick of the Gospel.[21]

Venerable Francis was speaking the truth in love.

The following letter from an earlier century to the mother of a novice is a masterpiece. Leaders or coordinators of basic Christian communities emerging from the charismatic renewal probably sometimes feel like writing a similar letter to one or both parents of a young person who has moved into a household.[22]

Rome, 28 January 1554

The sovereign grace and eternal love of Christ our Lord be always with us to our help and favour.

I have received a letter from Your Ladyship dated the twelfth of this month in which you show a desire that your son,

95

Ottaviano, should be moved to Naples, for the sake of your health which you think would be improved by seeing him.

I think Your Ladyship will already have understood that in anything in which I can serve and comfort you without going against the will of God our Lord, I shall be most ready to do so. . . . Now because I think it would be against the divine will I cannot consent to have him brought to Naples now until he is more resolute and Your Ladyship calmer and more content with your son's choice. I cannot think that for the bodily or spiritual health of Your Ladyship the presence of your son is necessary; because, to believe this, would not only be a slur on Your Ladyship but also on God's high Majesty, for it would then appear that God had no other way of healing Your Ladyship in body and soul than our falling into disorder and committing sin, for at this time to bring Your Ladyship and your son together would bring him into temptation. . . .

May His divine and sovereign goodness grant us all grace always to know His holy will and to follow it out perfectly.

Ignatius Loyola ²³

Notes to Chapter 7

1. St. Jerome (c. 342-420) studied Scripture under St. Gregory Nazianzen. In 382 he was secretary to Pope Damasus in Rome. He is remembered chiefly for his work in revising the existing Latin versions of the Scripture. Almost the whole of the Latin Bible called the Vulgate was either translated or worked over by St. Jerome.
2. Letter no. 33 in *Letters from the Saints.*
3. *Ibid.*, p. 4.
4. *Letters of Mother Seton to Mrs. Julianna Scott*, Rt. Reverend Msgr. Joseph B. Code, p. 8.
5. St. John of the Cross, *Ascent of Mount Carmel*, II, 22, 9.
6. Poverty, chastity and obedience.
7. *Monumenta Historica Carmeli Teresiani* ed. Eulogio Pacho *et al.* Rome, Teresianum, 1973, I 17-19.
8. Regarding posthumous appearances, like all visions, they can come from one of

three sources. They can be genuine like the visions of Moses and Elijah who appeared with Jesus at the transfiguration on Mt. Tabor, or they can come from our own psyche and be an hallucination or they can come from Satan. To categorize all visions or all posthumous appearances as being demonic in origin would condemn what happened on Mt. Tabor or such happenings as the posthumous appearance of C.S. Lewis described in J.B. Phillips' *Ring of Truth*.

9. Bernard Lonergan, S.J., "Belief Today," a paper read to a meeting of the American Graduate Commission of Pax Romana (Pittsburgh, March 16, 1968) reprinted in *Catholic Mind*, May 1970, and appearing under the title "Belief: Today's Issue" in *A Second Collection*, Westminster Press, Philadelphia, 1974, pp. 87-99.

10. In a footnote to his introduction to this judgment, Allison Peers says that the term "judgment" used here recalls a burlesque ceremony held in Spanish universities before a candidate received a doctor's degree. The candidate would be eulogized in fun and then attacked by professors and other students. This is why Peers thinks Teresa adopts a light, ironical tone in this judgment.

11. *Complete Works of St. Teresa*, edited by Allison Peers, Vol. III, pp. 266-268.

12. *The Normal Christian Church Life*, Watchman Nee, International Students Press, Washington, D.C., 1969, p. 31. Nee is speaking of the "local church" and we are speaking of a religious community or community within the church although the institutional element of the world-wide Church could probably find Nee's thoughts of value.

13. *The Letters of St. Teresa*, Benedictines of Stanbrook Edition, Vol. II, pp. 190-199.

14. "Communities like the new charismatic communities have been common throughout the history of the Church. As renewal movements have appeared and grown, the people involved have collected to form communities within the Church where they could live a life permeated by the movements' ideals—renewal communities. The ascetic movement produced the earliest monasteries and convents; the mendicant movement produced the great religious orders of Franciscans and Dominicans. Today, renewal communities are developing not only within the charismatic renewal, but also as part of the movement of *communidades de base* in the Latin countries of Europe and America. It seems to be almost a sociological law: renewal movements produce renewal communities." Stephen B. Clark, *Unordained Elders and Renewal Communities*, Paulist Press, 1976, p. 4.

15. Refer to Chapter 2, footnote 15.

16. See above, footnote 12.

17. *Faithful Servant* (Spiritual Retreats and Letters of Blessed Claude La Colombiere) Letter 51. Mme. Acarie, Blessed Mary of the Incarnation, a leading figure in the renewal of the Church in France in the seventeenth century also was initially

not attracted to Teresa of Avila's account of her life with its visions and other phenomena. Mme. Acarie, however had a vision herself—of none other than St. Teresa—who requested that Mme. Acarie bring Teresa's reformed Carmelites to France. This came to pass.

18. *Collected Letters of St. Therese of Lisieux*, edited by Abbe Combes, Letter CXXI to Celine.

19. At the time Therese was suffering from the tuberculosis which took her life.

20. *St. Therese*, Letter CCXXV, (Combes).

21. *Spiritual Letters to Clergy and Religious*, Vol. 2, pp. 110-111.

22. A network of households forms the basic structure of most of the Christian communities arising out of the Charismatic renewal. Each household is a group of committed Christians living under the same roof and accepting a common discipline. For an account of one such community see Mary Ann Jahr "An Ecumenical Christian Community: The Word of God Ann Arbor, Michigan," *New Covenant*, February 1975, pp. 4-8.

23. *Letters from the Saints*, pp. 139-140.

CHAPTER 8

The Saints and Prayer

One thing is certain, Saints prayed. They prayed a lot. Just as Jesus would go apart into a desert place or up a mountain to spend hours communing with His Father, all those who love Jesus have done likewise. They have taken to heart Jesus' words that one "ought always to pray and not lose heart" (Luke 18:1), and to *daily* ask for one's bread. St. Paul counseled "pray constantly" (1 Thess. 5:17), and this theme of continual prayer is expressed elsewhere: "Be constant in prayer" (Rom. 12:12); "Pray at all times in the Spirit, with all prayer and supplication" (Eph. 6:18); "I desire then that in every place the men should pray . . ." (1 Tim. 2:8); "Continue steadfastly in prayer . . ." (Col. 4:2).

Early in the life of the Church the use of short but frequent prayers was common. These brief prayers have been variously called aspirations, ejaculatory prayers or brief elevations of the soul. The Prayer of Jesus, a prayer form of the Eastern Church is this kind of prayer. Most people baptized in the Spirit seem to find this prayer form second nature as they find themselves saying "Praise You, Jesus!" or "I love You, Jesus" over and over throughout the day. St. Teresa of Avila recommended this: "In the midst of our occupations we should retreat within ourselves, be it only for an instant, as a reminder of Him who keeps us company." (*Way of Perfection*, Ch. 31.)

The tradition of spending some portion of the day in meditation or contemplation is an old one also. This is the kind of prayer Jesus

99

spoke about when He said to go to an inner room, shut the door and pray to the Father in secret (Matt. 6:6).

Strictly speaking, meditation is not prayer at all but rather is preparation for prayer or pious reflection. It is often called the first degree of mental prayer or discursive prayer. In meditation one applies memory, imagination, and intellect to a pious subject such as some aspect of the life of Jesus. Hopefully a period of such reflection will precipitate a conversation with Jesus or will elicit acts of the will, acts of love, acts of contrition. ". . . Meditation is simply a thought that we welcome again and again, that we harbour intently in our minds, in order to prompt our wills to give way to emotions which are holy or to make resolutions which are good." (St. Francis de Sales, *The Love of God*, Bk. 6, Ch. 1.)

Discursive prayer eventually gives way to affective prayer, and then to various types of infused prayer. This means that the kind of prayer in which the mind is active with thoughts gradually yields to a kind of prayer where the heart expresses ardent love for God. The head begins to dwell in the heart. With the passage of time one may begin to experience a form of prayer which is a loving attention towards God. The will, the memory and thoughts are captivated by God and He teaches and refreshes and infuses into the one praying, a loving knowledge of Himself. The names or categories may vary, but what is certain is that one's prayer life eventually becomes more simple, more passive, and less active.

The prayer of many people consists of simply being before the Lord and making acts of love. Some could give the same description of prayer that it is said the uneducated simple farmer gave the Cure of Ars when he asked him what he did while he sat for hours in church. The peasant replied, "I look at Him and He looks at me." Prayer in tongues is often used as an aid to recollection at the beginning of one's prayer time and used again and again in conjunction with aspirations when one's mind wanders or is disturbed by distractions.

Prayer is not all sitting and loving. It is often a time of suffering, of breaking, of changing and of growing. It is a time of bringing our life into the Lord's presence for Him to shape it and mold it. "Prayer is not being too heavenly minded to be of any earthly use," writes Rev. William Davies in *Gathered Into One*. "It means thinking about the issue involved in the presence of God and acknowledging that He knows best. It means emptying one's mind in His presence of all prejudice. It means asking God to enable one to listen to His voice. . . ." [1]

The chief thing I think the Saints can teach us about prayer is fidelity and perseverance. Sometimes prayer is full of consolation and an hour seems like ten minutes. But occasionally prayer is arid like a desolate landscape and ten minutes seem like an hour. Do we remain faithful and sit or kneel there content with whatever prayer the Lord sees fit to send us, or do we give up before the allotted time we have set aside for daily prayer is over?

Last year a friend of mine complained to a priest she knew, that sitting in church for an hour a day, which had been pure heaven for months, was now a chore. The priest told her that many people stay with Christ for the joyful mysteries [2] but leave Him when the sorrowful mysteries begin. Without fidelity during the sorrowful mysteries, one won't reach the glorious mysteries.

St. Francis of Assisi often spent the night in prayer, sometimes repeating an aspiration such as "O God, Thou art my God and my All!" St. Vincent de Paul (1580-1660), the friend of the poor, one of those through whom the Church in France was renewed in the seventeenth century, spent five or six hours daily in prayer. St. Francis Xavier (1506-1552), Jesuit missionary to the Far East, a Saint who seems to have manifested many charismatic gifts including prophecy, spent much of the night in prayer. St. Peter of Alcantara has been a favorite of night watchmen because of his incredible vigils. St. Colette of Corbie was a Poor Clare abbess of the fifteenth century and contemporary of St. Joan of Arc, St.

Vincent Ferrer and St. John Capistran. For more than three years she devoted herself to prayer, living as a recluse, walled into two rooms attached to her parish church of Notre Dame in Corbie, until the Lord revealed to her that she was to leave her anchorhold and work for the reform of the Franciscan order. St. Ignatius Loyola, the founder of the Jesuits, when asked how he would feel if the pope suppressed his order, replied, "A quarter of an hour of prayer and I should think no more about it!"

Many of the Saints wrote about prayer. The works of the Fathers of the Church, St. Ambrose, St. Augustine, and St. Gregory the Great are full of teachings on prayer. St. Bonaventure, St. Thomas Aquinas, and St. Catherine of Siena wrote about prayer. The two leaders of the Carmelite reform, St. Teresa of Avila and St. John of the Cross each wrote several books on prayer, tracing its normal development in a soul generously given to God. There have been so many Saints who have left us teaching on the when, where, how and why of prayer that it would be impossible to list them all here.[3]

One thing all Christians baptized in the Spirit have in common is that they are led to pray or pray more than they did before. Praying is like breathing. If we don't breathe, and breathe often, we die. If we don't pray, and pray regularly, we die spiritually. It is possible to be baptized in the Spirit and still wind up spiritually dead some time later. One common way we can begin to kill the life of the Spirit within us is to pray only when we feel like it. The Saints counsel us to establish regular habits of daily prayer which we remain faithful to whether we feel like it or not.

Think of how many books have been published recently on nutrition and good eating habits and how avidly they are read by so many people. We should just as eagerly read the advice of Saints on how to maintain and increase spiritual health. Customs may change but spiritual biology remains pretty much the same. Humility, charity and patience are in style in any age. We must guard against getting so caught up in the "newness" of what God is doing today, that we forget that there is also an "oldness" to what He is doing. He has been gathering people to Himself since the beginning of time and we can only benefit from the reflections of those who have gone before. The teaching of the Saints on prayer is available for us to profit from. To disdain it because it is "old" would be foolish as well as prideful.

This chapter concludes with prayers written by four quite different people: Elizabeth of the Trinity and Charles de Foucauld, both candidates for canonization, St. Gertrude the Great and Symeon the New Theologian, a great reformer and teacher of the Eastern Church. Symeon (949-1022) is famous in the Eastern Church but has remained for the most part unknown in the West until recently. Hilda Graef [4] points out that Pourrat in his classic four-volume *History of Spirituality* only gives Symeon a footnote. Symeon should be of special interest to those seeking to integrate the charismatic renewal with traditional spirituality.

For Symeon the mystical life was not to be considered extraordinary. He stressed the conscious possession of grace which he describes as the "baptism of the Holy Spirit." He writes: "He who knows that signs and wonders happen within him is truly a God-bearer." Symeon felt that the Christian must know that he has received the pledge of the Spirit; for the Son of God has come to earth to "unite us to himself consciously through his Holy Spirit." Symeon advised those who had not yet received what he called "the pledge of the Spirit" to make efforts to obtain it.

Symeon apparently ran into conflict over his teaching with the Church of his day. After living for a time as a monk in the famous monastery of the Studios near Constantinople, Symeon joined St. Mamos, a smaller monastery in the neighborhood. He was ordained a priest and was elected abbot at the age of thirty-one. Controversy arose when Symeon began saying that the teaching authority of the Church belonged to those who had experienced revelations rather than to ecclesiastical authorities. Also, regarding the sacraments, what mattered to Symeon was the subjective experience not the objective action involved in their celebration. Tears of compunction were for him a "second baptism" more efficacious than the first baptism of water and oil.

In 1009 Symeon was finally condemned by the patriarch and the Holy Synod, and exiled from Constantinople. He went to Chrysopolis where he was joined by a group of his disciples. Symeon was later rehabilitated but his experience points out the importance of seeing that the baptism in the Spirit is *not* another sacrament and understanding that baptism in the Spirit belongs to life in the Spirit while the sacraments belong to the means or economy of salvation.

Fr. Simon Tugwell reasons that in spite of terminological similarity, Symeon is much closer to Wesley than to the Pentecostals. "His concern for spiritual efficacy leads him seriously to underrate sacramental objectivity (he does this in connection with ordination and confession too, though his doctrine of the eucharist is objective and realist in the extreme). He leaves himself wide open to the charge of mystical subjectivism, as his critics and enemies were quick to point out." Tugwell concludes, "However, if we discount this, making the necessary allowances, I think we shall find that he has much to teach us." [5]

I have included Symeon because of his great devotion to the Holy Spirit. This prayer to the Third Person of the Trinity is one of the most beautiful ever written. The prayer of Sr. Elizabeth of the Trinity is one often said by many Catholics, particularly religious.

Sister Elizabeth died in 1906 at the age of twenty-six after a religious life of five years in the Carmel of Dijon. For one not yet declared venerable, Elizabeth's widespread influence is amazing. There are a number of books on her life and writings, including one by Hans Urs von Balthasar. Elizabeth is characterized by her powerful sense of the indwelling of the Blessed Trinity.

Charles de Foucauld was killed in Africa ten years after Sr. Elizabeth died. His prayer of abandonment, which characterized his whole life, has become as well known as Sr. Elizabeth's prayer to the Trinity.

The last prayer is one of many similar prayers written by St. Gertrude the Great of Helfta in Saxony (c. 1256-1302). St. Gertrude, to whom St. Teresa of Avila had a great devotion, deserves to be better known. A nameless orphan at the age of five, she was left with the Benedictine nuns at Helfta where she spent the rest of her life. She has often been confused with her abbess, Gertrude von Hackenborn. Sr. Mary Jeremy, this Saint's biographer, writes:

> The only woman in Germany called "the Great," St. Gertrude of Helfta is at once known and unknown. Many churches are dedicated to her; she is quoted in books on mysticism; her role in the development of the devotion to the Sacred Heart is acknowledged. Besides these perennial reminders of the saint, there are some references to her in unlikely places; Mauriac, writing in the Saturday Evening Post series "Adventures of the Mind," quotes from her Exercise; Maritain in his correspondence with Jean Cocteau writes, "St. Gertrude wanted to recover all love for Jesus," and then adds a long passage from her *Legatus;* two German scholars, H. Grossler and W. Preger, insist that the saint was really a pre-Reformation Protestant, basing their argument chiefly on her devoted study of the Scriptures. . . . Ledos, her French biographer observes, their efforts to claim her for themselves are a tribute to the attraction exerted by her . . . spirit.[6]

PRAYER TO GOD, THE HOLY SPIRIT [7]

Come, true light,
Come, eternal life,
Come, secret of hiddenness.

Come, delight that has no name.

Come, unutterableness.

Come, O presence, forever fleeing from human nature.

Come, everlasting jubilee.

Come, light without end.

Come, awaited by all who are in want.

Come, resurrection of the dead.

Come, mighty one, forever creating, recreating, and renewing with a mere wave of Thy hand.

Come, Thou who remainest wholly invisible, for none ever to grasp or to caress.

Come, Thou who flowest in the river of hours, yet immovably stayest above it, who dwellest above all heavens, yet bendest to us who are bowed down.

Come, most longed-for and most hallowed name: to express what Thou art,
    to comprehend how Thou art, and how Thou existest is forever denied to us.

Come, perpetual joy.

Come, unwitherable wreath.

Come, O purple raiment of our Lord and God.

Come, girdle, clear as crystal and many-colored with precious gems.

Come, inaccessible refuge.

Come, Thou whom my poor soul desireth and hath desired.

Come, lonely one, to the lonely one—for lonely I am, as Thou canst see.

Come, Thou who hast made me solitary and forlorn on earth.

Come, Thou who hast become my longing, for that thou hast ordained that I must needs long for Thee whom no human breath has ever reached.

Come, my breath and my life.

Come, joy, glory, and my incessant delight.

I give Thee thanks that without merging or losing Thyself in my nature, Thou art yet one spirit with me, and while Thou remainest God, high above everything, Thou hast become everything to me.

Ineffable nourishment, never to be withdrawn, pouring forth unceasingly into the lips of my spirit and aboundingly filling my inner self!

I give Thee thanks that Thou hast become for me a day without evening and a sun without setting:

Thou, who hast no place to hide, as Thou fillest the universe with Thy power.

Never hast Thou hidden from anyone; we, however, hide from Thee always, if we dare not appear before Thy Face.

And where also shouldst Thou hide, Who hast nowhere a place to rest?

Or why shouldst Thou hide, Who dost not shrink nor shy away from anything in all the world?

Ah, Holy Lord—make an abode in me, dwell in me, and till my departure leave me not, leave not your servant;

That I too, may find myself after death in Thee, and reign with Thee, O God, who reignest over everything.

Remain with me, O Lord, do not forsake me.

Strengthen me interiorly, so that I may be unmoved at all times; and protect me by dwelling in me: that, although dead I may live in contemplating Thee, and although poor, may be rich in the possession of Thee.

Thus I shall be mightier than all kings:

Eating and drinking Thee, and at chosen hours wrapping myself in Thee, I shall enjoy unspeakable bliss.

For Thou art all Good, all Beauty, all Beatitude,
And Thine is the glory of the universe, Thine, with the Father and
the Son, for ever and ever. Amen.

Symeon, the New Theologian

PRAYER OF SISTER ELIZABETH OF THE TRINITY [8]

O my God, Trinity Whom I adore! Help me to become utterly
forgetful of self, that I may bury myself in Thee, as changeless and
as calm as though my soul were already in eternity. May nothing
disturb my peace or draw me out of Thee, O my immutable Lord!,
but may I at every moment penetrate more deeply into the depths
of Thy mystery!

Give peace to my soul, make it Thy heaven, Thy cherished
dwelling place, Thy home of rest. Let me never leave Thee there
alone, but keep me there, all absorbed in Thee, in living faith,
adoring Thee and wholly yielded up to Thy creative action!

Oh my Christ, Whom I love, crucified by love, fain would I be the
bride of Thy heart; fain would I cover Thee with glory and love
Thee . . . until I die of very love! Yet I realize my weakness and
beseech Thee to clothe me with Thyself, to identify my soul with all
the movements of Thine Own. Immerse me in Thyself; possess me
wholly; substitute Thyself for me, that my life may be but a
radiance of Thine own. Enter my soul as Adorer, as Restorer, as
Savior!

O Eternal Word, Utterance of my God! I long to pass my life in
listening to Thee, to become docile, that I may learn all from Thee.
Through all darkness, all privations, all helplessness, I crave to
keep Thee ever with me and to dwell beneath Thy lustrous beams.
O my beloved Star! so hold me that I cannot wander from Thy
light!

O Consuming Fire! Spirit of Love! descend within me and reproduce in me, as it were, an incarnation of the Word; that I may be to Him another humanity wherein he renews His Mystery!

And Thou, O Father, bend down toward Thy poor little creature and overshadow her, beholding in her none other than Thy Beloved Son in Whom Thou hast set all Thy pleasure.

O my "Three," my All, my Beatitude, Infinite Solitude, Immensity wherein I lose myself, I yield myself to Thee as Thy prey. Bury Thyself in me that I may be buried in Thee, until I depart to contemplate in Thy Light the abyss of Thy greatness!

PETITION TO JESUS [9]

O tender Jesus, full of pity and mercy, who never despisest the sighing of the wretched, to thee I betake myself, imploring thy clemency. Speak thou for me, supply thou for me; for I confess unto thee all my sins. By the sinless tears of thy most glorious eyes, wash away all the stains of my sinful eyes. By the gentle pity of thy blessed ears, wash away all the iniquities of my sinful ears. By the thrilling energy of the sweet words of thy blessed lips, wash away all the offences of my polluted lips. By the perfection of thine actions and by the wounds in thy hands, wash away all the offences of my impious hands. By the aching weariness of thy blessed feet, and by the cruel holes of the nails, wash away all the defilement of my sinful feet. By the pure intention of thy most holy thoughts, and by the glowing love of thy pierced Heart, wash away all the guiltiness of my evil thoughts and of my wicked heart. By the matchless innocence of thy life, and by thy unspotted holiness, destroy all the foulness of my corrupt life. By the priceless fountain of thy most Precious Blood, wash away, cleanse and efface every defilement of my heart and soul, that by thy most holy merits I may be found clean from sin, and be henceforward enabled to keep all thy commandments perfectly and spotlessly. Amen.

St. Gertrude, the Great

PRAYER OF ABANDONMENT [10]

Father,

I abandon myself into your hands; do with me what you will. Whatever you may do, I thank you: I am ready for all, I accept all. Let only your will be done in me, and in all your creatures—I wish no more than this, O Lord.

Into Your hands I commend my soul; I offer it to you with all the love of my heart.

For I love you Lord, and so need to give myself,

To surrender myself into your hands, without reserve,

and with boundless confidence.

For you are my Father.

Brother Charles of Jesus

Notes to Chapter 8

1. William R. Davies, *Gathered Into One*, The Faith Press, Morehouse-Barlow Company, Inc., New York, 1975.
2. This is a reference to a Roman Catholic prayer form, the Rosary. The mind dwells on events in the life of Jesus or Mary while certain vocal prayers are repeated.
3. See Fr. O'Connor's footnote in the chapter on "Pentecost and Traditional Spirituality" in his book *The Pentecostal Movement in the Catholic Church*, on p. 183 for a list of sources on this subject. See also Louis Bouyer's notes on the great classics of the spiritual life at the end of *Introduction to Spirituality*.
4. Hilda Graef, *The Story of Mysticism*, pp. 129-134.
5. Simon Tugwell, O.P., *Did You Receive the Spirit?* Darton, Longman & Todd, London, 1972, p. 53.
6. Sister Mary Jeremy, O.P., *Scholars and Mystics: St. Gertrude the Great*, Henry Regnery Company, Chicago, 1962, p. iii.

7. M.L. Shrady, ed., *Come, South Wind, A Collection of Contemplatives*, Pantheon Books, 1957, pp. 134-136.

8. M.M. Philipon, *The Spiritual Doctrine of Sister Elizabeth of the Trinity*, The Newman Press, Westminster, Md., 1935, pp. 53-54.

9. *Prayers of St. Gertrude and St. Mechtilde*, H.F. Steel Book Shop, Philadelphia, Pennsylvania, 1917.

10. Supplied by the Little Sisters of Jesus, Washington, D.C.

CHAPTER 9

Voices and Visions

A certain female visionary told the fifteenth-century priest John Gerson that, while contemplating God, her mind had been annihilated and then re-created. Gerson asked her, "How do you know?" She answered, "I experienced it!" Such encounters inclined Gerson to belittle even the revelations of Sts. Bridget of Sweden and Catherine of Siena. Gerson also relates that someone was always receiving a revelation about becoming the pope. "One man in particular believed himself predestined first to become pope and then the Anti-Christ, so that he contemplated killing himself in order to save Christendom!"[1]

During certain periods in history, especially those of widespread revival and reform, for every Teresa of Avila, there were hundreds or perhaps thousands of pseudo-visionaries causing havoc in the Church and making God's Word and Christianity a thing of ridicule.

Sometimes a person would claim a vision of Jesus or His Mother and would insist that he or she had been entrusted with a message for mankind. In such cases the Church made a scrupulous investigation. The fact that she made any investigation at all shows how open the Church has always been to the possibility of divine intervention and explains the Catholic Church's watchful openness to the charismatic renewal—an occurrence which has astounded many Protestants and classical Pentecostals.

One case the Church investigated was that of St. Margaret

Mary Alacoque (1647-1690). Margaret Mary belonged to an enclosed French order, the Visitation nuns, who were founded by St. Francis de Sales. Margaret Mary was the contemporary of Corneille, Racine, Moliere and Fenelon, in her native France and of Milton and Donne in England. From revelations made to her by our Lord in 1673-75, Margaret Mary spread devotion to the Sacred Heart of Jesus. Here in her own words she describes one of the visions:

> The Blessed Sacrament was exposed, and I was experiencing an unusually complete state of recollection, my senses and faculties utterly withdrawn from their surroundings, when Jesus Christ, my kind Master, appeared to me. He was a blaze of glory—his five wounds shining like five suns, flames issuing from all parts of his human form, especially from his divine breast which was like a furnace, and which he opened to disclose his utterly affectionate and lovable heart, the living source of all those flames. It was at this moment that he revealed to me the indescribable wonders of his pure love for mankind . . . [2]

A book came out in London five years before Margaret Mary was born, under the title: *The Heart of Christ in Heaven towards sinners on earth: or, A Treatise demonstrating the gracious disposition and tender affection of Christ in His human Nature, now in glory, unto His members, under all sorts of infirmities, either of sin or misery*. This book was written by Thomas Goodwin, the Congregational minister who attended Oliver Cromwell on his deathbed. In a reference to this book, an English writer, Msgr. Ronald Knox, once remarked: "Devotion to the Sacred Heart of Jesus, commonly thought of as a popish superstition from the middle of the seventeenth century, is in fact a form of piety which can commend itself to all Christians."[3] The Catholic Church approved devotion to the Heart of Jesus but that does not mean that the Church passed judgment on Margaret Mary's private revelations. Devotion to the Sacred Heart was in the hearts of many people before Margaret Mary's time. Goodwin's book is one example. Another is St. John Eudes (1601-1680) who composed a Mass and office of the Sacred Heart in 1668-69, and a feast of the Sacred Heart was first celebrated by Eudist communities on October 20, 1672. St. Margaret Mary's first revelation at Paray didn't occur until December 27, 1673.

It may come as a surprise, even to some Catholics, that the Church does not require that Catholics believe everything attributed to the Saints. Even such public facts as the revelations of the Sacred Heart or the happenings at Lourdes are not matters of divine faith. Catholics do not have to believe that Jesus appeared to Margaret Mary or that the mother of Jesus appeared to a little girl named Bernadette Soubirous at Lourdes, France in 1858. The Catholic Church investigated the events at Lourdes (as can be seen in the movie, "The Song of Bernadette," often shown on TV) and decided to *allow* pilgrimages and devotion to Mary under the title "Our Lady of Lourdes." No new doctrine emerged from the devotion. The episodes just re-emphasized the value of prayer and penance. The American bishops said in 1973:

> Even when a "private revelation" has spread to the entire world, as in the case of Our Lady of Lourdes, and has been recognized in the liturgical calendar, the Church does not make mandatory the acceptance either of the original story or of particular forms of piety springing from it.[4]

In other words, Catholics are not bound to believe that the Blessed Mother of Jesus appeared at Lourdes (1858), Fatima (1917), Guadalupe, Mexico (1531), Beauraing (1923-33), La Salette (1846), Paris (Miraculous Medal, 1830), Banneux (1933), or anywhere else where the Church allows devotions. Allowing a cult does not mean that the Church binds us as a matter of faith to believe in the apparitions or the messages of these visitations. All the Church says when she allows such devotion is that she can find no natural explanation for the occurrence which precipitated the devotion (such as the apparitions at Lourdes or Guadalupe) and there is nothing connected with the devotion that is contrary to faith or morals.

Margaret Mary Alacoque, Bernadette Soubirous and Catherine Laboure, all visionaries, were canonized after their deaths. It is certainly true that the visions and the messages that went with them brought the three to public notice, but they were not canonized because they had visions which were instrumental in initiating new devotions (not doctrines). They were canonized for the same reasons as anyone else. It was shown that they fulfilled the duties of their state in life and heroically practiced the virtues associated with their state. This point becomes clearer if we recall the fact that the Church approved of the devotion to Our Lady which grew out of apparitions at La Salette in France in 1846. The boy and girl who claimed to have seen the Blessed Mother there did not live unusually saintly lives and have not been canonized.

Christianity has always been a religion of "voices and visions." In the Acts of the Apostles there is Stephen's vision of the glory of God (Acts 7:55), the angel who spoke to Philip (Acts 8:26), the voice of the Lord in Paul's conversion (Acts 9:4-5), the vision of the Lord to Ananias (Acts 9:10), the vision of Cornelius (Acts 10:3-6), Peter's trance and subsequent vision (Acts 10:10-16), the angel that came to Peter in prison (Acts 12:7), and so on. Paul talks about being caught up to the third heaven in 2 Corinthians 12:1-7. Lives of Christian men and women from the time of Peter and Paul until now show us that such occurrences did not cease with the early Church but have continued as an integral part of the life of the Spirit.

Visions or voices (theologians sometimes term these "locutions") either pertain to one's own particular relationship with the Lord and growth in union with Him or they have to do with the Lord's work and are given for the building up of Christ's body. Paul's experience of being rapt up into the third heaven was a gift of grace for him and a personal event in his walk with the Lord. It was a way that the Lord consoled him in the midst of the "weaknesses, insults, hardships, persecutions and calamities" that Paul tells us about immediately after discussing the grace of consolation granted him by the Lord. Peter's trance and vision of the sheet and food was not a grace of consolation but instead was given for guidance. The Holy Spirit was teaching him that salvation was also for the gentiles.

Likewise, when Francis of Assisi heard the voice of the Lord speaking to him from the crucifix at San Damiano, he was receiving guidance. He was being told to repair the Church which was falling down. By contrast, the vision of the Trinity that a number of Saints experienced seems to have marked their reaching a degree of spiritual maturity and was a perfecting, strengthening grace rather than guidance.

The Church has accumulated a body of wisdom over the years as to what should be our attitude with regard to voices and visions. The teaching could pretty well be summed up under two words— detachment and discernment. The Church counsels us not to seek after consolations and not to seek after extraordinary experiences. We are to seek after the Lord. If we experience a grace of consolation or a word of guidance during our prayer time, we are to accept it with gratitude but not become attached to the experience. Many people today are experiencing consolations from the Lord and are rejoicing in a personal relationship with Him as a result of the action of God known as the charismatic renewal. St. Bernard was opposed to seeking pleasant spiritual experiences for the consolation they would bring, but he did not disdain them. "If God in Scripture is compared to a honeycomb, why seek the comb without the honey!"

Discernment is one of the gifts of the Spirit and the Church has always taught the importance and necessity of this gift with regard to life in the Spirit. Spiritual writers stress the fact that visions, locutions, revelations and other spiritual apprehensions do not necessarily come from God. They can come from Satan or a person's own fancy. Therefore there arose within the Church the tradition of submitting one's spiritual life to a spiritual director or one spiritually more mature. In the Byzantine Church the tradition of spiritual paternity (*pater pneumatikos*) goes back to the desert fathers. The Russian Church has the *startsy* tradition. The *starets* [5] is an elder who guides one young in life in the Spirit, and keeps the initiate safe from self-delusion. In the *Ascent of Mount Carmel*, St. John of the Cross, a spiritual director in the Western Church, who was writing at a time of renewal and revival in the Church, had this to say:

> I am appalled at what happens in these days—namely, when some soul with the very smallest experience of meditation, if it be conscious of certain locutions of this kind in some state of recollection, at once christens them all as coming from God, and assumes that this is the case, saying: "God said to me . . . ;" "God answered me . . . ;" whereas it is not so at all, but, as we said, it is for the most part they who are saying these things to themselves. (*Ascent*, Book II, Chapter 29, par. 4)

Despite the fact that St. John of the Cross urged caution and discernment, he admitted the possibility of authentic divine communication and took the subject seriously enough to classify visions and locutions into three kinds.[6] Visions may be corporeal, imaginative or intellectual; locutions may be auricular, imaginative or intellectual. In corporeal visions (apparitions) or auricular locutions (voices) there is real perception by the external senses (eyes or ears). In imaginative locutions or visions there is divine action on the imagination. Tanquerey (*The Spiritual Life*) gives the example of the angel appearing to St. Joseph in his sleep. St.

Teresa of Avila had several imaginative visions of Jesus when she was awake. In intellectual visions or locutions divine action affects the intellect; an example of this would be Teresa's vision of the Holy Trinity which she describes in her *Autobiography*.

John of the Cross further subdivides intellectual locutions into three types: successive, formal and substantial. These are discussed in the *Ascent of Mount Carmel*, Book II, Chapters 28-31. He defines the substantial locution as one where the words of the Lord effect a change in the person, and gives the example of a very fearful soul to whom the Lord says, "Fear thou not," and the person immediately feels great fortitude and tranquillity. St. John points out that Jesus healed the sick and raised the dead by no more than a word and it is in this manner that he gives certain souls substantial locutions. According to E. Allison Peers, who is a recognized translator and authority on St. John of the Cross and St. Teresa of Avila, St. John of the Cross has been criticized for telling people not to fear these locutions. St. John goes so far as to say that with this kind of locution, neither the devil nor the understanding can intervene, and he writes, ". . . one of these words works greater good within the soul than all that the soul itself has done throughout its life." [7]

Voices and visions are not the only phenomena we encounter in lives of Saints. St. Philip Neri corresponded with St. Catherine dei Ricci (1522-1590) and with their relationship we encounter the phenomenon of "bilocation." With Catherine, we encounter "stigmata" and "ecstasy." When she was twenty years old Catherine began to experience a series of ecstasies in which she beheld and enacted the scenes which preceded our Lord's crucifixion. She lost consciousness at noon every Thursday and came to at four o'clock on Friday afternoon. This happened every week for twelve years.

Evidence was also submitted at the process of canonization to the effect that Catherine's body bore the wounds of Christ, the stigmata. St. Philip Neri, who (according to Butler's *Lives of the*

119

Saints) "was always most cautious in giving credence to or publishing visions," stated that Catherine appeared to him in Rome and talked with him—and all the while she was in her convent at Prato. This is not the only instance of bilocation in the life of a Saint. St. Catherine dei Ricci also exercised prophecy. She predicted an attempt against the life of St. Charles Borromeo, at the time that he was the Archbishop of Milan.

And bilocation, ecstasy, stigmata, voices and visions are not the sum of the phenomena found in some Saints' lives. St. Joseph of Cupertino, a Franciscan (1603-1663) "flew," or to be more accurate, he levitated. St. John Bosco (1815-1888) was guided by prophetic dreams and protected by a mysterious large dog which would appear only in time of need. Angela of Foligno remained twelve years without taking any nourishment and St. Catherine of Siena for about eight years. This phenomenon is called "inedia." St. Peter of Alcantara slept only about an hour and a half a night for forty years. St. Catherine of Siena and St. Frances of Rome exhibited "hierognosis." They were able to recognize immediately any person, place or thing that was holy, blessed or consecrated and to distinguish it from things that were not. St. Aloysius Gonzaga knew the date of his death in advance. (This is one of the most common phenomena to be found in lives of Saints.) St. Bernardino Realino (1530-1616), an Italian Jesuit, was found praying with a radiance emanating from him which lighted up the room. Several times St. Catherine of Siena received Communion without the host being brought to her. The host left the priest celebrant's hands and traveled through the air to her mouth. St. Mary Magdalen dei Pazzi (1566-1607), a Carmelite, experienced frequent ecstasies and her body levitated. Even when not in ecstasy her body exhibited an incredible agility, swiftness of speed in movement and a seeming exemption from normal physical laws. St. Madeleine Sophie Barat, foundress of the Religious of the Sacred Heart, died in 1865. When her body was disinterred in 1893, the coffin had decayed but the body was intact.

What are we to make of such things? Are such phenomena a necessary or common accompaniment of sanctity? What is the attitude of the Church on the subject? The answer will help us to have a rule of thumb when encountering phenomena sometimes associated with religious experience today.

The Church and the Saints themselves teach that neither voices, nor visions, nor dreams, nor raptures, nor bilocation, nor levitation, nor stigmata, nor prolonged fasting, nor ecstasies are integral to Christianity. Neither are they necessarily signs of holiness. They can be signs of mental illness and often are signs of weakness or immaturity in the spiritual life. The Saints write that such things should not be sought after and if experienced, should be treated with great detachment. Perhaps the thing to keep in mind is that there are many canonized Saints who never exhibited unusual phenomena and those who did were canonized in spite of it.

Accounts of over three hundred stigmatics have been recorded. A stigmatic is someone who bears on his or her body the wounds of Christ. St. Francis of Assisi is the first and perhaps the best known stigmatic Saint. Some people have even conjectured that St. Paul bore the wounds of Jesus. They arrive at this conclusion from Colossians 1:24: ". . . in my flesh I complete what is lacking in Christ's afflictions for the sake of his body, that is, the Church . . ." and from Galatians 6:17: ". . . I bear on my body the marks of Jesus." In our own century there have been some stigmatics, Teresa Neumann (1898-1962), and Padre Pio (1881-1968), a Capuchin Franciscan, being perhaps the two best known.

Many doctors now hold that the stigmata are a result of suggestion and so should have no miraculous significance. Even if this were so, it is impressive that someone, body and mind, should be so united with Jesus in his suffering that His wounds by suggestion appear on the body. And whether stigmata are the result of

121

suggestion or are caused by a direct action of God as Dr. Rene Biot says in his book, *The Enigma of the Stigmata*, does it matter?[8] Fr. Crehan, in the preface to Fr. Thurston's book, *Surprising Mystics*, says: "If, as some doctors now claim, stigmata can be produced by the subject's own devout meditation on the Passion of Christ, that does not prevent God from producing them when He will by infusing in other souls such a knowledge of the Passion that stigmatization follows perforce." [9]

Fr. Thurston's book is quite interesting and helps to place religious phenomena in perspective. Fr. Thurston was the man who revised Butler's *Lives of the Saints* and in doing so he came across many borderline cases of pious people the Church hesitated to canonize. In order to be canonized a person must have practiced virtue in an heroic degree. Fr. Thurston decided to study the lives of those in whom the phenomena appeared without the sanctity. He believed that in doing so the behavior patterns of real sanctity could better be appreciated. The result was *The Physical Phenomena of Mysticism* which appeared in 1952 and *Surprising Mystics*, which came out in 1955.

Saints (and other people not canonized) whose lives exhibited phenomena, such as seeing visions, stigmata, levitation and ecstasy, and charisms, such as prophecy, have been called "mystics." Sts. Teresa of Avila, John of the Cross, Catherine of Siena and some others are called "great mystics." It would take too long (and it would be outside the scope of this book) to trace how the word "mystic" came to be used by Catholic spiritual writers and theologians. [10] As an example of how the term is presently used we quote from a popular book *Mystics of Our Times* by Hilda Graef.

. . . we must define what we mean by a "mystic." Christian theologians consider that a mystic is a man who is united to God in an experimental fashion. That is to say, he does not only know by faith that God dwells in him through His grace and through the sacraments, but he "experiences" this divine

Presence within him in such a way that he is really aware of it.
. . .[11]

In other words, mysticism could be defined as the experiential awareness of the Holy Spirit's action in one's life.

Contemporary Catholic spiritual writing and the introductions to books on Saints reveal a strange state of affairs. We find Saints being divided into those who were mystics and those who were not. And there does not seem to be agreement as to which Saints go in which category. Poor St. Ignatius Loyola gets placed in either list depending on the writer, as Miss Graef remarks:

> Why then do so many people not think of, say, St. Ignatius of Loyola as a mystic? This is due to the fact that he and many other saints like him are more noted for their active works. These were, indeed, the outcome of their intense mystical life, but this was, quite naturally, unknown to a wider public. We know of the mystics mostly through their own or their disciples' writings. Where these do not exist, we simply have not the material from which to judge whether they were mystics or not. . . .[12]

There have been reputed mystics who were never canonized, for example, Tauler, Thomas a Kempis, Julian of Norwich, Blosius, Osuna, Gertrude More, Benedict Canfield, Brother Lawrence and de Caussade. As for Saints being or not being mystics, I would suggest that they all were mystics and that all Christians should be mystics. This simply means that to be a Christian should mean to live by and in the Holy Spirit with some awareness of His presence. Depending on our temperament, our sensitivity, our degree of suggestibility (most stigmatics have been women), and our tendency towards introspection or our ability for self-reflection, the action of God will neverberate to a greater or lesser degree.

Recognized mystics who were canonized left behind writings describing their spiritual journey. But, just because a Saint was perhaps less introspective or perhaps just reticent, does not mean that a Saint like Vincent de Paul was not a mystic. On this subject Louis Bouyer in his *Introduction to Spirituality* writes:

> . . . Jacques and Raissa Maritain . . . have . . . pointed out quite rightly that this mystical development of every Christian life carried to holiness will be more or less conscious according to the innate tendency and capacities of the subject for reflex consciousness of what is going on within him. Thus Saints at the first sight do not seem to be mystics actually live a mystical life without talking about it and to a certain extent, without being aware of it.[13]

In his paper, "The Role of the Holy Spirit and the Gifts of the Spirit in the Mystical Tradition," Dr. Vinson Synan writes:

> . . . the experiences and teachings of St. Francis of Assisi, St. Teresa of Avila, St. John of the Cross, St. Francis Xavier, St. Bernard, and St. Catherine of Genoa, to name a few, have convinced me that we are on most points indeed soul-brothers. I therefore end by suggesting that modern Pentecostals and charismatics should make a serious study of the great saints of the Catholic mystical tradition with at least as much interest in those who were canonized as in those who were excommunicated or burned at the stake.[14]

It is encouraging to have Dr. Synan suggest that people from other than Catholic traditions should study some Catholic Saints. The ones he mentions exercised charismatic gifts, received mystical graces, and experienced mystical phenomena.

However, two things could be said here. First, the writings of Saints who are considered mystics need to be read against the background of their lives. We need to know, for example, that Teresa traveled about establishing convents, that she participated in recreation in the community, and other such facts, otherwise we would be left with the mistaken impression that all she did was have visions. Secondly, I would enter a plea for a study of all the Saints, not just those who are considered mystics.

Notes to Chapter 9

1. Huizinga, *The Waning of the Middle Ages*, pp. 175, 178, as cited in Gannon and Traub, *The Desert and the City*, p. 121.
2. Vincent Kerns, translator, *The Autobiography of Saint Margaret Mary*, p. 46.
3. *Ibid.*, p. xi.
4. National Conference of Catholic Bishops, *Behold Your Mother*, Nov. 21, 1973, p. 38.
5. See "'The Russian 'Startsy:' Monks of 'Holy Russia'" by Elisabeth Behr-Sigel in *Concilium*, Vol. 37, "Prophets in the Church."
6. St. Augustine is the originator of the classical categorization of visions.
7. E. Allison Peers, translator and editor, *The Complete Works of St. John of the Cross*, pp. 205-206.
8. Dr. Rene Biot, *The Enigma of the Stigmata*.
9. Herbert Thurston, S.J., *Surprising Mystics*, p. viii.
10. See Appendix I.
11. Hilda Graef, *Mystics of Our Times*, Deus Books, Paulist Press, Glen Rock, New Jersey, 1963, p. 10.
12. *Ibid.*, p. 12.
13. Bouyer, *Introduction to Spirituality*, p. 303.
14. Vinson Synan, "The Role of the Holy Spirit and the Gifts of the Spirit in the Mystical Tradition" in *One in Christ*, 1974-2, p. 192.

CHAPTER 10

In Praise of Saints

There is much talk these days about "gifts of the Spirit." Two gifts that Saints seemed to possess in abundance were common sense and a sense of humor. Coming in all sizes and shapes, the immense variety of Saints can teach, inspire, console, correct and amuse us. Joined with us in communion through Jesus, they are our brothers and sisters. Some were inclined to introspection as well as teaching, and they left us records of their walk with God. As for others, we can only judge their interior life or mystical experiences from the fruits of their activity. Some were popes and bishops, some were theologians, some were illiterate, some were married, many were women, and all loved the Lord intensely. All had a personal relationship with Jesus Christ.

Some taught school, some built schools, some founded hospitals, some cared for orphans, some died for their belief in Jesus, some were itinerant preachers, some lived in caves, some lived in the desert, some Saints lived in convents and St. Anthony of Padua lived in a walnut tree the last weeks of his life [1] but all the Saints were conscious that they lived and worked through the power of the Holy Spirit.

When I think of Saints, I think of Catherine Laboure swallowing the relic of Vincent de Paul; Francis of Assisi praying for a Scripture; Therese of Lisieux spitting in the inkwell; Alphonsus Liguori playing the harpsichord; Thomas More playing with his daughters; Catherine of Genoa caring for her husband's illegitimate daughter;

127

John Vianney, the Cure of Ars, questioning the apparitions at La Salette; Mother Cabrini sending some of her sisters out to measure property with a tape measure; Gabriel of Our Lady of Sorrows appearing to Gemma Galgani laying his hand on her hand to relieve the pain; Clare of Assisi pulling up the covers of her sleeping sisters; Mother Seton brushing snow off her sleeping sisters; Anthony of Padua washing pots and pans; Mme. Acarie in her old age being persecuted by Berulle; Don Bosco weeping and yearning for the early days of the oratory; Philip Neri going about with half his beard shaved and Hilda of Whitby nurturing Caedmon.

How about this remark contained in one of Madeleine Sophie Barat's letters: "Our Society has not been established to prove that women can become men, even though that may be less difficult in a country [France] where so many men become women."[2] The Cure d'Ars was never at a loss for words. He once asked a very talkative lady if there was any month in the year in which she talked less than usual except February. Visiting a well-known pantheist [one who tends to identify God with nature] when the man was sick in bed and desirous of converting him to Christ, St. Clement Hofbauer pinned a note to the blanket saying "A piece of divinity is ill."

It is probably a good thing that Sts. Joan of Arc and Bernadette of Lourdes suffered martyrdom, for without that they might not have been canonized! Both were rather outspoken and could be caustic at times. Joan was burned at the stake and Bernadette suffered a lingering and painful martyrdom of an incurable illness which killed her when she was thirty-five. Theodore Maynard says Bernadette was possessed of "peasant shrewdness—salty, practical and tart."[3] After the apparitions at Lourdes and after entering the convent, one of Bernadette's sufferings was to have to retell the events of the apparitions for bishops or anyone she was sent to the parlor to speak to.

Bernadette did her best to dodge these encounters. Once when reproved for being reluctant to meet with a bishop and reminded that there was a "forty days" indulgence for kissing his ring, Bernadette, with an irritation that to us would seem expressive of modern discomfort and embarrassment with indulgences, quickly reeled off an ejaculatory prayer which had an attached indulgence: "Jesus, Mary and Joseph, I give you my heart and my soul! There, that gives me a hundred days!"

Another time a visitor asked Bernadette where or how he could see Sister Marie-Bernard (Bernadette's name in religion). Bernadette said to him, "Well, if you watch that door, you'll see her go through it," and then she vanished through the door.

Joan of Arc was kept in a civil prison and looked after by men instead of women. She was not allowed an advocate and so had no one to advise or encourage her, and she was only nineteen. Occasionally Joan was defiant and caustic in answering questions. This is a selection from the trial testimony:

Question: What figures do you see?
Joan: I see their faces.
Question: These Saints which appear to you, have they hair?
Joan: Wouldn't you just like to know! (C'est bon a savoir!)
Question: Of what form was Saint Michael when he appeared to you?
Joan: I saw no crown on him, and of his clothes I know nothing.
Question: Was he naked?
Joan: Do you think God cannot afford to clothe him?
Question: Had he hair?
Joan: Why should it have been cut off? [4]

We are usually appalled when reading of the incredible austerities of certain Saints. Sometimes just thinking of Saints conjures up visions of hair shirts, fasting, iron chains and so on. It is true that some Saints were known as ascetics and some were famous penitents but most Saints tried to tread the mean between extremes of over-preoccupation with health and recklessness regarding it. St. Thomas Aquinas' remedy for melancholy was a hot bath, and a good night's sleep. St. Paul advised Timothy to take a little wine for his stomach. In writing to one of her sisters St. Teresa told her to take care of her body because it must serve the soul. St. Francis of Assisi confessed towards the end of his life that he had been too hard on Brother Ass (his name for the body) and St. Ignatius admitted that in the period following his conversion he also had been too hard on his body. But as Fr. Aloysius Roche pointed out in one of the best books ever written on Saints,[5]

> absorption in any pursuit almost inevitably implies a certain amount of self-neglect. . . . The indiscretions of the Saints must be judged for what they were, namely indiscretions. Generous as God's grace made them and ardent and impetuous as some of them were by nature, they felt called upon to give themselves and to sacrifice themselves even to imprudence. . . . The Saints did not play for safety. Had they done so there would be none of them. There would be no St. Vincent de Paul, no Father Damien, no Martyrs, no Confessors; and St. Peter would never have jumped into the sea. [6]

Fr. Roche also reminds us that in earlier ages mankind accepted as normal conditions which we would consider as privations today. Mediaeval castles did not have glass windows and were cold and drafty. Highland chieftains slept on the moors in winter with no extra covering except the plaid. We can read in Scott of a man who rebuked the effeminacy of his son for making a snowball to serve as a pillow.

Bernadette, Gemma Galgani, Therese of Lisieux, Aloysius Gonzaga and Anthony of Padua died young but other Saints lived a long life. At their deaths, St. Philip Neri was eighty; St. Alphonsus Liguori was ninety-one; St. Vincent de Paul was seventy-nine; St. Madeleine Sophie Barat was eighty-six. Pope John XXIII who called Vatican Council II died at eighty-two.

Saints nurtured and encouraged other Saints. St. Vincent de Paul patiently directed St. Louise de Marillac who had a taste for varied devotions and who was given to being fearful. St. Vincent simplified Louise's prayer life and helped her to concentrate more on God's mercy than His judgment, which for one with her temperament, brought great freedom. Blessed Claude de la Colombiere brought comfort and assistance to St. Margaret Mary Alacoque at the time of the revelations of the Sacred Heart. St. Camillus, who founded a nursing order, was guided by St. Philip Neri. St. Catherine of Siena spiritually instructed her "director," Blessed Raymond of Capua. The experience of striking of St. Philip Benizi (1233-1285) in the face launched St. Peregrine on the way to sanctity. (St. Philip Benizi was a well-known preacher and head of an order known as the Servites. He was an effective peacemaker among the warring cities of northern Italy. Once, while trying to bring peace among Guelfs and Ghibellines, Philip was struck on the face by a Ghibelline named Peregrine Laziosi. Philip turned the other cheek and the manner in which he accepted the blow so impressed Peregrine that he was converted to Jesus. He lived a life of prayer and service to others, and was canonized.) St. Peter Claver (1580-1654) would not have ministered to slaves were it not for the influence of the saintly doorkeeper St. Alphonsus Rodrigues, in the college where he was stationed. (St. Alphonsus had been married, lost his wife and children and became a Jesuit brother at age forty-four.) St. Lioba, known for her beauty and intelligence, assisted St. Boniface in his missionary work in Germany in the eighth century.

St. Gerard Majella (1726-1755) knew the founder of the Redemptorist order which he entered, St. Alphonsus Liguori. Dominic Savio lived and studied under St. John Bosco a few years and died a Saint at fifteen. John Bosco wrote a biography of Dominic as well as one of St. Joseph Cafasso who was Don Bosco's teacher and adviser for over twenty years. When St. Aloysius, a Jesuit student, lay ill approaching death at twenty-three, he was ministered to by St. Robert Bellarmine who was a friend of St. Francis de Sales and St. Bernadino Realino. Another young Jesuit who died the year Aloysius was born was St. Stanislaus Kostka (1550-1568). He knew and was inspired by St. Peter Canisius and was received as a novice by St. Francis Borgia.

We have seen that the Franciscan St. Peter of Alcantara influenced St. Teresa of Avila.[7] Other Saints that Teresa of Avila knew and consulted were St. John of the Cross, St. Francis Borgia, St. Louis Bertrand and St. John of Avila. Louis Bertrand was a blood relative of St. Vincent Ferrer. St. John of Avila (d. 1569) was a renowned preacher and evangelist. During one of his sermons, St. John of God (1495-1550), a founder of a nursing order, was converted. According to the dictionary of Saints of the Benedictine monks of Ramsgate, "the fervour of his [John of God's] conversion produced in him such extravagant behaviour that he was taken for a madman."[8] However, John finally settled down and founded a hospital.

John of God's post-conversion behavior is a little reminiscent of St. Benedict's experience. The august "Father of Western Monasticism" was so zealous that the first community of monks that he lived with tried to kill him off by poisoning him!

Benedict would have some hard things to say today to "prayer meeting hoppers," traveling prophets or "spiritual lone rangers." These are people who make no commitment to any prayer group and don't stay around any group or community long enough for their gifts or spiritual state to be discerned. One of the ingredients of Benedictine spirituality is stability. Benedict wanted monks to live their whole life in one house or monastery. They were not to wander from house to house. Those that did, Benedict called "gyrovagues."

These spend their whole lives tramping from province to province, staying as guests in different monasteries for three or four days at a time. Always on the move, with no stability, they indulge their own wills and succumb to the allurements of gluttony. . . . Of the miserable conduct of such men it is better to be silent than to speak.[9]

Saints not only begat Saints, they sometimes came in groups. St. Francis de Sales (1567-1622), Bishop of Geneva, knew St. Jane de Chantal, St. Vincent de Paul, St. Robert Bellarmine, Mme. Acarie (Blessed Mary of the Incarnation), and St. Charles Borromeo. He also corresponded with St. Peter Canisius whose catechism he used in instructing converts. The first Capuchin to be canonized, St. Felix of Cantalice, knew St. Charles Borromeo and St. Philip Neri. St. Ignatius's roommates, Francis Xavier and Peter Faber, became Saints.

Ignatius turned to the Lord while reading lives of Saints, particularly about St. Francis of Assisi and St. Dominic. (What better recommendation could there be for devotional reading!) The Cure d'Ars kept a volume of lives of the Saints in his bedroom. One factor in the conversion of St. Augustine was the reading of the *Life of Antony*, the Egyptian hermit who was one of the founders of monasticism.[10] Blessed John Colombini (c. 1300-1367) was converted while reading about St. Mary of Egypt.[11] Author Robert Leckie describes it this way:

> Blessed John Colombini was . . . terrible tempered. . . . He was a successful merchant of Siena who married Biagia Cerretani. He came home one night, tired out, and Biagia didn't have dinner ready. Blessed John lost his temper. Biagia, never very tactful, said something about possessing his soul in patience and pressed a book of saints' lives into his hand. John threw the book on the ground. Suddenly ashamed, he picked it up and began reading. The story of the life of St. Mary of Egypt fascinated him so that he forgot his dinner and kept Biagia waiting. . . . Thereafter John Colobini's life underwent a change. He put an end to his trading career. . . . He took a

leper home to nurse. Biagia liked the new John less than the old.[12]

Much the same thing happened in reverse almost three hundred years later. In 1588, Pierre Acarie went into a rage when he found his twenty-two year old wife reading a new romance, *Amadis*. He got a pile of spiritual books from his confessor and ordered Barbe, his wife, to read them. In doing so she met the Lord in a powerful way and was transformed. While remaining a dutiful wife she was a moving force in the reform and revival of religious life in France. "Of all the husbands who have attempted to dictate what their wives should read, Pierre Acarie deserves the palm," wrote Seldon Delany in *Married Saints*.[13] In the same book there is recorded a famous exchange (I don't know how true) between St. Louis IX of France and his wife. The queen expressed exasperation at her husband's simple way of dressing. After all, he was the king! King Louis said he was most willing to comply as it was his duty to please his wife. Since that obligation was reciprocal, however, he agreed to royal dress only if the queen would dress humbly and unostentatiously. The queen refused to make the exchange and Louis heard no more about it.

With renewed interest in the area of headship and submission, it is interesting to note that Louis never engaged in any serious business without first asking his wife's permission. His feelings about the poor and about war are indicated in this instruction to his son Philip the Bold: "If it becomes needful for you to make war, be very careful that the poor people who had no part in the injustice that led to it should be preserved from all hurt, either by fire or otherwise. . . ."[14]

Occasionally Saints grieved each other. St. Leonard of Port Maurice (1676-1751), a Franciscan, was a victim of misinformation concerning the Passionist Congregation founded by St. Paul of the Cross (1694-1775). St. Leonard presented a petition to the pope for the disbanding of the Passionists. When he recognized his mistake, St. Leonard apologized and was forgiven by the Passionists. Both he and St. Paul of the Cross were canonized in 1867. By special indult St. Leonard has a place in the Passionist liturgical calendar.

Three hundred years earlier, another Franciscan, St. John Capistran (1386-1456), caused suffering in the life of the reforming Poor Clare Abbess St. Colette of Cobie. The sister who kept an account of St. Colette's life says St. Colette described the anguish St. John Capistran caused her in these words: "I feel as if someone had split my heart across the middle, filled it with burning salt, and sewed it up again." St. John Capistran had been working with St. Bernardine of Siena in Italy for the reform of the Franciscan Order. St. John came to France to see St. Colette to get her to accept a plan for restablishing unity among the Franciscans some of whom by this time were living the primitive, more ascetic rule, while others were living a mitigated rule. St. John wanted Colette to merge her life's work of establishing convents of the primitive observance with the mitigants. He came armed with new constitutions for her which he had worked on with the pope. For three days St. Colette and the nuns in her community traversed their cloisters and choir on their knees, begging God to protect His work. St. John finally admitted to St. Colette that God had revealed to him that he was in error and he would not interfere with her work again.

Saints are to be praised for their attitudes and thinking which were often advanced for their day. St. Francis de Sales was a student in 1590 in Padua when an epidemic of typhoid broke out and he almost died. When asked about the disposition of his body, should he die, de Sales asked that his body be given to the medical students. He felt his body had been useless during lifetime and he wanted it to be of use after his death.

One of de Sales' gifts was practical wisdom. The following excerpt is from one of his letters to a Madame Brulart whose husband obviously didn't share her enthusiasm for the Lord. This and similar letters by de Sales contain excellent teaching for this kind of mixed marriage:

> You must yield to their will [her father and husband] and bend to the utmost without breaking through your good rules,—such submission is acceptable to Our Lord. I have told you before, the less we live according to our own taste, the less we choose for ourselves, the better and more solid our devotion will be. There are times when we must leave our Lord to please others for love of Him. . . . Perhaps you have given your good husband and father some grounds for being annoyed at, and interfering with, your religious practices? Perhaps you have been rather too eager and busy. . . . If so, that is why they react upon you now. We must strive, if possible, that our devotion should be troublesome to no one. . . . I have often admired the intense resignation of St. John Baptist, in remaining so long near our Lord, without eagerly seeking or following Him; even after His Baptism letting Him go without cleaving to His bodily Presence. (Letter 85. Blaise Edition, XV, Rivingtons.)

A famous saying attributed to St. Francis de Sales illustrates that although he never complained about peoples' bad manners he was human and did suffer because of them. "Do you really want me to pretend that black looks exhilarate me and that I can bear smoke puffed in my face without sneezing?" St. John Chrysostom admitted that he liked a compliment but wouldn't fish for one. "Not to feel pleased at being praised is, I am inclined to think, what has never happened to any man."

Saints even influenced the vocabulary of their day and days to come. St. Fiacre was a seventh century Irish hermit who settled in France. He has been considered the patron Saint of gardeners because of the vegetables he grew at his hermitage and he is most often depicted holding a shovel or spade. Around 1620, cabs for hire appeared in Paris and a cab stand was near the Hotel Saint-Fiacre. From this came the name "fiacre" for the French four-wheeler. The "oratorio," a musical form usually with a Scriptural subject, employing recitatives, arias and choruses, derives from religious gatherings planned by St. Philip Neri (1515-1595) in Rome and held in what was called the Oratory.

Not only did Saints often beget Saints, the institutions or buildings connected with Saints or the communities they founded sometimes graciously served as shelters for Saints of a later age. The Portinuncula, the cradle of the Franciscan order, belonged to the monks of the Benedictine Abbey of Mount Subasio who had abandoned it. When St. Clare and her cousin ran away from home to join Francis, he lodged them with Benedictine nuns at the monastery of San Paolo. When Clare's fifteen-year-old sister, Agnes, joined her the women moved to another Benedictine Abbey, that of Sant'Angelo. Here they stayed four months until the Bishop gave them San Damiano. In opening their home to the two first Poor Clares the good Benedictine nuns lost more than some living space. They lost some of their peace. Clare's relatives appeared at the first refuge and tried to persuade her to come home. The Abbey of Sant'Angelo had its stillness shattered also by Clare's relatives, this time they were trying to abduct Agnes and take her back home. It is recorded that while Clare knelt to pray, Agnes's body became so heavy, the horsemen who came with her uncle could not lift her. The local bishops supported and protected Clare, her cousin Pacifica, and her sister Agnes. This is interesting in view of the recent practice of parents kidnapping young people from various types of religious group and then attempting to have them deprogrammed.

When the sisters of St. Joseph of Cluny, founded by Blessed Anne-Marie Javouhey, arrived in Martinique they settled in a building that had formerly been an Ursuline convent. St. Frances Xavier Cabrini and her new community in Italy in about the year 1890 moved into a deserted Franciscan friary which had been empty since its suppression by Napoleon. St. Gabriel of Our Lady of Sorrows (1838-1862) was born in Assisi, was named Francis (Gabriel was his name in religion), was baptized at the same font in San Rufino as was St. Francis, and he lived the last four years of his life as a Passionist, in a monastery at Isola which had belonged to the Franciscans. The Franciscans had lived at Isola for six centuries until they were expelled under the law of Joachim Murat, King of Naples.

The common sense and practicality of Saints is praiseworthy. St. Hildegard (1098-1179) planned a drainage and water supply for a monastery. Centuries later, St. Veronica Giuliani (1660-1727), a Poor Clare noted for the abundance of mystical phenomena associated with her life, installed a system of water pipes in her convent. Anne-Marie Javouhey (1779-1827) not only established schools, hospitals and leper colonies in Bourbon, Senegal and the entire French empire in South America and Africa, she colonized the Mana district in Guinea.

The care of Saints for one another seems to have extended beyond the grave. St. Norbert (c. 1080-1134), when he was praying about what rule his community should adopt, had a vision of St. Augustine who advised him to adopt his rule.[15] When St. Jane de Chantal lay dying she had St. Jerome's epitaph on St. Paula read to her. Then she had the death of St. Francis de Sales read and the death of St. Monica written by Monica's son, St. Augustine. Jane was asked if she hoped to be met by St. Francis de Sales who had died nearly twenty years earlier. Jane answered: "Yes, I trust to that, he promised me that he would. . . ." When St. Clare of Assisi lay dying she said to her sister Agnes, who was also later canonized, "Do not cry, dear sister. I am not leaving you for long, for you will soon rejoin me." Agnes died three months later.

Saints who left writings behind show a deep understanding of the presence and role of the Holy Spirit in their lives, and they understood the significance of baptism. St. Louis Mary Grignion de Montfort (1673-1716) became known for spreading devotion to

Mary, the mother of Jesus. He is best known for a treatise he wrote entitled "True Devotion to the Blessed Virgin." But the essence of that devotion in de Montfort's own words is:

> I have said that this devotion may most justly be called a perfect renewal of the vows or promises of holy Baptism. . . . In Baptism, we ordinarily speak by the mouth of another, namely, by our godfather or godmother, and so we give ourselves to Jesus Christ not by ourselves but through another. But in this devotion we do it by ourselves, voluntarily, knowing what we are doing. (Part II)

Thomas Merton wrote the life of a Trappistine foundress, Mother M. Berchmans,[16] *Exile Ends in Glory*. The year 1907 found Mother Berchmans, a native of France, in a poor isolated convent on a hill in northern Japan. She was experiencing numerous interior trials and temptations against faith. On the feast of the Assumption she wrote a prayer to Our Lady in her own blood. This is an excerpt from that prayer.

> I consecrate . . . above all else . . . to you, my dearest Mother, that little spark of divine love which Jesus placed in my heart on the day of my Baptism, and which lies buried under the ashes of my pride. Take care of it, sweet Mother. Make it grow. Stir up this fire into a mighty blaze that will quickly burn me up and cause me to die, as you died, of love, for I desire no other death but yours, dearest Mother.[17]

Moving to the category of interesting trivia we might mention the fact that St. Patrick (c. 385-c. 461) the patron of Ireland was not Irish (by birth). St. Patrick's father was a deacon and his father's father was a priest. Apparently celibacy was not yet a requirement for clergy in the Western Church at the time of St. Patrick's grandfatṇer. Marie-Louise Trichet assisted St. Louis Mary Grignion de Montfort in the foundation of a community of women known as the Daughters of Wisdom. St. Louis died in 1776.

139

Marie-Louise died forty-three years later on the same date, at the same hour and in the same house as her friend St. Louis.[18]

Saints' lives were so conformed to that of their Divine Master that all of them in some way "died" during their lifetime, so that they might rise with Him. ("If we have died with him, we shall also live with him" 2 Tim. 2:11.) We tend to remember St. Francis of Assisi as the joyful Saint of the peace prayer, the Canticle of the Sun, the birds and the makeshift viol. But the last year of his life the stigmatized Francis suffered in his body the passion of His Lord. He was nearly blind and had excruciating headaches. He was plagued with gastric disorders, was weak from loss of blood and he suffered in his heart the pain of the betrayal of some of his friars.

St. John of the Cross, age twenty-five when St. Teresa of Avila, age fifty-two, asked him to begin reform among the men of the Carmelite Order, was eventually imprisoned in 1577 by friars opposing the reform. John was kept in a cell in a monastery in Toledo, Spain. The cell was about ten by six and so low he could barely stand up. Every day he was taken to the dining room (refectory) to get bread and water and every member of the community took a turn scourging him on his bared shoulders.

The incarceration lasted about nine months. The friars eventually tired of scourging him and John finally escaped. He went back to working for establishment of the reform. The last year of his life, 1591, found St. John of the Cross again persecuted by friars. This time they were friars of his own reform. The reformers were in conflict over a variety of issues, St. Teresa was dead, and St. John fell out of favor. St. John was stripped of his offices, former penitents were intimidated into calumniating him and he died in obscurity. "Indeed all who desire to live a godly life in Christ Jesus will be persecuted . . ." (2 Tim. 3:12). One could well say to the Lord with St. Teresa, when she fell off a horse into a stream, "If that's how you treat your friends, no wonder you have so few of them."

St. Vincent de Paul, a man of immense activity, spent his last year confined to bed with his useless legs ulcerating. He had to pull himself up by means of a cord attached to one of the joists of his room. His friends, including St. Louise de Marillac, died before he did. St. Alphonsus Liguori and St. Julie Billiart endured being expelled from the communities they had founded. St. John Bosco lived long enough to weep over the loss of the close family spirit in the community he founded. Cornelia Connelly (not yet canonized), foundress of the Society of the Holy Child Jesus, who had only become a nun because her husband, an Episcopal minister, wanted to be a Catholic priest, was persecuted by her husband who also alienated the affection of her children. The attitude of the Saints towards the suffering they endured is perhaps best expressed by the fact that St. John of the Cross wrote the first thirty stanzas of his *Spiritual Canticle* while imprisoned in Toledo. St. Francis of Assisi, when he was blind, suffering and in pain, wrote *The Canticle of Brother Sun.*

We praise the Lord for Saints because they are signs to us of His loving care. In the time of Alphonsus Liguori, and in the area of Italy in which he lived, people in cities had sufficient clergy for their needs. However, the poor who did not live in the cities did not have the gospel preached to them. By means of prophecy and visions God led Alphonsus to provide for their needs. By means of dreams and visions St. John Bosco began to see more clearly that he was to care for poor boys in Turin. The Holy Spirit inspired St. Vincent de Paul to lovingly provide for galley slaves and for the orphans whose legs would purposely be broken by the adults who owned them so that as cripples they would inspire pity and make more money begging in the streets of Paris. God created the world and loved what He created so much that He sent His Son into the world. Saints are a continuation of that love. What would English letters be without the poet Caedmon and what would have happened to Caedmon had not St. Hilda been inspired to encourage him? The Lord sent St. Frances Xavier Cabrini to America to be a sign of His loving care to the hoards of Italian immigrants huddling together in New York City and elsewhere.

We praise the Lord for the immense variety of Saints who shine like gems in His crown. We honor the Saints for their cooperation with grace and their yieldedness to the Spirit.

The Spirit is free, He blows where He will, and chooses whom He will for His plans and for His pleasure. Salvation, new life, the gifts of the Spirit and union with God are offered to all. But heaven has many mansions and God is not a "great Democrat." Mary was chosen to be the mother of the Lord; no other woman will ever have that privilege. Jesus chose twelve men as His first apostles. There have been other apostles in other centuries but no other men had the privilege of belonging to that first select group the Lord personally chose. Even in that group, Peter was singled out in a way the others were not. Why? Did Mary merit her role? Did Peter win a contest? No. It simply pleased God to do what He did. He gives His graces and special calls to whom He pleases and all is freely given.

Our place in the Body is part of God's plan and He wills that some be heads, some be hands, some feet, some apostles, some prophets, and so on. Our place in His Body—our ministry—is part of God's plan in gathering a holy people to Himself. Our place in His heart, our degree of union with Him, is His mysterious will and pleasure. At the last supper, all present were apostles, but some were seated nearer to Jesus then others. St. Peter had been singled out in one way. St. John the Divine was chosen to rest his head on the Lord.

Notes to Chapter 10
1. Clausen, *St. Anthony*, p. 113. If everything in this chapter were to be footnoted the citations would probably run to a hundred. All incidents in this chapter are to be found "somewhere" in the books listed in the bibliography.
2. Aloysius Roche, *A Bedside Book of Saints*, p. 73. Also told in *Saint-Watching* by Phyllis McGinley, p. 117.

3. Theodore Maynard, *Saints for Our Times*, p. 258.

4. Regine Pernoud, *Joan of Arc*, pp. 187-188.

5. Roche, *op. cit.* This book appeared in 1934. Although it assumes some slight familiarity with the Saints on the part of the reader, it is most entertaining and, most important, it was obviously a labor of love and one catches the enthusiasm of the author.

6. *Ibid.*, pp. 50-52.

7. Teresa knew Peter of Alcantara personally. At least two other Franciscans influenced her through their writings. Francisco de Osuna wrote, among other things, six *Alphabets* (so called from the alphabetical arrangement of the different sections). Teresa tells us in her writings that she meditated on the *Third Spiritual Alphabet* of Osuna. Bernadino de Laredo was a disciple of Osuna and a Franciscan lay brother. In 1535 in Seville he published a treatise on prayer called *The Ascent of Mount Sion*. Louis Bouyer says that Teresa adopted Osuna and Laredo's psychological orientation. (Louis Bouyer, *A History of Christian Spirituality*, Vol. 2, p. 539.)

8. The Benedictine Monks of St. Augustine's Abbey, Ramsgate, *The Book of Saints*, Adam & Charles Black, London, 1966, p. 383.

9. St. Benedict's *Rule for Monasteries*, Chapter 1.

10. Bouyer, *A History of Christian Spirituality*, Vol. 1, pp. 469.

11. St. Mary of Egypt, according to the Benedictine monks already cited, was a fifth century Egyptian who became an actress and then lived as a courtesan at Alexandria. After her conversion it is said that she went into a desert beyond the Jordan.

12. Robert Leckie, *These Are My Heroes*, Random House, New York, 1964, p. 66.

13. Delany, *Married Saints*, p. 195.

14. *Ibid.*, p. 123.

15. Cornelius Kirkfleet in his *History of Saint Norbert* says (1916) in a footnote, after describing this vision: "Much has been written about this Rule of St. Augustine which is followed by many religious Orders. Did the Saint really write this rule? Is it perhaps his famous letter of the year 423 to the Sisters of Hippo? That it was first intended for women seems beyond doubt . . ." p. 103. Bouyer in Volume One of *A History of Christian Spirituality* (1960) says that in contemporary patristic studies there are few literary problems as intricate as that of the "Rules of St. Augustine." The *Regula tertia*, it has been established, is an adaptation to monasteries for men of Letter 211, written by Augustine to the superior of a monastery for women. The letter is probably authentic but the adaptation may not be. (pp. 495-496).

16. Mother Berchmans has not yet been canonized.

17. Merton, *Exile Ends in Glory*, p. 177.

18. C.C. Martindale, S.J., *The Queen's Daughters: A Study of Women Saints*, p. 145.

143

CHAPTER 11

Saints and Charisms I

Make love your aim, and earnestly desire the spiritual gifts, especially that you may prophesy. (1 Cor. 14:1)

If it is given to you to read, accept this poor little gift [her commentary on the Song of Songs] from her who desires for you, as for herself, all the gifts of the Holy Spirit. St. Teresa of Avila, Doctor of the Church.[1]

A question Catholics frequently ask is whether or not the Saints manifested or exercised any charismatic gifts. When that question is asked, people usually have in mind the charisms listed by St. Paul in 1 Corinthians 12: tongues and interpretation of tongues, word of wisdom, word of knowledge, faith, healing, working of miracles, prophecy, and discernment of spirits. This does not mean that Catholics limit the term "charism" to this list. Dr. Walter J. Hollenweger, author of a ten-volume work in German on the Pentecostal movement, wrote two years ago: "As amongst German Protestant Neo-Pentecostals, Catholic Pentecostals similarly see in community work, journalism and run-of-the-mill management, even in music, poetry, and theology charisms of the Holy Spirit." [2] Yves Congar, in an article in 1974,[3] reminds us that Vatican II freed the charisms from a restricted meaning (tongues, prophecy, the gift of healing and the other "nine gifts"). He says these are particular forms of charisms but that St. Paul speaks also of charisms concerning marriage, and the vocation of virginity, the gift of consolation, and so on.

In this chapter I will be limiting the discussion to the nine ministry/spiritual/charismatic gifts.[4] The reason for this is that most people know that the charisms Fr. Congar lists, as well as others, are evident in Saints' lives. The charism of virginity is one of the best known. The "nine gifts" are relatively new in the experience of most Catholics and that is what prompts this investigation. It might be pertinent here to mention also that classical spiritual theology includes these under "extraordinary gifts," because up to now, except during the time of the early Church, they were rarely seen except in Saints' lives. Today, however, they are being exercised and experienced by so many hundreds of thousands of people that they are again becoming "ordinary" to the life of the Church.

Tongues and Interpretation of Tongues

Scholars call tongues *glossolalia*. Before going into possible instances of this gift in the lives of some Saints it might be good to say a few words about the gift itself. St. Paul said: "Now I want you all to speak in tongues. . ." (1 Cor. 14:5) and "I thank God that I speak in tongues more than you all" (1 Cor. 14:18). "For one who speaks in a tongue speaks not to men but to God. . ." (1 Cor. 14:2).

Tongues seems to have been an ordinary way of private prayer in the early Church. It was and is a way of praising God and is for speaking to God not to men. It is a way of speaking to God with the heart and is prayer of the heart not the mind. Although some people feel an emotional uplift when praying in tongues, it is not ecstatic speech and is under the control of the one praying. Tongues is making sounds unto the praise and glory of the Lord. The sounds to a listener seem like a foreign language.[5] The utterances emerge from a heart that cannot find the proper words to express its love and gratitude to God.

The Pentecostal narrative in Acts 2 has looked to most people as though the apostles are miraculously speaking foreign languages in order to convey the good news to the international gathering of people in Jerusalem. According to a footnote in the New American Bible, "to some of the hearers, however, the language is unintelligible, and they conclude the apostles are drunk." The apostles may have been exercising the gift of tongues as we experience it today—as nonrational speech. The New American Bible suggests that the multitude received the charism of interpretation and that is how they could understand what was said.[6] The accusation of drinking only makes sense if the sounds the apostles made were not recognizable as rational speech.

Whatever the tongues were at Pentecost, tongues in the experience of most people is nonrational speech (or singing). St. Paul gives rules for the regulation of the gift of tongues when it is used in the Christian assembly. "When you come together. . . . If any speak in a tongue, let there be only two or at most three, and each in turn; and let one interpret" (1 Cor. 14:26-27). This is because unbelievers participating in a prayer meeting where people are speaking in tongues (nonrationally) are going to think the people are mad.[7] Therefore in public, people should seek to prophesy, which will convict an unbeliever—or seek to use tongues with interpretation sparingly.

From my own experience I have seen that tongues plus interpretation have the same effect on a group as prophecy. St. Paul says they are of equal value. "He who prophesies is greater than he who speaks in tongues, *unless** some one interprets, so that the church may be edified" (1 Cor. 14:5). This equality has been pointed out by Bittlinger [8] and others. It should be mentioned in passing here for those unfamiliar with how the charismatic gift of interpretation is exercised, that interpretation is not translation. A person giving an interpretation of tongues has the same "sense"

---

* Italics mine.

as does one who prophesies that "this" is what God wants said, but with interpretation there is no recognition of a known language with a subsequent translation.

The early Christians exercised spiritual/charismatic/ministry gifts and so understood St. Paul and each other when they discussed their use and their value. The little research which has been done so far on the subject of the history of the nine gifts from apostolic times until now,[9] shows that the general use of the charisms by "ordinary" Christians petered out for the most part and they were seen only in lives of "extraordinary" Christians (Saints and heretics!). Tongues was and still is considered one of the signs of demon possession! [10]

Works of spiritual theology written after tongues had disappeared *in the form* in which it was known in the early Church cannot be expected to portray the spiritual/charismatic/ministry gifts in a way which will be helpful to us today. It does not look like St. Thomas Aquinas prayed in tongues the way St. Paul did or the way some of us do today. Therefore, this must be taken into consideration when reading St. Thomas on tongues. The question: "Did the Saint or spiritual writer have firsthand experience of what they were writing about?" is to be kept in mind when reading modern theology as well as the writings of Saints.

It is with all this in mind that we look to the Saints to see evidence of tongues and interpretation and other of the nine gifts. We will not be as interested in what they may say about tongues as we will be in whether or not we can find if they had the experience. I think our own experience of speaking in tongues devotionally, its use in the assembly with interpretation, and its regulation by elders, can serve as a valid tool of investigation.

Let me clarify by using an analogy. Suppose a gift poured out by God in the early Church was a sense of balance and this was manifested by riding bicycles. Then for unknown reasons, hidden in history (perhaps they lost their bicycle wrench), the practice of riding bicycles all but stopped. Then in modern times some people take up bicycles again and everyone begins to wonder what happened "between then and now." My contention is that most bicycle riders would know by experience that the essential ingredient in cycle riding is balance and that in going through history they would look, not only for instances of cycle riding, but also, and more importantly, for examples of manifestation of the facility of physical balance. My guess is that in this analogical tale the modern bicycle-riding investigators would find numerous instances of other activities requiring balance: tightrope walking, gymnastics (balance beam), ice hockey, circus performing (bareback riding, human pyramid) and ballet. The excited bicycle-riding investigator will exclaim: "This is it! I know because my spirit recognizes and witnesses to the same Spirit. This is the same gift!"

I suspect that God does not give gifts to His people only to withdraw them. I think his gifts just get recycled. As civilization evolves or progresses God's gifts disappear in one form only to reappear in another—much the same way as H_2O can be water, ice or steam. I surmise that when those who have had experience exercising charismatic gifts as they were known in St. Paul's day take the time to delve into lives of Saints and Church history, numerous instances of tongues speaking or its analogue will be found.

Here are two examples from primary sources,[11] both from the writings of St. Teresa of Avila. This passage from Chapter XVI of her *Autobiography* certainly seems like it is a description of the essence of tongues speaking.

Let us now go to speak of the third water with which this garden is watered. . . . The water of grace rises to the very neck of the soul, so that it is unable to go forward, and has no idea how to do so, yet neither can it turn back: it would fain have the fruition of exceeding great glory. . . . Nor does the soul . . . know what to do: it knows not whether to speak or to

149

be silent, whether to laugh or to weep. This state is a glorious folly, a heavenly madness. . . . It is now, I believe, some five, or perhaps six, years since the Lord granted me this prayer in abundance, and granted it me many times, yet I never understood it or knew how to describe it. . . . Many words are spoken, during this state, in praise of God, but, unless the Lord Himself puts order into them, they have no orderly form. The understanding, at any rate, counts for nothing here; the soul would like to shout praises aloud, for it is in such a state that it cannot contain itself. . . . O God, what must that soul be like when it is in this state! It would fain be all tongue, so that it might praise the Lord.

The next passage is taken from the record Teresa kept of her experiences in founding reformed convents. These accounts are called the *Book of the Foundations*. In this excerpt from Chapter XXVI, Teresa is talking about the foundation of the convent of St. Joseph in Avila, Spain in 1576. The passage seems to include a description of tongues as well as other charismata.

Of the first nun who entered this house, I will say something, as this will give you pleasure.

She was the daughter of most Christian parents. . . . When she reached an age for marriage, her parents discussed together with whom they should marry her. . . . She told them that she had made a vow not to marry. . . . As they had already betrothed her, and realized that this would be an affront to her suitor, they beat her and inflicted such treatment on her (even throttling her and trying to strangle her) that it was only by good luck that they did not kill her. . . .

Thirteen or fourteen years before Father Gracian went to Seville, when no one knew anything of the Discalced Carmelites, she happened to be with her father and mother and two women who were their neighbors when there entered a friar of our Order, dressed in frieze, according to their present custom, and with bare feet. They say that he had an open and venerable countenance, but he was so old that his long beard looked as if it were made of silver. He came quite near her and began to speak a few words in a language which neither she nor anyone else could understand. When he had finished speaking, he made the sign of the Cross over her three times and said: "Beatriz, God make thee strong." Then he went away. While he was there, nobody moved, so astonished were they at the sight. The father asked her who he was, but she herself had supposed that it must be someone he knew. They then got up quickly to look for him but never saw him again. The incident made the girl very happy, and all the others were astonished, saying that it was God's doing, and as a result of it they held her in high regard, as has been said. . . . Years passed—fourteen, I believe, . . . One day she went to hear a sermon . . . the preacher was . . . Father Master Gracian. When she saw him in his habit, with his bare feet . . . she at once remembered the friar whom she had seen before, for the habit was the same, though the face and age were different. . . .

The next two examples of what look like descriptions of tongues are taken from papers compiled during the canonization process of a French parish priest of the last century, John Vianney, also known as the Cure d'Ars. These papers serve as the basis for the biography by Abbe Trochu. The incidents he records are documented. John Vianney was very sought after as a confessor. People waited days to go to him for confession as his counsel was very wise and he also was able to read hearts. He often knew peoples' sins before they confessed them. He also showed a knowledge of their future as well as their past.

Seven weeks after the accident Mme. Meunier came to

confide to M. Vianney her fears as to the salvation of her husband. He had no sooner opened the shutter than he said: "My child, you think that some members of your family are damned but I do not think so." . . . Having said this, M. Vianney withdrew once more into the recesses of the confessional. The penitent heard him speaking softly to himself, for nearly five minutes, as if he were conversing with someone who remained invisible to her. Then drawing near to the grate: "Poor breadwinner." Mme. Meunier had not yet told him that she had five children and that the death of her husband left them penniless.[12]

Soeur Marie Francois, of the third Order of St. Francis of Saint-Serlin, went to confession to him [the Cure] during Holy Week in 1849 or 1850. Her accusation concluded, she asked: "Father, what is it God wants of me?" "Ah! my child . . ." a faint gentle voice murmured from behind the grating.

"That was all. After that," the Sister relates, "M. Vianney spoke as if to himself, for the space of five minutes and in a tongue unknown to me; at any rate I could not understand him. In my astonishment I looked into his face. He seemed to be out of himself, and I thought that he beheld the good God." [13]

Glossolalia, as we have said, is not a language (unless we would want to call it heavenly language). However, there are rare occasions when listeners will claim that the tongues speaker is speaking in a known language he has not learned. Anthropologists call this *xenolalia* or *xenoglossia*. William J. Samarin, professor of Anthropology and Linguistics at the University of Toronto, defines xenoglossia as ". . . the demonstration of knowledge of a language not learned in the normal way." [14] Donald Gee, a renowned British Assemblies of God teacher, in speaking of this phenomenon, also supports the fact that tongues is ordinarily nonrational speech.

Although its [tongues] chief purpose was for communion with God in prayer and praise . . . Divine Providence . . . could . . . cause . . . the language uttered to be the mother-tongue of an unbeliever, as on the Day of Pentecost. *This was apparently incidental, however, and was not inherent in the gift.* [15] *

As to whether there are examples of xenoglossia in lives of Saints it is hard to say at present. As Stanley Burgess, an Assemblies of God historian, pointed out in a paper [16] he gave in 1973 at the Society of Pentecostal Studies, secondary sources have perpetuated errors. Dr. John Kildahl, a psychotherapist and author of the book *The Psychology of Speaking in Tongues*, writes:

Biographies of the great missionary saints of the time of the Middle Ages—Vincent Ferrer, Francis Xavier, and Louis Bertrand—long perpetuated the notion that these individuals possessed the gift of tongues in the sense that they could speak existing foreign languages of which they had little or no knowledge. They supposedly had been given this gift in order to convert the non-European pagan peoples of the world to Christianity.

More careful study of the facts indicates that the biographers were subject to the power of the myth. Xavier, for example, in his letters to his superiors and other associates, told of his difficulties in attempting to master such Oriental languages as Japanese. He wrote that he used both sign language and interpreters to assist him in preaching the gospel in Japan and China.[17]

In a book, *Saints, Their Place in the Church*, Fr. Paul Molinari says that the material containing the processes of beatification and canonization of Saints lies in Vatican archives "woefully neglected." [18] Hopefully, research into this source material in the

---

* Italics mine.

future will answer some of our questions about xenoglossia and other related matters.

Stanley Burgess,[19] and following him, Vinson Synan,[20] and after him, Williams and Waldvogel,[21] call the phenomenon of the Pentecost event *heteroglossolalia*, which Dr. Synan defines as a phenomenon in which "each person hears his own language when the speaker is communicating in his native tongue." [22] Here, as with xenoglossia, errors have been perpetuated in secondary sources. The reporting of a Pentecost miracle (heteroglossolalia) is another legend in St. Anthony of Padua's life along with the mistakes made about his name, nationality, and the vision of the Child Jesus. In 1228 St. Anthony went to Rome and preached before Pope Gregory IX (former Cardinal Ugolino, great friend and protector of St. Francis) and many cardinals. His preaching was so inspired it captivated his hearers. Here is what a respected Franciscan scholar, Sophronius Clasen, O.F.M., has to say of this event. "In later times, it seemed quite incredible that his sermon should have such an effect, and men began to say instead that on this occasion the miracle of Pentecost was renewed." [23] In my reading of primary and secondary sources I have come across no examples of heteroglossolalia.

One of the blessings of glossolalia so far not mentioned is singing in tongues. Another look at Church history will probably reveal many analogues of singing in tongues as well as praying in tongues. What is called "jubilation" is probably an analogue of singing in tongues. A description of jubilation can be found in *Hungry for God* by Ralph Martin:

> Numbers of music historians, in their attempts to understand the roots of Western music, have researched the common practice of congregations and individual Christians of this period using wordless singing as a means of praising God. Most of the Church Fathers laud this practice. Jubilation (L. jubili—shouts or sounds of joy), "wordless praise," "wordless

psalms," and the "singing of alleluia," were some of the terms used to describe this singing of wordless hymns. Augustine, perhaps, defines it best. He states that jubilation is a breaking forth into a singing of a vowel sounds. [sic] He furthermore states: "What is jubilation? Joy that cannot be expressed in words; yet the voice expresses what is conceived within." (Enar. in Ps. 94,3; 99,4.)

. . . Jubilation, in a free, improvised Spirit-led form appears to have been a major part of the life of the Christian Church at least till the first part of the seventh century. . . .[24]

A classic of spiritual theology is *The Graces of Interior Prayer* by A. Poulain, S.J. (1912). In this book Fr. Poulain speaks of a state of prayer which he calls the "quietude of jubilation." He describes it this way: "The soul . . . feels a need to overflow in ardent colloquies, or even to break out into singing." [25]

Many, if not most of the Saints prayed a form of prayer called the "rosary." Rosary beads consist of five sets (decades) each of ten small and one larger bead; a crucifix with two large and three small beads is ordinarily added. An Our Father is said on the large beads and Hail Marys on the small beads. The method of saying the rosary is to recite the prayers while meditating on a mystery of faith such as the nativity or the crucifixion. Now it is impossible to think what the words of the prayers mean if the mind is dwelling on a mystery of faith, and so many people mechanically rattle off the prayers but they are praying because their mind is with the Lord in some way. I believe the rosary said in this manner is analogous to the gift of devotional or private tongues.

This perhaps becomes clearer as the rosary is explained by a Methodist minister. In his book *Five For Sorrow, Ten For Joy*, J. Neville Ward gives this explanation of the rosary:

It seems hard to believe that one can meditate on a theme

while mentally repeating certain prayers even though these are so thoroughly known that little effort is required. As one becomes familiar with the Rosary the prayers gradually recede, to form a kind of "background music," and the mystery is before the mind as though one is looking at a religious picture or icon. The balance frequently changes, and the prayers occupy the foreground of the mind for a time, and this may lead to a form of simple attention to God which is more like contemplation. If one finds one's mind being led into a stillness and concentration of this kind it is good to let it happen. It is just a fact of Christian history that the saints put their money on contemplation rather than meditation for producing the longing for God. . . .

This movement of the mind between meditation and contemplation and petition and praise is a feature of this way of praying that gives it great flexibility and may well explain in part why it appeals to so many people so different in religious makeup.[26]

Of course, while the mind is doing the moving about that Reverend Ward describes so well for us, the mouth and vocal chords are engaged in speaking words. The listener would say the words have meaning because they are words to well-known prayers. The speaker or one praying would truthfully admit the words have no meaning, for the mind is engaged elsewhere.

As a little girl I used to attend novena services [27] with my Catholic grandmother. I can still recall vividly what it was like if we came late to the service. The congregation and priest would be reciting a "litany." All litanies sounded the same, very much like a locomotive gathering up steam. If it were a novena to the Blessed Mother, for example, the priest would give one of her ancient titles, "Star of the Sea" or "House of Gold." The people would then respond with "Pray for us." You would hear perhaps two hundred or more voices rising and falling saying: "Pray for us. Pray for us. Pray for us." From the back of the Church you could barely hear the priest inserting his lines. Litanies were usually followed by a Benediction service in which much incense was used. When I think of the novenas that were a part of my childhood, I think of incense, adoration and the rhythmic rise and fall of many voices.

Eight years ago I spoke to a woman in her eighties who had just been to her first prayer meeting. She said she felt quite at home. She likened the praying in tongues to reciting litanies and the singing in tongues to the old Latin Benediction hymns like "Tantum Ergo." "You know," she said wisely, "the Holy Spirit never likes a vacuum." She was referring to the fact that novenas had just about gone the way of the Latin mass.

It was only in recent years that for Catholics the liturgy was changed from Latin to the vernacular. For hundreds of years not only did the faithful attend a Sunday service (Mass) that was in a foreign language, priests had to say daily prayers (the Divine Office) in Latin, and so did many communities of sisters, especially sisters belonging to comtemplative orders. Many of the priests and religious did not understand what they were praying but I imagine that if in some way their heart was united with the Lord while they were reciting the Latin they couldn't understand, that this was comparable to tongues.

Reciting the Office in Latin was the occasion when St. Teresa of Avila sometimes received the gift of understanding a language she had not learned. (Teresa spoke Spanish.) In her own words (contained in her *Autobiography*) we have her describe this phenomenon:

> Thus, when in this state of Quiet, I, who understand hardly anything that I recite in Latin, particularly in the Psalter, have not only been able to understand the text as though it were in Spanish but have even found to my delight that I can

penetrate the meaning of the Spanish.[28]

Another Saint, according to a primary source, who received assistance from God in saying the Divine Office was St. Catherine of Siena (1347-1380). Her life was written by Blessed Raymond of Capua who was her friend and confessor and who, after her death, became a reforming general of the Dominicans. Here is what happened in Raymond's own words:

. . . I must tell you, reader, that this holy virgin knew how to read without being taught by human beings. I say "read;" she could never speak Latin, but she could read the words and say them properly. She told me that when she decided to learn to read so that she could say the Divine Praises and the Canonical Hours, a friend of hers wrote the alphabet and tried to teach it her, but after spending many fruitless weeks over it she decided not to waste any more time over it and to turn to heavenly grace instead. One morning she knelt down and prayed to the Lord. "Lord," she said, "if you want me to learn to read so that I can say the Psalms and sing your praises in the Canonical Hours, deign to teach me what I am not clever enough to learn by myself. If not, thy will be done: I shall be quite content to remain in my ignorance and shall be able to spend more time in meditating on you in other ways."

Then a marvel happened—clear proof of God's power—for during this prayer she was so divinely instructed that when she got up she knew how to read any kind of writing quite easily and fluently, like the best reader in the world. When I realized this I was flabbergasted, especially when I discovered that though she could read so fast she could not read separate syllables; in fact, she could hardly spell the words. I believe that the Lord meant this to be a sign of the miracle that had taken place.

From then on Catherine began to hunt for books on the

Divine Office and to read the Psalms and anthems and the other things fixed for the Canonical Hours.[29]

Three studies on the history of the charisms [30] credit the Benedictine Abbess, Hildegard of Bingen (1098-1179), with the gift of tongues. A recent paper by Dr. George Williams of Harvard and Edith Waldvogel, a Harvard Ph.D. candidate, says that Hildegard ". . . sang in unknown words with such facility and winsomeness that her utterances were called concerts in the Spirit." [31]

What is known as the "Jesus Prayer" in the Eastern Church is comparable to glossolalic prayer. The commonest form of the prayer is: "Lord Jesus Christ, Son of God, have mercy upon me, a sinner." A shortened form—the Name of Jesus only—is frequently used also. This prayer of the invocation of the Name thousands upon thousands of times a day was used by numerous holy people of the Eastern Church and has become popular in recent years in the Western Church. The prayer of the holy Name of Jesus is breathed continually. Saints of the Eastern Church especially associated with the Jesus prayer were: St. Gregory the Sinite (d. 1346), St. Maximus the Kapsokalyvia (14th c.), St. Theoleptus (d.c. 1310), St. Gregory Palamas (c. 1296-1359), St. Nilus Sorsky (Nilus Maikov, 1433-1508) and St. Macarius of Corinth (1731-1805). St. Seraphim of Sarov (1759-1833) recommended the prayer. From the Middle Ages onward the monks of the Byzantine East used a rosary in association with the prayer of Jesus. Perhaps the best known and most valuable book on this prayer form is *The Prayer of Jesus* by a monk of the Eastern Church. In concluding his work on this subject the monk writes:

After Pentecost the apostles became capable of announcing the name "with authority." Here we have a "pentecostal" use of the name of Jesus, a use which is not the apostles' monopoly, but which remains open to all believers. Only the weakness of our faith and charity prevents us from renewing

159

in the name of Jesus the fruits of Pentecost, from driving out devils from imposing hands on the sick and curing them.[32]

Simone Weil (1909-1943, a French mystic, considered a Saint by many moderns despite her refusal to receive the sacrament of baptism) described in a letter to a French priest, her experience of repetitive prayer:

> Last summer, doing Greek with T_____, I went through the Our Father word for word in Greek. We promised each other to learn it by heart. . . . Some weeks later, as I was turning over the pages of the Gospel, I said to myself that since I had promised to do this thing and it was good, I ought to do it. I did it. The infinite sweetness of this Greek text so took hold of me that for several days I could not stop myself from saying it over all the time. A week afterward I began the vine harvest. I recited the Our Father in Greek every day before work, and I repeated it very often in the vineyard.[33]

During the fourth week of the *Spiritual Exercises*, St. Ignatius recommends a method of prayer which he calls "rhythmical recitation." Reminiscent of the "Jesus Prayer" and what came to be known as the "Hesychast tradition," Ignatius connects his method of praying with breathing. One word of the "Our Father," "Hail Mary" or any other prayer is to be said with each breath. Either the mind may give full attention to each word, or (while breathing and saying the words of the prayers rhythmically) Ignatius proposes that the mind may dwell on concepts other than the meaning of the words. The mind may give full attention "to the person whom he is addressing, or to his own unworthiness, or to the difference between the greatness of this Person and his own lowliness" (*Exercises*, Fourth Week). Certainly we can see here a similarity to tongues. Commenting on this recommended method of Ignatian prayer, Michael Foss writes in his book *The Founding of the Jesuits*: "This [method of prayer] is novel, though whether it is effective or not is hard to say. The mind seems to play little part in these proceedings." [34]

Notes to Chapter 11

1. *Minor Works of St. Teresa*, "Introduction to the Conceptions of the Love of God," translated by the Benedictines of Stanbrook, Thomas Baker, London, 1913, p. 112.

2. Walter J. Hollenweger, *New Wine in Old Wineskins*, Fellowship Press, Gloucester, England, 1973, p. 47. The first section of this little book is a revision by the author of the first chapter of his book, *The Pentecostals*. (Augsburg Publishing House, Minneapolis, 1972; S.C.M., London, 1972). *The Pentecostals* is an abridged English version of the ten-volume study in German by the author.

3. Yves Congar, "Charismatiques, ou quoi?" *La Croix*, 19 Janvier 1974 as cited by Kilian McDonnell, O.S.B. in "The Holy Spirit and Christian Initiation" in *The Holy Spirit and Power* edited by McDonnell, Doubleday & Company, Inc., Garden City, New York, 1975, pp. 62-64.

4. These three adjectives are most commonly used to designate the nine gifts. In many places in the text of this book I use all three together to help to ensure that I will be understood by people of varying traditions. These gifts are not the "sanctifying gifts," the "seven gifts" mentioned in Isaiah which Catholics usually memorize in preparation for the sacrament of confirmation. Also, in singling out these nine gifts it is understood that the term "charism" is not restricted to them.

5. Whether or not tongues is a real language the speaker has not learned has been a matter of some controversy among those who speak in tongues. I agree with Frs. Kilian McDonnell and George Montague that in most cases scientific investigation would find that it is not. At the annual meeting of the Catholic Biblical Association in 1973 Fr. Montague called tongues "preconceptual prayer."

6. Fr. Montague says that S. Lyonnet in "De Glossolalia Pentecostes eiusque significatione," *Verbum Dei* 24 (1944) considers the Pentecost miracle one of hearing as well as speaking. Each listener heard each speaker speaking the listener's language. Fr. Montague fails to see this interpretation as necessary. Since the community was engaged in praising, ". . . it would certainly not be surprising that occasional words in the other language known to the listeners would be heard and this. . . without any accompanying miracle of hearing." (George T. Montague, S.M., "Baptism in the Spirit and Speaking in Tongues: A Biblical Appraisal" in *Theology Digest*, winter 1973, p. 353 and note 77 p. 360.)

7. 1 Corinthians 14:22 is usually translated: "Thus, tongues are a sign not for believers but for unbelievers, while prophecy is not for unbelievers but for believers." This is immediately followed by these lines: "If, therefore, the whole church assembles and all speak in tongues, and outsiders or unbelievers enter, will they not say that you are mad? But if all prophesy, and an unbeliever or outsider enters, he is convicted by all, he is called to account . . ." (1 Cor. 14:23-24). The J.B. Phillips translation of 1 Corinthians 14:22 reverses the order of the words so it reads: ". . . 'tongues' are a sign of God's power, not for those who are unbelievers but to those who already believe." Phillips says in a footnote: "This is the sole instance of the translator's departing from the accepted text. He felt bound to conclude, from the sense of the next three verses, that we have here either a slip of the pen on the part of Paul, or, more probably, a copyist's error."
8. Arnold Bittlinger, *Gifts and Graces*, p. 101.
9. The material in this field, as in others, is proliferating faster than one can keep up with it and the fact that it is scattered in so many varied publications makes the problem more acute. Some of the work I am familiar with includes: "A History of Speaking in Tongues and Related Gifts" by George H. Williams and Edith Waldvogel in *The Charismatic Movement*, edited by Michael P. Hamilton, Eerdmans, Grand Rapids, 1975; Morton T. Kelsey, *Tongues Speaking*, Doubleday & Company, Inc., Garden City, 1968; Chapter III, "A Peculiar History," Robert G. Gromacki, *The Modern Tongues Movement*, Presbyterian and Reformed Publishing Company, Nutley, N.J., 1973; Chapter II, "A Historical Survey of Speaking in Tongues," Watson E. Mills, *Speaking in Tongues, Let's Talk About It*, Word Books, Waco, Texas, 1973; "Glossolalia in Historical Perspective" by John T. Bunn and "Glossolalia as a Vocal Phenomenon" by Samarin. The last-mentioned article is good for a clarification of terms. The same author has written an analysis of tongues in book form, *Tongues of Men and Angels*, (New York: Macmillan, 1972). I might point out a really excellent article on "Catholic Pentecostals" in the Mills book by Don Patterson, Th.D., Associate Professor of Religion at Baylor University. An interesting contribution is a paper "Lesser-Known Sources in the Roman Catholic Tradition for Charismatic Piety" by Stanley Burgess (Assemblies of God), Associate Professor of History at Evangel College in Springfield, Mo. Depending on one's persuasion he is a "reformation historian" or a "revolt historian." (This is how the author was introduced.) This paper was presented at the Society of Pentecostal Studies in November 1973. It is distributed on a cassette by Logos Tapes, Hazlet, N.J., 07730. The author says in an introductory statement that the paper is a progress report (really of his own investigation) and not a final word. It is encouraging to see research into our common heritage by a classical Pentecostal. The paper is however flawed by a few errors. There is given a definite impression that the

Church canonizes because of miracles and tongues speaking. This is not true. There is also a difference between the posthumous miracles required during the canonization process (after the candidate is dead) and those recorded during the person's lifetime. The author seems unfamiliar with the distinction. There are also minor factual mistakes. For example, Clare of Montefalco is called the founder of the Poor Clares, wh'le the foundress actually was Clare of Assisi.

A paper which cites Burgess' paper is "The Role of the Holy Spirit and the Gifts of The Spirit in the Mystical Tradition" by Vinson Synan in *One In Christ*, 1974, Vol. 2. This paper is a contribution to the Roman Catholic-Pentecostal Dialogue. Dr. Synan accepts Burgess' conclusion that scholars need to go beyond the *Acta Sanctorum* to the contemporary documents to get the truest picture of mystical charismatic phenomena. (See Appendix I for a critique of this terminology.) I wonder why Burgess concluded, as he did in his paper, that the Bollandists haven't succeeded in removing all the errors in the Saints' lives they have worked on. As I only had access to the tape and not the footnotes I don't know the answer. I don't feel the average scholar is equipped to deal with hagiography.

Another source is the series of articles on tradition which have been appearing in *New Covenant*, a magazine serving the Catholic charismatic renewal and the renewal at large, P.O. Box 102, Ann Arbor, Michigan, 48107. These articles appear under the general heading "A Charismatic Heritage." They include: "Healing and Worship in the Fifth Century Church," March 1975; "Charisms in an Age of Upheaval," April 1975; and "A Brotherhood of Love in the Thirteenth Century," May 1975. All three articles are by Eddie Ensley. None of the above sources, with the exception of *New Covenant*, is Catholic. Material in this area by Catholics is mostly written "by the way" and is scattered through books and articles primarily on other subjects. *Healing* by Francis MacNutt, O.P., contains general references to Saints and the tradition of healing shrines. There is limited reference to Saints and charisms in *The Pentecostal Movement in the Catholic Church* by Fr. Edward O'Connor, C.S.C. Two books by the Dominican priest, Simon Tugwell, contain assorted references to relevant subject matter, *Did You Receive the Spirit?* and *Prayer*, Vol. 2, Templegate Publishers, Springfield, Ill., 1975. The reader might want to consult the bibliography to the present volume under the heading "Mystical Phenomena." Basic works on Catholic spiritual theology often contain references to miracles associated with Saints but sometimes the citations are undocumented and are of little value. One of the best contributions by a Catholic is an article by a Carmelite nun, Teresa Del Monte Sol, "Pentecostalism and the Doctrine of Saint Teresa and Saint John of the Cross" in *Spiritual Life*, Spring, 1971.

10. So in the *Rituale Romanum*, the official Catholic book of public services, issued in 1614 and with occasional subsequent revisions, the general rules concern-

ing exorcism state: "Especially, he [the priest authorised to perform an exorcism] should not believe too readily that a person is possessed by an evil spirit; but he ought to ascertain the signs by which a person possessed can be distinguished from one who is suffering from some illness, especially one of a psychological nature. Signs of possession may be the following: ability to speak with some facility in a strange tongue (ignota lingua loqui pluribus verbis) or to understand it when spoken by another; the faculty of divulging future and hidden events; display of powers which are beyond the subject's age and natural condition; and various other indications which, when taken together as a whole, build up the evidence." (*The Roman Ritual*, Complete Edition, translated and edited by Philip T. Weller, The Bruce Publishing Company, Milwaukee, 1964, Part XIII, Ch. I, para. 3, p. 641.)

11. By primary sources I mean writings by the Saints themselves or firsthand accounts by witnesses. The translations of the *Autobiography* and *Foundations* are by E. Allison Peers.

12. Abbe Francis Trochu, *The Cure d'Ars*, p. 538.

13. *Ibid.*, pp. 529-530.

14. William J. Samarin, "Glossolalia as a Vocal Phenomenon" in *Speaking in Tongues, Let's Talk About It*, by Watson E. Mills, Editor, p. 130.

15. Gee, *Concerning Spiritual Gifts*, The Gospel Publishing House, Springfield, Missouri, no date, p. 58. Also cited in William J. Samarin, *Tongues of Men and Angels*, p. 110.

16. Stanley Burgess, "Lesser-Known Sources in the Roman Catholic Tradition for Charismatic Piety," presented at the Society for Pentecostal Studies, November 1973.

17. John P. Kildahl, *The Psychology of Speaking in Tongues*, Harper and Row Publishers, New York, 1972, pp. 15-16. A different explanation is given by the Jesuit historian, Fr. James Broderick, S.J., who regards the attribution of xeno-glossia to Xavier as stemming entirely from the evidence of one unreliable witness (*Saint Francis Xavier*, the Wicklow Press, New York, 1952, p. 457).

18. Molinari, *Saints, Their Place in the Church*, p. 33.

19. Burgess, *op. cit.*

20. Synan, *op. cit.*

21. Williams and Waldvogel, *op. cit.*, p. 69.

22. Synan, *op. cit.*, p. 200.

23. Clausen, *St. Anthony*, p. 88.

24. Ralph Martin, *Hungry for God*, Doubleday & Company, Garden City, New York, 1974, pp. 165-166. This is a quotation from original research done by Eddy Ensley.

25. A. Poulain, S.J., *The Graces of Interior Prayer*, p. 184.

164

26. Ward, *Five for Sorrow, Ten for Joy*, pp. 12-13.

27. The word "novena" comes from the Latin *novenus*, meaning "ninth." A novena is a prayer for some special intention or occasion extended over a period of nine days. Novenas were private devotions made by individuals or they were sometimes Church services. Novena devotions I attended as a child consisted of a litany, a sermon and benediction.

28. *Autobiography*, Chapter XV, Peers Translation, Image, p. 158.

29. Blessed Raymond of Capua, *The Life of St. Catherine of Siena*, Pt. 1, Chapter XI, p. 97.

30. Kelsey, *Tongues Speaking*, p. 47-48; Gromacki, *op. cit.*, p. 18; Williams and Waldvogel, *op. cit.*, p. 70.

31. Williams & Waldvogel, *op. cit.*

32. *The Prayer of Jesus*, by a Monk of the Eastern Church, Desclee Company, New York, 1967, p. 111.

33. Simone Weil, *Waiting for God*, Harper Colophon Books, Harper & Row, New York, 1973, p. 71.

34. Michael Foss, *The Founding of the Jesuits*, p. 96.

CHAPTER 12

Saints and Charisms II

Faith

St. Paul says in Galatians 2:20, ". . . the life I now live in the flesh I live by faith in the Son of God, who loved me and gave himself for me." This and similar passages show us that faith is essential and integral to the Christian life. Then what is Paul talking about when he includes faith in his list of the gifts of the Spirit in 1 Corinthians 12:9? This is the special faith Jesus was talking about when He said: "if you have faith as a grain of mustard seed, you will say to this mountain, 'move hence to yonder place,' and it will move . . ." (Matt. 17:20). It is special faith which enables a person to know that that which he prays for will be or has been granted. It is the faith Jesus exhibited when He said, "Lazarus, come out" (John 11:43) and to the paralytic "take up your bed and go home" (Matt. 9:6). Jesus knew that His Father had heard His prayer and issued a command based on that knowledge.

This special gift of faith is sometimes categorized as a "gift of power"[1] or a "sign gift"[2] and as such is usually grouped with two other gifts also considered sign or power gifts. These are gifts of healing and the working of miracles. These gifts attract attention to the Christian message. They display striking evidence not to be denied that Jesus Christ is truly Lord of heaven and earth.

There are numerous instances of the charismatic gift of faith contained in primary sources concerning Saints' lives. One has already been alluded to in the chapter on relics. This is one of the times when the miracle of the multiplication of food is recorded in the life of St. John Vianney. We have the incident from a book based on testimony given during the investigation that paved the way for the canonization of this French parish priest of the last century. One day, in The Providence, the orphanage founded by St. John Vianney, there was only enough flour to make three loaves of bread.

"We felt anxious," says Jeanne-Marie Chanay, "because of our children. Catherine [Catherine Lassagne was in charge of the orphanage for twenty-two years] and I thought that if M. le Cure [John Vianney] would pray to the good God, he could obtain that the handful of flour that was left should yield an ovenful of loaves. We went to inform him of our predicament. 'You must make the dough,' he said. So I set to work, not without a certain apprehension. I began by putting a very small quantity of water and flour in the kneading trough, but I saw that the flour remained too thick. I added some water and more flour, without my small stock being exhausted.

"The trough was full of dough, as on a day when a whole sack of flour was emptied into it. We baked ten big loaves, each weighing from twenty to twenty-two pounds, and the oven was filled as usual, to the great astonishment of all present.

"We told M. le Cure what had happened; his reply was; 'the good God is very good! He takes care of His poor.' " [3]

In saying "You must make the dough" the Cure d'Ars manifested the charismatic gift of faith. The cure knew God had heard his prayer and he issued a command based on that knowledge.

Another example of this charismatic gift comes from the life of a Saint who served the Lord more than seven hundred years earlier. St. Bernard of Clairvaux (1090-1153) joined the abbey of Citeaux under St. Stephen Harding. A few years afterwards he was sent to found another monastery, which he did, at Clairvaux. He served as an adviser to popes and kings and established sixty-eight Cistercian houses. His correspondence is said to have been enormous, though only a small fraction survives. A translator of Bernard's letters has this to say about a letter written around the year 1119:

> This is one of the most characteristic of Bernard's letters and it is interesting from an historical point of view as the first shot fired in the great controversy between the congregation of Cluny and the Cistercian reform. It is also interesting from the circumstances under which it was written. The monk, William, Bernard's secretary at this time, tells us that while Bernard was dictating in a secluded corner out of doors, where he could not be overheard, heavy rain began to fall. But when he tried to protect the letter *Bernard told him to write on** for it was God's work, and yet, although rain fell all around, the letter remained dry *in imbre sine imbre*.[4]

Just as Jesus said, "take up your bed," to the paralytic, St. Bernard exercised special faith when he told William to write on.

The Gift of Healing

Along with the power or sign gifts of faith and working of miracles, there are healing gifts, often connected with the ministry of evangelism. Sign gifts, as we said earlier, attract attention and prepare people to hear the good news. People are more disposed to being evangelized after seeing God work in power.

> And Jesus went on from there and passed along the Sea of Galilee. And he went up into the hills, and sat down there. And great crowds came to him, bringing with them the lame, the maimed, the blind, the dumb, and many others, and they put them at his feet, and he healed them, *so that the throng wondered,** when they saw the dumb speaking, the maimed whole . . . (Matt. 15:29-31).

The testimony collected for the canonization process of St. John

---

*Italics mine.

Vianney lists a good number of healings. Some were instantaneous and some were gradual like the following example:

In 1855, a girl of Montchanin (Saone-et-Loire) of the name of Farnier, came to Ars to beg from M. Vianney the cure of her paralyzed leg. "My child," the saint told her, "you disobey your mother far too often, and answer her back in a disrespectful manner. If you wish the good God to cure you, you must correct that ugly defect. Oh! What a task lies before you! But remember one thing: you will indeed get well, but by degrees, according as you try to correct that defect." As soon as Mlle. Farnier returned home she endeavoured to show more obedience and respect to her mother. Her crippled leg, which had been four inches shorter than the other, insensibly grew longer, and at the end of a few years her infirmity had wholly vanished.[5]

Signs such as this healing drew people to the parish church in Ars to hear John Vianney preach the good news and contributed to the conversion and transformation of the entire town.

The history of Saints reveals that sometimes a healing or miracle occurred as a sign from God that He approved of an endeavor or work a Saint was engaged in and it served to silence criticism or opposition. St. Colette of Corbie was a great Poor Clare abbess of the fifteenth century. An account of her life was written by her confessor, Father Pierrede Vaux and another was compiled by her secretary, Sister Perrien de la Baume. Both of these friends of Colette swore in the presence of witnesses that what they wrote was true. There are numerous incidents recorded of the gifts of healing and miracles being manifested in Colette's life. Especially when Colette's work for the Lord was threatened with scandal, someone would be healed as a sign from God that Colette was about His business. Here is one account as told by a Poor Clare who has consulted the primary sources.

. . . canons and parish priests had tried to defame her

[Colette]. God was swift to defend her, and with miracles. Just at the time of the building scandal, Father Pierre de Vaux tells us, the town bailiff was suffering from a violent attack of what was then called quatern ague. (It was perhaps a variant of malaria.) Colette saw him pale and shivering. . . . She intended to assure the sick man of her prayers for his recovery. Instead, on a sudden inspiration, she heard herself say: "Have courage, monsieur! You must get well without delay, for you have to help us finish the monastery." She made the sign of the cross over him, and he was instantly cured.[6]

St. Teresa of Avila recorded instances of healing when she wrote her own life story.

. . . there was a person very ill with a most painful malady, which, as we do not know its exact nature, I shall not now describe. His sufferings for two months had been intolerable and he was in such torture that he would lacerate his own body. My confessor . . . . told me that I must certainly pay him a visit. . . . I went and was moved to such pity for him that I began with great importunity to beg the Lord to cure him. . . . On the very next day, my relative was completely free from that pain.[7]

The lives of some Saints, however, as well as our present experience, teach us that suffering has a place in God's mysterious design for His people. St. Paul left Trophimus ill at Miletus (2 Tim. 4:20). If St. Paul could cure at will, he would certainly have seen that his friend Trophimus was healed. Also, instead of (or along with) praying over Timothy's stomach, St. Paul prescribed that Timothy take a little wine for the ailment (1 Tim. 5:23). St. Luke in Colossians 4 is described as "the beloved physician," not "the unemployed physician!" When she lay dying, St. Bernadette, who was used by God to discover the healing spring at Lourdes, was told by the sisters that they wanted to take her to Lourdes so she

171

could be healed. She repeated with great certainty, "The spring is not for me. The spring is not for me."

Working of Miracles

Donald Gee, in *Concerning Spiritual Gifts*, remarks that this gift is in the middle of the list in 1 Corinthians and just takes its place among other, what we would regard as more ordinary, manifestations of the Spirit. He feels we are wrong in thinking this way on two counts: first, because we don't expect the miraculous enough; and second, because we do not see enough of the miraculous in the ordinary.[8] Saints seem to have done both. Francis of Assisi was entranced with the miracle of the beauty of nature. As for expecting the miraculous, excerpts from his life such as the taming of the wolf of Gubbio, show that he expected the power of God to be operative.

St. Peter raised Dorcas to life (Acts 9:40). St. Paul brought Eutychus back to life (Acts 20:10). St. Colette of Corbie restored to life a dead child, Colette Prucet, named after the woman used by God to bring her back to life. Three other such miracles of raising the dead were attested to and figured in the beatification proceedings of St. Colette.[9]

Saints seemed at times to have miraculous empathy with or control over nature. Three primary sources on the life of Francis of Assisi recount the famous story of the time Francis preached to the birds.[10] Francis came to a place called Pian dell' Arca three miles south of Assisi, and found that the trees and fields there were full of birds. He asked his companion to wait for him and he "ran eagerly" towards the birds.

> . . . not a little surprised that the birds did not rise in flight, as they usually do, he was filled with great joy and humbly begged them to listen to the word of God. Among the many things he spoke to them were these words that he added: "My brothers, birds, you should praise your Creator very much and always love Him; He gave you feathers to clothe you,

wings so that you can fly, and whatever else was necessary for you. . . ." At these words, as Francis himself used to say and those too who were with him, the birds, rejoicing in a wonderful way according to their nature, began to stretch their necks, extend their wings, open their mouths and gaze at him. And Francis . . . went on his way and returned, touching their heads and bodies with his tunic.[11]

St. Bonaventure, a theologian who was himself a Franciscan, wrote a life of Francis. He reports at least fifteen similar incidents. There was a hare in the town of Greccio that followed Francis like a little dog. Sheep who loved him accompanied him at St. Mary of the Angels, the Portiuncula.[12]

It is said of St. Julie Billiart (1751-1816), the foundress of the Sisters of Notre Dame de Namur, that once when she was leaving the town of Plessier, a mad dog rushed at her and the sisters who accompanied her. The dog had already bitten several people. Julie told her sisters not to be afraid. Then she bent towards the dog and said, "Let us pass, my friend. We are little servants of the Lord and we are going to do His work." They passed safely on and the dog remained quiet for that short time and then became as dangerous as before.[13]

Perhaps the most famous dog in hagiography is "Grigio" (Gray), Don Bosco's protector. His existence is well documented since few Saints' lives have the amount of primary source material available as that of Don Bosco, St. John Bosco (1815-1888). Two popes, Pius IX and Leo XIII ordered him to write his memoirs. For the last twenty-four years of his life practically his every word and every detail of his life were recorded by Don John Lemoyne. Primary sources attest to the fact that many attempts were made on Don Bosco's life by Waldensians, Carbonari and others. Whenever there was danger a huge gray dog appeared out of nowhere to protect him.[14]

The gift of the Spirit of the working of miracles is a burden on one through whom the Spirit works in this manner. After Jesus multiplied loaves and fish for the multitude who were following Him "because they saw the signs which he did on those who were diseased," He had to withdraw to the hills because the crowd wanted to make Him king (John 6:15).

The list of recorded miracles in the life of Don Bosco is lengthy. After consulting the sources Dr. Phelan, one of this Saint's biographers, tells us an incident which reveals how heavy the Saint felt the responsibilities of this gift:

> One day he [Don Bosco] jokingly told an enthusiastic Salesian who had just preached a successful mission, "I would like to obtain the gift of miracles for you from God." "Nothing could be better," was the happy reply, "then I could more easily convert sinners." "If you had this gift," Don Bosco said, suddenly becoming very serious, "you would quickly, and with tears, ask God to take it from you."[15]

The "Word of Wisdom" and the "Word of Knowledge"

These two gifts of the Holy Spirit appears first in order in St. Paul's list of the nine gifts. Many writers on the subject of these two charisms refer to the distinction between these gifts but also their relationship, by repeating the ancient definition: "wisdom is knowledge rightly applied." This definition obtains whether we are talking about natural or supernatural wisdom or knowledge. Perhaps it would be good to look at what the charisms of wisdom and knowledge are not, before we attempt to see what they might be and then seek examples in Saints' lives.

The charisms of wisdom and knowledge are not: 1) natural common sense, a Ph. D. or high I.Q.; 2) special knowledge that someone has been cured of a specific illness during a healing service, or other special knowledge:[16] 3) permanent endowments always there to be drawn upon. Certainly it is true in a broad sense that everything is a gift of God: good health, a high I.Q. or inherited wealth. But by the charisms of wisdom and knowledge we do not mean, for example, an Einstein who has been baptized in the Spirit. The Pentecostal writer Donald Gee wrote about the three common misunderstandings of these gifts. Of the first he wrote: ". . . highly educated people in the natural, and believers with a lot of Bible knowledge in the spiritual, can sometimes do extremely foolish and fanatical things."[17] Regarding the second, he wrote: "We shall be . . . foolish if we try to drive the 'word of knowledge' into mystical channels of remarkable revelations concerning men and things."[18] Steppen Clark writes the same thing: "St. Paul, when he is speaking about the utterance of knowledge almost certainly does not mean a special knowledge of facts that a person could not have known oterwise."[19] And of the third misunderstanding of these charisms Gee wrote:

There are some who regard themselves as having "the gift of wisdom," and they apparently consider themselves as endowed with an infallible sagacity that can be tapped to order at any time! In the mistaken sense in which such folk mean it, there is no such gift. It is the gift of the *"word* of wisdom," and implies a spoken utterance through a direct operation of the Holy Spirit at a given moment, rather than an abiding deposit of supernatural wisdom.

Believers do not become reservoirs of *this* kind of wisdom. All the "treasures of wisdom and knowledge" are hid in Christ (Col. 2:3). Severed from His grace a counsel of utter foolishness can be given even by one who at other times has had truly supernatural flashes of the spiritual gift. Its manifestation is subject to the divine sovereignty, and dependent upon the Spirit-filled believer walking in unbroken communion with the Lord.[20]

The charisms of wisdom and knowledge are teaching gifts for the body of Christ. Just as the charism of prophecy (one of the nine gifts) relates to the office of prophet, the charisms of wisdom and knowledge relate to the offices of teacher and other "leadership" offices in the Church dealing with government and guidance. The charismatic/spiritual/ministry gift of wisdom comes by revelation. "Something flashes," says Gee. "There is a sense of the divine. . . . One is deeply conscious that the supremely right thing has been said, and the true course of action indicated."[21] According to Stephen Clark, the utterance or word of wisdom is concerned with the best way to live. "It is an expression of God's guidance in how to live as a Christian."[22] Clark describes the utterance of knowledge more in terms of doctrinal teaching. "It is the Spirit inspiring someone to speak an understanding of a truth of the mystery of Christ."[23]

St. Catherine of Siena, who had no formal education, had revelations and gave teaching which was taken down by secretaries. Her confessor, Blessed Raymond of Capua, also recorded much of what she taught. In his account of St. Catherine's life, Raymond tells us that on one occasion Catherine told him how she understood Jesus' prayer in the garden. "She said that the words, 'My Father, if it be possible, let this chalice pass from me . . .' were not to be understood by the strong and perfect in the same way as by the weak who are afraid of death." Catherine tells Raymond that Jesus was not asking for a cancellation or postponement of His death. He was not asking for respite but for quick fulfillment. "He was not referring to the chalice of His future Passion, but to that of the present and past." To Judas at the time of betrayal Jesus had said "That which thou dost, do quickly." Raymond responds to this interpretation by telling St. Catherine that ". . . the Doctors . . . agree in saying that the Saviour was speaking as a real man, whose senses were naturally afraid of death, and as the head of the elect, the weak as well as the strong, so that the weak would not despair if they felt any fear of death . . . ." Catherine gives Raymond this reply:

If the works of the Lord are studied attentively, they will be found to be so full of meat that everyone will find the part of the meat that suits him and fits in with his salvation. If the weak find comfort for their weakness in this prayer of the Lord's, it seems necessary that the strong and perfect too should be able to find an increase of their strength in it; which would not be the case if this kind of interpretation could not be made. It is better, therefore, for it to be interpreted in several ways so that everyone can have his share in it. If it was interpreted in one way only, it would only suit one kind of person.

Raymond, a man of great learning, gives a one line comment following on the above. He says, "When I heard this I was silent in admiration of her grace and wisdom."[24] The Church a few years ago recognized the gifts of wisdom and knowledge reflected in Catherine's teaching (as recorded in her *Dialogue*, in her letters and in such places as Raymond's *Life*) and declared her a Doctor of the Church.

Blessed Anna Maria Taigi (1769-1837) was an Italian housewife. Before marriage she had been a wool-winder in a factory and a chambermaid. She had seven children and when one of the daughters was widowed, Anna Maria brought the six fatherless grandchildren into her home. She also took in her parents in their old age. She became renowned for words of wisdom and knowledge which were manifested as she counseled and taught the many who came to her door. Three popes held her in great esteem and sought her advice.

Wisdom and knowledge and other charisms were obvious in the life of St. Seraphim of Sarov (1759-1833). He was a monk and a priest who spent ten years alone in a hut in the woods before going back to the monastery where he finally entered into the period of elderhood which spanned the last seven years of his life. St. Seraphim embodied the idea of the Eastern Church that the head should dwell in the heart. He himself said: "It is the sign of a reasoning soul when a man sinks his mind within himself and his workings in his heart."[25]

In all of the Saints' lives that I investigated I found evidence of manifestations of words of wisdom and knowledge. This should not be surprising as most of the Saints gave teaching to the people around them in one way or another. This also leads me to speculate regarding a link between holiness and spiritual gifts. I would agree with the Carmelite Sister Teresa Del Monte Sol when she concludes that genuine holiness is always accompanied by a liberal exercising of spiritual gifts. (This is not to say that there are not some very unholy people exercising charisms.) She writes:

> The association of spiritual gifts and virtues . . . has sometimes been emphasized to the point of distorting the value of spiritual gifts and their relationship to holiness. It is often remarked regarding the gifts that they are not necessarily a sign of holiness. It is true that the gifts are not to be *equated* with holiness. Nonetheless, it is also true that there will never be a case of genuine holiness where there are not highly developed spiritual gifts. Holiness, be it remembered, means *wholeness*; full development of the entire person— personality, virtue, and *gifts*. God never raises a person to great holiness in isolation from others, no matter how humble, unimportant or hidden his role in life, and since the gifts are given us for others, in every case of genuine holiness there will be spiritual gifts in evidence.[26]

The Church only canonizes those whose lives evidence eminent holiness. It is therefore no surprise that Saints' lives reveal that these holy men and women were not strangers to the charisms. Catherine of Siena and Bridget of Sweden are best remembered as prophets. St. John Vianney and St. Seraphim of Sarov were famous for discernment and also were known as healers. Founders and foundresses such as St. Madeleine Sophie Barat, St. Dominic, St.

Benedict and others instructed their young communities with words of wisdom and knowledge. St. Ignatius of Loyola's chief gift to the Church was his understanding of discernment of spirits. Colette of Corbie worked miracles such as raising the dead to life. The Saints' lives confirm a prophecy of Jesus: "Truly, truly, I say to you, he who believes in me will also do the works that I do; and greater works than these will he do, because I go to the Father" (John 14:12).

Notes to Chapter 12

1. Gee, *Concerning Spiritual Gifts*, p. 35.
2. Stephen B. Clark, *Spiritual Gifts*, Dove Publications, Pecos, New Mexico, 1969, p. 13.
3. Trochu, *The Cure d'Ars*, p. 204.
4. Bruno Scott James, *St. Bernard of Clairvaux Seen Through His Selected Letters*, pp. 7-8.
5. Trochu, *op. cit.*, pp. 521-522.
6. Sister Mary Francis, *Walled in Light*, p. 173.
7. *Autobiography*, XXXIX, Peers translation.
8. Gee, *op. cit.*, pp. 39-40.
9. Sister Mary Francis, *op. cit.*, pp. 112-113.
10. Celano, *The Fioretti* and St. Bonaventure.
11. Thomas of Celano, *The First Life of St. Francis*, Chapter XXI as contained in *English Omnibus of the Sources for the Life of St. Francis*, pp. 277-278.
12. Brady and Brown, revision with introduction, appendices, and comprehensive bibliography covering modern research, of *St. Francis of Assisi* by Omer Englebert, p. 189.
13. James Clare, S.J., editor, *The Life of Blessed Julie Billiart* by a member of the same Society, p. 318. According to this biography, the episode just related comes down to us from one of the travelers. The sister who wrote this book likens the incident to things found in the *Fioretti*. There are no footnotes in this book which says it depends on the life of the Saint by Rev. Pere Clair. The revised edition of eleven years later (1909) says the revision is based on consultation of the process of beatification [Julie had at that time been declared Venerable and Blessed but not yet Saint] and the collection of Julie's letters. This incident is repeated in another biography with no footnotes: *As God in the Furnace* by Sister Mary Fidiles (1957) pp. 154-155.

14. Edna Boyer Phelan, *Don Bosco*, pp. 298-299. This is a reliable and very readable biography by a Phi Beta Kappa from Radcliffe and a Ph.D. Dr. Phelan has consulted the primary sources.

15. *Ibid.*, p. 289.

16. What has just been described is often called a "word of knowledge" at charismatic conferences. In my opinion this is incorrect. A sense that someone has been healed of this or that would seem more to pertain to the gift of prophecy.

17. Gee, *op. cit.*, p. 30.

18. *Ibid.*, p. 117.

19. Clark, *Spiritual Gifts*, p. 11.

20. Gee, *op. cit.*, pp. 25-26.

21. *Ibid.*, p. 24.

22. Clark, *op. cit.*, p. 10.

23. *Ibid.*

24. Blessed Raymond of Capua, *The Life of St. Catherine of Siena*, Chapter V, pp. 187-188.

25. G.P. Fedotov, *A Treasury of Russian Spirituality*, p. 258.

26. Teresa Del Monte Sol, "Pentecostalism and the Doctrine of Saint Teresa and Saint John of the Cross" in *Spiritual Life*, Spring 1971.

CHAPTER 13

Saints and Charisms III

Discernment of Spirits

Discernment of spirits (*diakrisis pneumaton*) is a "sifting through" [1] or a "judging through" [2] of interior experiences (one's own or those of someone else) in order to determine if they originate from God, Satan or ourselves. Scripture, writings of the Saints, and the classical spiritual tradition of the Church teach that God has a plan for our lives and He gives us guidance through promptings of His Holy Spirit. It is true that God speaks to us through laws (commandments, Church laws, public safety laws) but He also speaks personally to us and He wants us to listen to Him and do His will as Jesus did. In our seeking out of God's will for us here and now, however, it is possible to mistake inspirations from Satan for impulses that come from the Holy Spirit. We can also mistake our own natural instincts for God's will. On the other hand, if God expects us to obey Him and do His will, He is not going to make it impossibly difficult to figure out what His will is. Otherwise it would defeat His purpose.

I once heard a great man of God describing what happened to him shortly after being baptized in the Spirit. He had urges to do all kinds of good things. He got up early in the morning and visited the sick before going to work. Then he spent the rest of his free time in a ministry with young people, teaching them about Jesus. He joined the local parish council. He began to acquire a reputation for being a wonderful servant of God. In reality, he was worn out.

He was not faithful to a daily quiet time with the Lord and his relationship with his wife and children became strained. He finally realized that Satan could never have tempted him to adultery or drunkenness or some gross sin, but instead had lured him into involving himself in many good activities. In so doing he had damaged his relationship with God (by neglecting his prayer time), he had injured his relationship with his family, and he had dissipated his energy.

An example of an impulse simply coming from ourselves rather than from God or Satan would be the inclination of a naturally talkative, extroverted person to share at a prayer meeting. People with such natures need the experience of growing in community and growing in self-knowledge so they can begin to learn to discern when God is leading them to talk and when an impulse to speak is just a result of their own exuberant personality.

The charism of discernment of spirits, as we have said, has to do with being able to judge whether inspirations come from God or not. Many theologians make a distinction between the ordinary discernment that every Christian needs to exercise in his daily life, and extraordinary discernment evidenced in the lives of Saints, usually those who founded communities or who participated in some way in government and guidance in the body of Christ. Fr. Ed O'Connor distinguishes between the "charism" of discernment, which he says is given only to certain people, and the "function" of discernment, which has to be exercised by everyone in regard to his own inspirations.[3]

Both Donald Gee [4] and Stephen Clark [5] describe discernment of spirits solely in terms of its use for the body of Christ. Clark, following Scripture, calls discernment of spirits "the ability to distinguish between spirits," which is perhaps a more helpful way of speaking about discernment as it makes the meaning clearer. Clark calls this gift "the protection of the Christian community." He says:

This is the gift which allows a man to "distinguish between spirits," to tell whether an evil spirit is at work in a person or a situation or whether it is just a man's own spirit. This is probably the work of the Spirit by which Peter "saw" that Simon was "in the gall of bitterness and the bond of iniquity" when he tried to buy the power to confer the Spirit (Acts 8:23). . . .[6]

Donald Gee associates this gift with those called into a position of leadership or eldership in the Church. "The possession of such a gift of the Spirit must have usually marked a presbyter out as a man specially fitted by God to have charge of Assemblies. . . ." [7] Hugo Rahner speaks on the one hand of the "ability to distinguish between spirits" of 1 Corinthians 12:10 as an actual pneumatic gift and, on the other hand, of the *dokimazein* (testing) of 1 Thessalonians 5:21 and 1 John 4:1 expected of all Christians.[8]

Only some people are called to exercise discernment with regard to others. These are people with pastoral responsibility, who exercise headship in a Christian community and need this special gift. Most Saints as well as all "spiritual fathers" of the Eastern Church were renowned for this type of discernment. Some would reserve the term "charism" for this spiritual gift.

Every Christian however must exercise discernment with regard to the inspirations he or she receives. Depending on one's terminology, this would be ordinary discernment versus extraordinary discernment (manifested by elders) or it would be the "function" of discernment versus the "charism" of discernment. Everyone must discern the inspirations they receive. Some will need help in discerning their inspirations and God provides that help by leading them to those who are able to discern spirits in others.

There is another way discernment is exercised. This is "communal discernment" or the gift of discernment a Christian body as a whole possesses. One simple way this is seen is in the reaction of a mature prayer group, which has been together for quite some time, to a prophecy which is way out of line, usually given by someone who has just "walked in off the street" and is unknown to the group. The prophecy will produce a general unease and restlessness in the group indicating a common consensus that there is something not quite right about the prophecy, or at least indicating a need for further discernment before accepting the prophecy as a word from the Lord.

Before going to discernment in Saints' lives, two more clarifications might be helpful. The charism of discernment of spirits is not the same thing as the virtue of prudence. "Prudence passes judgment on the *action* in itself, but discernment judges the *impulse* to act, to determine its source" writes Fr. O'Connor.[9] Also, discernment is not usually concerned with the right or wrong of something. Rather, it judges what is "God's thing" among several "good things." The man in the example given earlier in this chapter was involved in ministry to youth, the parish council and visiting the sick. All good things. But he hadn't allowed God to order his priorities. His prayer life (union with God) and family life (union with wife and children) were "God's thing" for him before any of the other activities.

This brings us to the second clarification or digression. Ordinarily one would expect that the man would have known to care for his family and his primary responsibilities before taking on other activities, no matter how good. But in the world today one can't assume that, any more than one can assume that just because people go to church they have been evangelized and converted to Jesus Christ. Our experience in our Christian community at Mother of God has shown us that many people are in need of teaching about very basic fundamentals of Christian living. They need teaching based on the ten commandments, the kind of teaching people would have received when they were children had they been raised in a truly Christian family. There is no point in even discussing how to discern spirits with people who do not have their lives in order and who do not know how to exercise prudence. People without a basic Christian foundation in their lives can't begin to discern the source of their inspirations.

In Mother of God we reserve the term "spiritual direction" for that kind of counseling which helps people to learn to exercise ordinary discernment in their lives. We find that most people aren't ready for real spiritual direction for several years after joining the community. The first few years are spent laying a foundation in Christian living that should have been laid in childhood. In the world today most people's lives are not in order and baptism in the Spirit does not automatically put them in order. With God's help people need to work at getting their lives in order and clarifying their priorities so that eventually they will be able to hear all the voices in their lives and will be able to distinguish the Lord's voice from all the rest. For several years after baptism in the Spirit, most people need to meditate on the ten commandments and need to let their hearts dwell on the law of the Lord. They need not concern themselves much with discernment of spirits.

Discernment of spirits is mentioned in ancient Christian writings such as the second century *The Shepherd of Hermas*. It was included in teachings of St. Antony of Egypt (according to St. Athanasius), St. Cyril of Jerusalem, and St. Augustine. St. Thomas wrote little on discernment of spirits. Some teaching on the subject is found in Catherine of Siena's *Dialogue*. St. Bernardino of Siena (1380-1444) gave three sermons on the subject shortly before he died. St. Teresa of Avila (1515-1582) mentions discernment of spirits in her *Autobiography* (Chapter 39) and she says the gift helps the one possessing it to judge spirits by their fruits irrespective of such considerations as age and time spent in prayer.

When discernment of spirits is mentioned, the Saint that Catholics most readily associate with this charism is Ignatius Loyola. Besides being the founder of the Jesuits, Ignatius is also remembered for a retreat which he developed and for which he wrote a manual of instructions called the *Spiritual Exercises*. Ignatius taught and wrote about discernment of spirits and one of his great gifts to the Church is his understanding of this charism.

We will give two examples of St. Ignatius and the gift of discernment. The first example has to do with individual discernment of God's will for another individual. Ignatius' way of discerning God's will can be found in the *Spiritual Exercises*. An example of how Ignatius experienced and manifested this charism in helping another to discern spirits, is a letter he wrote on June 18, 1536. Ignatius was in Venice at the time and he was writing to a nun in Barcelona named Sister Teresa Rejadella. Sister Teresa's convent, Santa Clara, had been founded in 1233 as a house of Poor Clares, but since 1427 it had been under Benedictine rule. For a long time the rule had not been taken seriously. Sister Teresa had apparently written to Ignatius about herself and about reform of the convent in a letter that no longer exists. In part here is what Ignatius wrote to her:

> You . . . beg me to write to you what the Lord says to me and that I should say freely what I think. What I feel in the Lord I will tell you frankly with a right good will and if I should appear to be harsh in anything, I shall be more so against him [Satan] who is trying to upset you than against you. The enemy is troubling you in two ways, but not so as to make you fall into the guilt of sin which would separate you from your God and Lord. He does, however, draw and separate you from God's greater service and your own greater peace of soul. The first thing is that he sets before you and persuades you to cultivate a false humility; the second that he strives to instill into you an excessive fear of God with which

you are too much taken up and occupied.

As to the first point, the general course which the enemy follows with those who love and begin to serve God our Lord is to set hindrances and obstacles in their way. . . . He hides from us the many and great comforts and consolations which the Lord is wont to give to such souls, if the man who has newly embraced the Lord's service breaks through all these difficulties. . . . When . . . we make ourselves humble, he tries to draw us into false humility, that is, into humility which is exaggerated and corrupt. Of this your words are clear evidence, for after you relate certain weaknesses and fears which are true of you, you say, "I am a poor nun, desirous, it seems to me, of serving Christ our Lord"—but you do not dare to say: "I am desirous of serving Christ our Lord . . ." but you say: "I seem to be desirous? . . ." Ponder well how the martyrs . . . declared themselves Christ's servants. So you, standing before the enemy of the whole human race . . . do not say you are desirous of serving Our Lord—rather you have to say and confess without fear that you are his servant and that you would rather die than separate yourself from his service. . . . This is the way wherein we should walk, that the deceiver may in turn be deceived, applying to ourselves the teaching of Holy Scripture which says: "Beware that thou be not so humble that in excessive humility thou be led into folly" (cf. Eccles. 7:16).

. . . I shall speak, although briefly, of two lessons which the Lord usually gives or permits. . . . That which he gives is interior consolation, which casts out all trouble and brings one to the full love of our Lord. . . . With this divine consolation, all trials are a pleasure and all weariness rest. . . . This consolation does not always remain with us—it follows its due seasons according to the divine ordinance. . . . Our old enemy now puts before us all possible obstacles. . . . He often makes us sad, without our knowing why we are sad, nor can we pray with any devotion. . . . He strives to bring us into distrust of everything. . . . If temptation, darkness or sadness comes, we must withstand it without any irritation and wait with patience for the Lord's consolation which will shatter all troubles. . . .[10]

An example of communal discernment is contained in a document the Jesuits refer to as *Deliberatio primorum patrum* or "The Deliberation of the First Fathers." [11] The *Deliberatio* gives an account of the discussion had by St. Ignatius and his companions when they were trying to determine whether God wanted them to be a new religious order in the Church and, if so, what kind of order it ought to be. Ignatius and his friends had already had at least one previous experience of communal discernment. This was when they as a group felt that God was calling them to a life lived in poverty and chastity. Ignatius and six companions made a vow to live such a life at Montmartre in 1534. They included in the vow a promise to go to Jerusalem to evangelize the people there. Of the prior experience of communal discernment leading up to the Montmartre vow, Fr. John Futrell says:

We have the testimony of Simao Rodrigues that the decision to make the vow at Montmartre was arrived at only after lengthy and lively discussion. . . . Their discussions must have been a mutual declaration of calls of the Spirit, each one quite simply and openly declaring what he found to be the motions of the Holy Spirit within his own spirit. Through sharing their own interior experiences, the companions were enabled to arrive at a common judgment of their response to the word of God to them in the concrete situation in which they found themselves in 1534.[12]

The deliberations which resulted in the foundation of the Society of Jesus in 1539 are recorded in the *Deliberatio*. The communal discernment process took almost three months. The first question the soon-to-be Jesuits asked themselves was whether they should remain united or disperse. Bishops from various parts of Europe were asking for their services. The *Deliberatio* records that the men making the discernment together included French, Spanish, Savoyards and Portuguese. After much prayer and then group discussion, the men discerned that God had gathered them together and they should not split apart. They should be joined in mutual care and concern for one another. They concluded the discernment of this question with these words:

> We want it understood that nothing at all that has been or will be spoken of originated from our own spirit or our own thought; rather, whatever it was, it was solely what our Lord inspired and the Apostolic See [the Pope] then confirmed and approved.[13]

All the men had vowed themselves to a life of poverty and chastity. The next question they took up during these months of decision-making was whether they should make a vow of obedience to one of their own number. The deliberations broke down over this question so they set about to find another way to determine God's will. They considered going to a hermitage for thirty or forty days but gave up this idea for several good reasons. They then considered ways of preparing for their times of common deliberation. Spiritual preparations included Mass, prayer and trying to have a preference for obeying rather than commanding. Here is how the primary source material, the *Deliberatio*, describes their second preparation:

> None of the companions would communicate with any other about this matter at issue or inquire about his reasoning on it. The point of this preparation was to prevent anyone from being persuaded by another, and, therefore, biased more

toward obedience or the contrary. This way each would desire as more advantageous only what he derived from his own prayer and meditation.[14]

Ignatius and his companions in the end felt the Spirit leading them to obedience. The result of the months of prayer and discussion was the formation of the Society of Jesus. The *Deliberatio* concludes with the sentence: "On that day [the feast of John the Baptist], but not without long vigils, much prayer, and labor of mind and body preceding deliberation and decision, all our business was completed and terminated in a spirit of gladness and harmony." [15]

Prophecy

"Make love your aim, and earnestly desire the spiritual gifts, especially that you may prophesy," writes St. Paul to the Corinthians. "He who prophesies speaks to men for their upbuilding and encouragement and consolation," he says in the same letter (1 Cor. 14:1-3). Prophecy primarily speaks to the present and is first and foremost "forth telling." Only secondarily, and sometimes, is it foretelling.

Revelation from God comes in a variety of ways to those called to exercise this gift. It may be received in dreams and visions—this is especially common with the foretelling prophecy—or it may just come as an intellectual sense that a certain message is from God and is to be given to another person, or, more often, to a group of people, as at a prayer meeting. Prophecies at prayer meetings usually speak to the present and are seldom foretelling. A person giving a forthtelling prophecy at a prayer meeting yields to the Holy Spirit and speaks out a message without being sure the message he speaks is a prophecy until it is confirmed in some way.

The recipient of foretelling prophetic dreams and visions, unlike the recipient of prophecies for prayer meetings or assemblies, sometimes feels some degree of certitude that it is genuine prophecy but there is usually uncertainty as to how the foretold event will come about. I am *not* saying that any person having a prophetic dream accompanied by a feeling of certitude knows that it is genuine. What I am saying is that any *genuine* prophetic dream or vision usually carries with it the stamp of the divine and the feeling that what is foretold will come to pass.

The life of Blessed Dominic Barberi (1792-1849) is a good example of what we have been discussing. To place Dominic in context we need to go back to the founder of the Passionist Congregation to which he belonged, St. Paul of the Cross. Born in Italy, St. Paul of the Cross (1694-1775) prayed much for England. He called England "Mary's dowry" and "Isle of saints and martyrs." He refers to his urge to pray for England in his diary of 1720. Before his death he was favored with a vision of his spiritual sons in England.[16] At the time of his death the Passionists had no foundation in England.

Dominic Barberi, also Italian, entered the Passionist Congregation. In 1813, while a postulant, he heard an interior voice which, he said, left no shadow of a doubt as to its being from God. The voice told him he was destined to announce the truths of the gospel. He was left with a hazy impression that God would send him to work somewhere where he would not be just among Catholics.

About a year later Dominic reported in his diary:

> One day about the end of September, or the beginning of October, 1814, as the religious were taking their refection, I went for a few minutes into the church to pray before the altar of the Blessed Virgin, and while I was on my knees, the thought occurred to me—how was the prophecy of last year to be fulfilled? Was I to go as a lay Brother to preach, and to whom was I to go? China and America came into my head. While I was thus racking my brains, I understood (not by an internal locution as before, but by another mode of interior

communication which I cannot explain) that I was not to remain a lay Brother, but was to study, and that, after six years, I was to labor neither in China nor America, but in the north-west of Europe, and especially in England. The time was not explained to me, and neither was the manner in which I was to be sent there. I was so convinced of this being a divine communication that I would sooner have doubted my own existence than its truth. I was soon afterward sent off to Paliano, to be received as a lay novice, and yet I felt that I would, notwithstanding, become a cleric and a priest.[17]

This prophecy came true and Dominic's actions throughout his life until he finally reached England when he was almost fifty, showed that he took it seriously and acted accordingly. He had the students that he taught in Rome pray for England. At the Passionist General Chapter in 1833 he was present as a consultor and he pleaded for a foundation to be made in England. The request was postponed. When a group was selected to make a foundation in Belgium preparatory to making one in England, Dominic was not included. He remarked to a companion: "You will see; I shall be sent." And again: "They have already nominated those who are to go to Belgium, but the thing is not well done. Without me they will not set out—I have to go with them." [18]

The man chosen to lead the pioneers to Belgium asked to be relieved of his assignment and Dominic of the Mother of God (Dominic Barberi's name in religion) was appointed to take his place. After making a foundation in Belgium, Dominic went to England, and established the Passionists there.

On October 7, 1845, John Henry Newman, the future English cardinal, wrote to Henry Wilberforce:

> Father Dominic, the Passionist, is passing this way. . . . He is to come to Littlemore for night. . . . He does not know of my intentions, but I shall ask of him admission. . . . [Newman

became a Catholic] . . . Father Dominic has had his thoughts turned toward England from a youth, in a distinct and remarkable way. For thirty years he has expected to be sent to England and about three years since was sent, without any act of his own, by his superior.[19]

Blessed Dominic affected Newman's life and the lives of many others. His holiness and dedication drew many souls to follow Jesus, thus fulfilling the prophecy of St. Paul of the Cross and the revelation he himself had received.

The early Christian communities had to deal with the problem of false prophecy. In the *Didache* (probably written before the end of the first century) we can find a rule for discernment which still obtains today. There it is written: "Not every man who speaks in the spirit is a prophet, but only if his life is modelled on that of Christ." [20] This shows once again the link between holiness and the gifts. In the present experience of the charismatic renewal, if one who prophesies frequently is not seen to be maturing and deepening in his walk with the Lord, his prophecies will cease to affect the group.

All the Saints were, in some way, prophets. All Saints were living messages from God. Their lives were modeled on Christ and their lives said something to the Church. In God's plan of gathering to Himself a holy people, Saints served as signposts all along the way. They pointed new directions that read: "to the desert," "to the monastery," "to the city." Translated, all the directions really read: "Gather My sheep. Care for My sheep. Feed My sheep. Love My sheep. Die, as I did, for My sheep."

Notes to Chapter 13

1. John Carroll Futrell, S.J., "Ignatian Discernment," in *Studies in the Spirituality of the Jesuits*, April 1970, p. 47.

2. Gee, *Concerning Spiritual Gifts*, p. 51.

3. O'Connor, "Discernment of Spirits Part I," in *New Covenant* April 1975, p. 11.

4. Gee, *op. cit.*, pp. 49-55.

5. Clark, *Spiritual Gifts*, pp. 17-18.

6. *Ibid.*, p. 17.

7. Gee, *op. cit.*, p. 54.

8. Hugo Rahner, *Ignatius the Theologian*, p. 166.

9. O'Connor, *op. cit.*

10. H. Rahner, *Saint Ignatius Loyola, Letters to Women*, pp. 332-334.

11. The original Latin text is in *Monumenta Historica Societatis Jesu, Constitutiones*, I, 1-7. Vol. 63, Monumenta Ignatiana, Series Tertia, Tome I, pp. 1-7. Two English translations are: Dominic Maruca, S.J., "The Deliberations of Our First Fathers" *Woodstock Letters*, Vol. 95 (1966), pp. 325-333, and John C. Futrell, S.J., *Making an Apostolic Community of Love* (The Institute of Jesuit Sources: St. Louis, 1970), pp. 188-194.

12. Futrell, S.J., *op. cit.*, p. 67.

13. *Deliberatio primorum Patrum* as quoted in Jules J. Toner, S.J., *Studies in the Spirituality of Jesuits*, "The Deliberation That Started the Jesuits" Vol. VI, June 1974, No. 4, p. 193.

14. *Deliberatio*, Toner, p. 198.

15. *Ibid.*, p. 208.

16. Jude Mead, *Shepherd of the Second Spring*, p. 14. Although I am here citing a secondary source, this vision is well documented.

17. *Ibid.*, p. 27.

18. Urban Young, C.P., *Life and Letters of the Venerable Father Dominic* (Barberi), C.P., (London, Burns Oates and Washbourne, 1926), p. 132 as quoted in Mead p. 71.

19. *Ibid.*, p. 256, cited in Mead pp. 162-163.

20. *Didache*, XI, 8 (Funk, I,28,1.4), cited in H. Rahner, *Ignatius the Theologian*, p. 166. I compared this with the translation in the *Ancient Christian Writers Series* but prefer the text as quoted in Rahner. In A.C.W.S. the word "ecstasy" replaces the word "spirit."

CHAPTER 14

Why Saints?

The course in Church history that I took in college in the fifties was taught from the point of view of the popes and what happened during their pontificates. This was the history of the institutional element of the Catholic Church. It stressed Church councils and papal pronouncements. The two other elements of the Church, mystical and intellectual, were adverted to once in a while when treating occasional Saints or the thought of Thomas Aquinas, but by and large the emphasis was on the institutional.

However, Pius XII, the pope preceding John XXIII, said in his encyclical *Mystici Corporis* that Jesus is permanently the Head and Ruler of the Church. So although God shepherds His people through men who pastor in His name, He also directs the Church through the charismatic element—through men and women He Himself calls to perform certain services for the Church.

It should be possible to write a history of the charismatic element in the Church and its relation to the intellectual and institutional elements. A few books written on the popular level have attempted to do this in the past. One example is *Church History in the Light of the Saints* by Fr. Joseph Dunney which appeared in 1944. Another is *Holiness in Action* (1963) by Roland Cluny.

A history of God's intervention in history through His Saints from the time of the Ascension until now would probably begin with Paul being knocked off his horse and then presenting himself to Peter and the apostles to have his call confirmed. (Paul knew the

Holy Spirit did not bless lone rangers!) As for Peter, the appearance of the ministry of Paul must surely have been a "surprise of the Holy Spirit!" Such a history would go to the arena with the martyrs, to the desert with the Fathers, to the monasteries with Benedict, to the reform of the monasteries with Bernard, to the highways with Francis, to the "heretics" with Dominic, and so on.

Cardinal Suenens provides an example of this kind of writing in the chapter of his book *The Nun in the World*, that briefly treats the history of women religious. He recalls that the Ursulines, founded by St. Angela Merici, were approved in 1544 and were not subject to enclosure. They devoted themselves especially to the education of young girls, particularly poorer ones whom no one cared about. The freedom did not last long. In what the cardinal calls "a triumph of legalism," in 1566 the Holy See ordered the suppression of all female congregations not in enclosure and subject to solemn vows. The Ursulines who, up till then had dressed like everyone else, had to adopt a religious habit.

The Cardinal also recalls that the Visitation Order, founded by St. Francis de Sales and St. Jane de Chantal and named "Visitation" because the sisters were to visit the poor and sick in their homes, went the way of the Ursulines and were enclosed. The battle lost by de Sales was won by St. Vincent de Paul, comments Suenens. When de Paul organized his Daughters of Charity the institute was called a company and the novitiate a seminary. The residence was not called a convent but simply "house." They wore no habit but instead the gray serge dress of common people. Here are the instructions he gave his daughters:

> Should the local bishop ask you if you are in religion, you will say that by the grace of God you are not, not because you have not a high opinion of religious but because if you were you would have to be enclosed and that would mean goodbye to the service of the poor. . . . Should some muddle-headed person appear among you and say, "We ought to be religious.

196

It would be much nicer," then, my dear sisters, the Company is ripe for Extreme Unction, for who says "religious" says "enclosed" but the Daughters of Charity must go everywhere.[1]

Source material on de Paul reveals the "newness" of his work which he did not want spoiled by emulation of or contact with the old forms of religious life which were in need of reform. The Daughters of Charity were called by their family names without the pious changing of names (the past ten years has seen a return to this simplicity in many religious orders) and without reverential titles. Vincent did not want the Daughters to be familiar with convents nor did he want a religious to be their spiritual director.[2] This is just a taste of the radical thinking to be found in primary source material on Saints. Who knows what will turn up when Church historians and theologians begin to examine all the material concerning Saints that lies unused in Vatican archives? What will probably be revealed with great clarity will be the tough single-mindedness with which Saints pursued the mission entrusted to them by the Lord. We will probably see how very much the pioneering and prophecy of their lives stood in contrast to the rest of the men of their day.

One of the answers to the question "Why Saints?" or "What is a Saint?" is that all the Saints were in some way prophets. Some, such as St. Bernadette, Catherine Laboure, and Margaret Mary Alacoque were entrusted with actual messages to the Church from the Lord. Other Saints lived a message—their actual lives were prophetic. Francis of Assisi was prophetic in many ways, one being his hatred of money. New wealth in his day was endangering the souls of many.[3] St. Therese of Lisieux was prophetic. Her life has proved to be a source of consolation to untold thousands. Other than the fact that she lived in a convent, her life was very ordinary. She taught a "little way" of following the Lord. Her life said that anyone could experience the fullness of the Christian life.

Rahner gives a definition of Saints in his article on "The Church of the Saints." Rahner says: "The Saints . . . are as it were the 'official,' appointed ways of the Church's discovery of herself which have become publicly historical and which have been consciously adopted by the Church."[4] What Rahner is saying is that the Church says something about herself when she canonizes Saints. She says something about her nature. Holiness is essential. The holy life of the Saint lends credence to his prophecy, but holiness is not what is new and different in a Saint. As Karl Rahner says in his article, what is new is that the Saint is holy in "this" particular way at "this" particular time in history. "The Saints are the creative prototypes in the history of holiness, because they make visible and livable new gifts of God's Spirit and create new modes of Christian existence" writes Fr. Harvey D. Egan in Chapter One of *The Spiritual Exercises and the Ignatian Mystical Horizon*.[5]

Therese of Lisieux's biographer, Ida Gorres, reflected on the relationship of prophets to the Church as she read the writings of Julian of Norwich. Gorres then wrote:

> Julian of Norwich has helped me no end to see the subject of priest and prophet, i.e. office and charisma, more clearly; Her "shewings" are flashes, not lamps. The seer *needs* the Church, for she alone provides the background against which his visions really make sense—instead of being simply isolated, crazy arabesques. The priest has to keep the *whole*, whatever is enduring, universal, catholic—to the prophet is committed the *part*, the renovation, what is new—as well as what must be renovated. His is the *special* task. But the second cannot be accomplished without the first. Only against the "common" outline of the whole, within its proportions, can the flash-lit details be understood. No point in enlarging a photograph of an eyelid, for instance, unless people know the face.[6]

Not all that attempts to pass for prophecy at charismatic prayer meetings is genuine prophecy. What is genuine prophecy is in some way confirmed by the institutional element of the group. The canonization process might be looked upon in the same way. It is the institutional element, upon consultation with the intellectual element, confirming the prophecy that was the Saint's life. Prophecies are given to a particular prayer group or community at a particular time, and although the truth of that prophecy abides and is part of the history of a particular prayer group or community, that same prophecy, with its unique impact in time, cannot be repeated. So too the significance of a particular Saint's life remains in the Church as a permanent form. But, as Rahner says, ". . . the 'old' Saints are no longer topical."[7] ". . . even a dutiful son of St. Francis can today no longer prescind 'romantically' from the fact that since the time of St. Francis there has been an Ignatius; and even the sons of St. Ignatius are not the guardians of the 'final truth'. . . ."[8]

A history of the charismatic element of the Church will reveal a connectedness to the history. What has gone before prepares the way for what comes after. The lives of Sts. Norbert of Xanten and Robert of Arbrissel, for example, paved the way for Francis of Assisi. John Henry Cardinal Newman believed very much in the connectedness of the work of the Holy Spirit throughout the history of the Church. In *Apologia pro Vita Sua* he wrote:

> There is a time for everything, and many a man desires a reformation of an abuse, or the fuller development of a doctrine, or the adoption of a particular policy, but forgets to ask himself whether the right time for it has come; and, knowing that there is no one who will be doing anything toward it in his own lifetime unless he does it himself, he will not listen to the voice of authority, and he spoils a good work in his own century, in order that another man, as yet unborn, may not have the opportunity of bringing it happily to perfection in the next.[9]

One who was Newman's contemporary, Fr. Frederick Faber

(1814-1863) had this comment about Church history:

Each age has its own distinctive spirit. It has its own proper
virtues and its own proper vices. It has its own sciences,
inventions, literature, policy, and development. Each age
thinks itself peculiar, which it is, and imagines it better than
other ages, which it is not. It is probably neither better nor
worse. . . . This is the reason why the Church seems to act
differently in different ages. There is a sense in which the
Church goes along with the world. It is the same sense in
which the shepherd leaves the sheep which have not strayed
and goes off in search of the one that has strayed. Each age is a
stray sheep from God; and the Church has to seek it and fetch
it back to him. . . . God's work is never done in any one age. It
has to be begun again in every age. . . . Old methods are found
unsuitable, because things have changed. It is on this account
that theology puts on new aspects, that religious orders first
succeed and then fail, that devotion has fashion and vicis-
situdes. . . .[10]

Each age is a stray sheep from God and each age God goes about
gathering back to Himself. There is a "newness" about God's work
in each age. There was a newness about each Saint as he began to
emerge and go about whatever it was that God was asking of him.
"God is doing a new work in our day" (Isa. 43:19; Rev. 21:5) is often
heard on the lips of those touched by the Spirit in the charismatic
renewal. Experience of this newness, while rooted in tradition and
in the Church as institution, has given Catholics an understanding
of what Saints experienced.

The Saints were about a new thing. Sometimes they knew it,
and sometimes they accomplished the new thing following the
Lord blindly without being too sure what was emerging. For
example, in the beginning, neither Francis of Assisi nor Ignatius
Loyola intended to found religious orders. Francis, when he heard
the words, "repair My Church," did exactly that. He went about

physically rebuilding churches which were in disrepair. Despite their stumbling beginnings and their almost blind adherence to what they perceived as God's will, Ignatius and Francis went about the new thing God was asking of them. When Francis was asked about a rule for the large numbers of men who had left all to follow Jesus along with him, Francis was quite emphatic about the newnessof the thing God had him involved in. In the *Mirror of Perfection* it is recorded that some friars wanted Francis to base his rule on the wisdom of more established orders. Francis responded:

> My brothers! My brothers! God has called me by the way of simplicity and humility, and has in truth revealed this way for me and for all who are willing to trust and follow me. So I do not want you to quote any other Rule to me, whether of Saint Benedict, Saint Augustine, or Saint Bernard, or to recommend any other way or form of life except this way which God in His mercy has revealed and given to me.[11]

Ignatius did not wish members of the Society of Jesus discussing other orders. Charles de Foucauld, the inspiration of the Little Brothers and Little Sisters of Jesus, said something along these lines about seventy-five years ago. Although he said he venerated the Benedictine rule he said he felt called to initiate "little flocks" and the Benedictine rule was meant for big communities. But, also, he gave another reason for not adopting it:

> . . . to adopt it would be to precipitate myself back into those discussions about the interpretation of texts and the spirit and the letter, in which one can drown, and which lead good souls to spend their time thinking about unimportant nothings instead of using it to love God.[12]

For the Saints, what had gone before was revered but it never became an idol. Their eyes were on Jesus and their hearts burned with the gospel message. It is because the Saints allowed the Lord to do a "new thing" through them that they emerged as pioneers and prophets in and to their eras.

It is astonishing to discover that up to now theology has very little to say about Saints. At least three theologians have pointed this out. Two of them call attention to what they consider a deficiency in the Vatican Council document, *Dogmatic Constitution on the Church,* in this area of Saints.

The why and how of veneration of Saints in relation to modern man was not treated as a question by the council. The council's teaching on the subject was confined to reaffirming that we can and should venerate Saints. Karl Rahner likens this treatment of the issue at hand to that of a young man being told the wonderful qualities of a young woman by the girl's mother. The young man "hears the message and does not dispute its accuracy, and yet no love is aroused in him." Rahner feels that the deficiency in the *Dogmatic Constitution on the Church* in this area could not have been avoided.

> What we feel to be missing here could not in any sense have been put forward as a conciliar statement, at any rate not at present, because virtually speaking it has not yet attained any *conscious* position in the Church's explicit awareness of her faith.[13]

In a much earlier work, Rahner pointed out that if one glanced at an average modern dogmatic theology one would have to look in many different places to find anything on Saints. Saints are mentioned when the "holy Church" is discussed and Saints are spoken of in connection with the subject of the adoration due to Christ.

> What the Saints are for us and for the Church, why they play a role in our Christian existence even beyond their intercession, all this is left rather unexpressed somewhere on the periphery of our consciousness of faith. . . . The question treated is our veneration of the Saints and not the question of the Saints themselves . . . not in their significance for the

Church at the time when they were still pilgrims with us on this earth and gradually becoming Saints. . . . If theology has . . . a duty towards the Christian life, then this lack in theology is harmful to life.[14]

Fr. Paul Molinari served as a Peritus to the Theological Commission of the Second Vatican Council and he was secretary to the special subcommission which was responsible for Chapter VII of the *Dogmatic Constitution on the Church*, ("Eschatological Nature of the Pilgrim Church and its Union with the Church in Heaven"). In a book published in 1962, *Saints, Their Place in the Church*,[15] Fr. Molinari states there is "urgent necessity" for a systematic dogmatic treatise on the Saints. He suggests that it be inserted in the dogmatic treatment *De Ecclesia* (On the Church). He calls for an unveiling of the importance of the Saints and he reminds us that there is valuable material contained in the processes of beatification and canonization of Saints and that this material is in the archives practically unused.

Fr. Molinari recognizes the existence of Saints in the Church as a "valuable source for an increased knowledge of dogma, apologetics, and spirituality" but he remarks that "this treasure" could be examined more so that the full value would be recognized. "The realization of the undiscovered possibilities that lie beneath the more commonly known truths about the Saints can serve as a point of departure for noteworthy developments."[16] Fr. Molinari points out that the Saints enjoyed tremendous authority in the theological argumentation of former times. This is because they bore witness to Christianity with their lives. Fr. Molinari said, almost fifteen years ago, that the future treatise he was calling for and envisioning would endeavor to ". . . discover, reveal and explain the internal and providential nexus that exists between dogmatic teaching and theology on the one hand, and on the other, the concrete practical life of the Saints." [17]

Fr. Harvey Egan in his book on Ignatius' *Exercises* said in 1976:

The saints are not simply models for Christian imitation;

because they enflesh new modes of Christian existence, they should also be considered as sources for theological reflection.

. . .There is a "metaphysics of the saints" which has been too easily by-passed in theological reflection.

Although theologians readily grant the authority of the Bible, the Church Fathers, Papal pronouncements, the Councils, the Scholastics, etc. to be sources of theological reflection (and of course they should), they have failed to see that the saints should also have importance as a theological source.[18]

Saints are not just pioneers and they are not just prophets. Without holiness St. Vincent de Paul would have been just a social worker. Without holiness St. Francis de Sales would have been an ordinary bishop. Saints were not only prophets, they were holy prophets. They were spokesmen for God and messengers of the Lord to us, His people. In each generation of Church life they assisted God in calling His people back to Himself. So Saints are more than models for us to follow. They are more than intercessors.

Traces of a newer and deeper understanding of what Saints mean for the Church can be found in recent popular writing. For example, John Garvey in 1975 in *A Contemporary Meditation on Saints* wrote ". . . saints show us that in an important way revelation continues, and is not confined merely to scripture and the early church."[19] Writing in a magazine article in 1976, Rosemary Haughton described the effect on theology of five holy women, who were not theologians. "Men and women, often very unlikely ones, have shaped the Church's self-understanding. . . ." [20]

I have said that for me Saints are holy prophets. But I don't believe that says it all. The God who calls and then sends the prophets must be at the center of any understanding of Saints. Why God sent them and the fact that He sent them at all is of significance.

It is very easy to see the holiness of the Saints and to stop there. Some would say that the holiness is what is most important. *How* Saints were holy, or what message their life brought to the Church, or their service to God's people is secondary for those who exalt the holiness of Saints. It is true that all the Saints seem to have been loving, patient, kind, gentle and joyful. Their lives manifest all the fruits of the Spirit and reflect the holiness of God. And the holiness of the Saints gives credence to their message to the Church. Had Francis of Assisi lacked humility the Church would not have listened to the prophecy that was his life. But when we think of Mary, and St. Peter, and St. Paul, is our first reaction one of being struck by their holiness? I don't think so. My first thought is that Mary was the mother of Jesus, Peter was first among the apostles, Paul was a great missionary. We could do this test of association with any one of the Saints. The initial thought most people have when hearing about a Saint is one connected with their message or mission. I think that reflects something essential about the nature of Saints.

Saints were about the Father's business. Like Jesus, their food was to do the will of Him who sent them and to accomplish His work. Saints received a call from God and throughout their lives they were faithful to that call. In the process of being faithful to their vocation, Saints grew in holiness. Mary was called to be the mother of Jesus; Peter was called to catch men instead of fish. Francis of Assisi was called to repair the Church. God calls. Saints respond with their lives. And the body of Christ, the Church, God's people, benefit in some way from God's action through Saints.

In any age it could be said what Jesus said in John 5:17 still holds: "My Father is working still, and I am working." God is always Lord of the universe and Lord of His Church. He is always fathering, shepherding, guiding and protecting His people. Saints are able to say with St. Paul ". . . we are God's fellow workers" (1 Cor. 3:9). Saints participate in God's work in every age. They reverence God's work.

Catherine of Siena prayed much for the reform of the Church in the fourteenth century. The Lord told her that the beauty of the Church would be restored by prayers, tears and sweat.

> Take, therefore, thy tears and thy sweat . . . and, with them, wash the face of My spouse [the Church].
>
> I promise thee, that, by this means, her beauty will be restored to her . . . peacefully, by humble and continued prayer, by the sweat and the tears shed by the fiery desire of My servants. . . .[21]

Catherine wept over the state of the Church and she spent long hours in prayer. The Lord also asked for sweat. By allowing God's will to be done in her life Catherine served God's people. God worked through her to speak a word to the Church and to the pope.

I think if we can learn anything from Saints, it would be to seriously seek out God's call in our lives and then to remain faithful to that call. Another way of saying that would be to say that we must find our place of service in the body of Christ and we must live out that service with dedication to the will of the Father. I think of all the Saints, Ignatius Loyola understood this best and this was his greatest gift to the Church.

I think there are traces in theology which are leading to a deeper understanding of Saints and the charismatic history of the Church. The quotes from Rahner point this out. In the already mentioned article "The Church of the Saints" Rahner also says: "The heroic nature of the virtues of the (canonized) Saints cannot *alone* explain their special task in the Church."[22] We have mentioned that Rahner points out in *The Dynamic Element in the Church* that St. Paul makes no distinction between graces given for the benefit of the recipient and graces given for the good of others. Rahner asks the question ". . . how else could one truly sanctify oneself except by unselfish service to others in the one Body of Christ by the power of the Spirit? And how could one fail to be sanctified if one faithfully takes up and fulfills one's real and true function in the Body of Christ?"[23] In an article "The Charismatic Structure of the Church" Hans Kung shows the relation of the words "gift" and "call." He discusses the concept of charisma for St. Paul's ecclesiology. ". . . How can we give a brief theological description of . . . charisma? In the widest sense it is God's call to the individual person in view of a specific service within the community, including the ability to perform this service."[24] Saints were called by God to perform a specific service for the Church and they relied on God to give them the grace to carry out the task He gave them.

I think Saints have special importance for ecumenism. I see them as treasures to be shared. I see them as a form of healing for those who see the Church only in terms of institution and who are discouraged with the failings of the institution. I see them also as comprising another sort of history of the Catholic Church—a charismatic history.[25] It is perhaps the reading of this history which will help to bring us all closer together.

Jesus is the head of His body, the Church. He ministers to and loves and cares for His people through ordained ministers like St. Peter. But He also sometimes acts sovereignly—directly— through those He Himself appoints, like St. Paul. Saints are ways God cares for His Church. Saints are God loving His people. Through the life of St. Peter Claver, God said: "I love My black people who are enslaved." Through St. Frances Xavier Cabrini, God said: "I love My people from Italy who are poor and alienated in America." Through St. Therese of Lisieux, God said: "I love those people who live what they think are "ordinary" lives. No life is ordinary, and I call all those I have created to experience My love."

Saints are a way that God gathers His people to Himself. He gathers people into the life of the Trinity. He gathers people into the community on earth which is His body, the Church, the communion of Saints. From age to age He gathers to Himself a holy people as day and night they never cease to sing, "Holy, holy, holy is the Lord God Almighty, who was and is and is to come!"

Notes to Chapter 14

1. Leon-Joseph Cardinal Suenens, *The Nun in the World*, The Newman Press, Westminster, Maryland, 1962, p. 41.

2. Igino Giordani, *St. Vincent De Paul*, p. 73.

3. See Mario von Galli, S.J., *Living our Future: Francis of Assisi and the Church Tomorrow*, Franciscan Herald Press, Chicago, 1972, p. 83ff.

4. K. Rahner, *Theological Investigations*, Vol. III, pp. 102-103.

5. Harvey D. Egan, *The Spiritual Exercises and the Ignatian Mystical Horizon*, p. 3.

6. Ida Friederike Gorres, *Broken Lights*, The Newman Press, Westminster, Maryland, 1960, p. 139.

7. K. Rahner, *op. cit.*, p. 108.

8. *Ibid.*, p. 101.

9. Cardinal Newman, *Apologia pro Vita Sua* (uniform edition), p. 259.

10. Frederick W. Faber, *The Precious Blood*, pp. 27-28.

11. *Omnibus of Sources*, p. 1197.

12. Jean-Francois Six, editor, *Spiritual Autobiography of Charles de Foucauld*, p. 120.

13. K. Rahner, *Theological Investigations*, Vol. VIII, "Why and How Can We Venerate the Saints?", pp. 3-4.

14. K. Rahner, *Theological Investigations*, Vol. III, "The Church of the Saints," p. 92.

15. Paul Molinari, *Saints, Their Place in the Church*.

16. *Ibid.*, p. 32.

17. *Ibid.* p. 34.

18. Egan, p. 3.

19. John Garvey, *A Contemporary Meditation on Saints*, The Thomas More Press, Chicago, Illinois, 1975, p. 19.

20. Rosemary Haughton, "Five Women Who Shaped What We Believe" in *Sign*, May 1976, p. 18.

21. Algar Thorold, translator, *The Dialogue of the Seraphic Virgin Catherine of Siena*, The Newman Bookshop, Westminster, Maryland, 1943, p. 73.

22. Rahner, *Theological Investigations*, Vol. III, p. 98.

23. Rahner, *Dynamic Element*, p. 55.

24. Hans Kung, "The Charismatic Structure of the Church" in *Concilium*, Vol. 4, p. 59.

25. I believe Yves Congar was envisioning such a book when he wrote "The Holy Spirit is continually at work to effect interiorly what the hierarchical ministry does exteriorly. . . . He is not just a divine force giving supernatural efficacy both to the ministry and to the sacraments, but a Person sovereignly active and free. He is not made use of by others, but himself directs events. . . . The body of Christ is built up by the regular mediation, functional and hierarchical, of the appointed ministers, the sacraments and other rites of the Church, but also by the unpredictable, occasional and fraternal mediation of the various conjectures and unexpected happenings brought about by the Spirit and signs of his working, which he offers to souls ready to accept them. A whole volume could be filled with examples drawn from the lives of saints and men of God, from one's own experience and that of many others who have confided in us. . . . How often . . . in the history of the Church, important decisions about vocations, foundations, even canons of councils, have been taken as a result of a dream, a word, a consultation of Scripture, in short of an intervention of the type of 'evenment (sic). . . .' " [Fr. Congar's translator uses "evenment" for the French *evenement* which would be more normally translated as "event."] "This subject, which has never been studied as a whole, certainly deserves investigation. We ourselves are convinced, as a result of a few haphazard soundings, that there could be disclosed here one of the most constant and decisive elements in the Church's life."

Yves Congar, O. P., *The Mystery of the Church*, translated by A.V. Littledale, Helicon Press, Baltimore, 1960, pp. 177-180.

CHAPTER 15

Two Saints

John Bosco

St. John Bosco (1815-1888) or Don Bosco as he is often called, worked mainly with boys. The work had its beginnings in 1841 in Turin, Italy and a hundred years later there were about fifteen thousand priests and brothers attached to the Salesian Congregation (John Bosco chose St. Francis de Sales as his patron) and over ten thousand Sisters of the Congregation of Mary, Help of Christians. In his lifetime John Bosco wrote nearly one hundred books.

John Bosco had a prophetic dream when he was nine years old. He seemed to be in a big yard where there were many boys playing together. Some were involved in games but some were fighting and swearing. John shouted at them to stop and began to strike at them. A shining figure in white by his side told John that with gentleness and charity he would win their hearts, not with blows. The figure then promised to give John a teacher and she would teach him true knowledge. When John asked the figure who He was, the answer was "I am the Son of her whom your mother has taught you to salute three times a day." The boys in the yard vanished to be replaced by wild animals. A beautiful lady then told John that she would show him what to do with her children. The wild animals changed to lambs. When John asked the lady what it all meant she told him that he would understand later. The dream was over.

As he grew older John decided that the Lord wished him to

become a priest. He entered a seminary and during a retreat preceding his ordination for the priesthood he wrote these thoughts and resolutions:

> No priest goes either to heaven or hell alone; faithful or unfaithful, he carries many with him. When it is a question of . . . souls I will always be prepared to humble myself, to suffer and to act. . . . Since work is such a power against the enemies of the soul, I will not allow myself more than five hours' sleep.[1]

A major influence in John Bosco's life at this time was Joseph Cafasso, rector of the Ecclesiastical Institute in Turin, and later also a canonized Saint. Under Joseph's guidance John saw the slums and prisons of the city. The plight of young orphaned or homeless boys sorrowed John especially. With St. Joseph Cafasso's support John began to gather boys around himself, instructing them in the faith and the basics of education, taking them on picnics and arranging sports and games. John was especially suited for youth work for he seems to have possessed a God-given magnetic personality. He had a zest for living. And of all things, he was an accomplished acrobat, juggler and master of magic tricks.

As the group of boys increased in size they had to move from one location to another. It was on the occasion of another move that John told his boys that young cabbages in order to grow must be transplanted often. In winter and bad weather, facilities were a problem but in good weather John Bosco met with his boys in open fields, hearing confessions and taking the boys to a nearby church for Mass. Sometimes the owner of the field would complain of trampled grass. Sometimes nearby residents would complain of noise. Local clergy, with poor attendance at their own parish Sunday school or CCD equivalent, complained that John Bosco was running a free-lance school which infringed on their parochial rights.

Many people tried to get John to relinquish his work with boys but he was certain that God was calling him to devote his life to this work and he answered the call without reserve. He did not yield to criticism and pressure. When told that he couldn't possibly take adequate care of so many boys, John would answer that if Providence had given him boys, Providence would provide for them. He even predicted that one day he would have buildings and a church. This led some people to the conclusion that he was losing his mind due to overwork. The vicar general of the archdiocese saw through the insanity rumors but two clerics took matters into their own hands. After making arrangements with the insane asylum the two priests paid a call on John Bosco and asked him to come for a drive with them as it was such a lovely afternoon. John got his hat but insisted that the priests step into the waiting carriage ahead of him. Then he slammed the door and told the driver to hurry and whip up his horse. The driver raced to the asylum. The waiting attendants were surprised to see two clerics in the carriage instead of one but they locked up the two anyway despite their shouts that it was all a mistake. The attendants, who were used to this explanation, proceeded about their business. The story was told all over the archdiocese.

The archbishop gave John Bosco faculties to act as parish priest to the boys, many of whom were homeless or came from broken homes. John had permission to say Mass, preach and hear confessions. In April 1846 he was given the use of a large shed and this became the first permanent Oratory of St. Francis de Sales.

Then John came down with pneumonia and the doctor said he was going to die. The last sacraments were administered. Now something happened that will have special meaning for Pentecostals. A priest friend said to John: "Father John, ask God to cure you." But John replied: "May God's holy will be done!" His friend said, "That is not sufficient. Make the prayer more specific. Ask God for your recovery for the sake of those five hundred boys."

John obeyed and the next day he was convalescing!

John's widowed mother joined him in the converted shed and served as housekeeper for the remaining eight years of her life. In 1847 John began taking in homeless boys to live. Soon he had forty neglected boys rooming with him and his mother. To combat outside influences he opened workshops for shoemakers and tailors in 1853. This way he could train apprentices at home.

John Bosco discerned two kinds of boys, those who would be apprentices, and those who could be trained to help with the work and possibly go on to the priesthood. For years John had the problem of help. Enthusiastic young priests would join him but would eventually leave for one of several reasons. Perhaps they did not have John's patience with boys or they didn't like his methods. He had great influence over the boys, sometimes even reading their thoughts. Through love he won their obedience. The absence of punishment sometimes scandalized the educational experts of his day.

John Bosco called his system of education and Christian formation, a "preventive system." [2] He insisted on unremitting supervision. This loving watchfulness would ensure that the boys would avoid occasions of sin. John, and those he trained to follow him in the work, lived amidst the pupils. They were true fathers to the boys. This paternal supervision encouraged the development of the right kind of freedom.

In January of 1854, John Bosco had the nucleus of a religious order and he began to train young men for the work with boys. In that year, twelve-year-old Dominic Savio, with the recommendation of his parish priest, came to the oratory. The most important source for Dominic's life is the account written by St. John Bosco himself. Dominic was under John Bosco's wise guidance the rest of his short life. He died in 1857 at the age of fifteen and was later canonized and declared a Saint. Dominic organized a little group among the boys called the Company of the Immaculate Conception. Besides being a devotional group, they swept floors and had a special care for boys with problems. John recorded that once Dominic was missing for hours. He was found in chapel wrapt in prayer as he had been for almost six hours since early Mass. He died a joyful death, his last words being, "I am seeing most wonderful things!"

The government at this time was radical and anticlerical. The archbishop of Turin who supported John Bosco at the beginning of his work went into exile. The Jesuits and the nuns of the Sacred Heart were driven out of Italy. But John Bosco went on expanding and building. His fame began to spread and he was in demand everywhere for retreats and missions. In his homilies John never touched on politics or topics of the day. He preached Jesus Christ. In his day, over a hundred years ago, John Bosco showed no attachment to the enclosed confessional. His boys knelt beside him and confessed their wrongdoing with Fr. Bosco's arm around their shoulder. When asked why he was so successful with young people, John would say: "You can do nothing with young people, unless you have their confidence and love."

A great believer in the power of the press, John Bosco wrote a manual of mathematics and a history of Italy for use in schools. He also wrote a prayer book and manuals of Christian doctrine and a monthly newsletter. One day, John Bosco said to his novices:

My children, we are living in very disturbed times, and it looks like madness to be founding a new religious congregation at the very hour in which the world and hell are doing their worst to destroy those now in existence. But fear not. I am not relying on probabilities but on certainties: God is blessing our endeavor and His will is that it shall go on. What has not been done to thwart our designs? What has it all amounted to? Nothing at all . . . we are seeking nothing but the glory of God.[3]

Opposition to the work the Lord was accomplishing through John Bosco came from the state as well as from the institutional element of the Church. The state demanded that all teachers be certified through special examinations. John Bosco's clerics took the test. Novices were enrolled at the university and some won high honors. Some members of the clergy criticized John for having his men attend a "secular" university. This had to be done so high school teachers could be certified. Later other orders followed suit.

Turin finally had a new archbishop who was not pleased that John Bosco was creating the nucleus of a religious congregation. The archbishop had been hoping John's work would provide parish priests for the diocese. Orders were issued that John Bosco could not use any natives of the archdiocese for work of the oratory. So John Bosco had to go to Rome to plead his cause. The people whom he needed to plead his cause with Pope Pius IX were in one way or another indisposed. In each case John told the person to ask intercession of Our Lady, Help of Christians. John loved the mother of Jesus and had special devotion to her under this title. In each case there was a healing. One cardinal was cured of gout and another of influenza. The nephew of a third was cured of typhoid fever. The prelates in question interceded with the Holy Father in John Bosco's behalf and John went home to Turin with an approval for a period of ten years. Ten years later came final approval. When John was suffering these trials, he never condemned his adversaries. He would say: "Have patience, this too will pass!" or "They put themselves against the work of God without wanting to!"

There is extant a copy of a short talk John Bosco once gave to some students and to young men training to assist him in his work with boys. On the occasion of the blessing of a statue of Mary, the mother of Jesus, John Bosco said in part:

. . . we know that what we have now blessed is not the Madonna, but an object representing the Madonna. We know, too, that by reverencing this statue we mean to reverence the Virgin Mary, who is represented by this statue. The world judges us rashly, and especially those . . . who are averse to such practices which they brand as idolatrous; and to condemn us they quote that text of Sacred Scriptures which says: "Ye shall make no idols nor graven images!" We are not simpletons! . . . How, then, are we to interpret that passage of the Sacred Scriptures? This is how: "Thou shalt make no idols, nor graven images of animals or other things *in order to adore them.*" That is, we are forbidden to adore them, but not to venerate or reverence them. Adoration, which is the translation of the Greek word *Latria*, meaning supreme worship or servitude, is the worship we give to God alone. On the other hand, the service we pay to the Saints, called in Greek *Dulia*, from Doulos (servant), is a homage which is by no means adoration, because we know that the Saints were men like ourselves, and we, too, can become Saints. . . . Do we not find in the Bible instances of statues? Of course we do. . . . There in the temple of Solomon, in the very Sanctuary of the Lord, what do we find to the right and to the left? Ah! yes, there were two cherubim. And who was it that placed them there? Idolaters, perhaps? No, it was Solomon himself, and that by order of the Lord. If then, this was commanded by God Himself, surely it is not in any way contrary to the Law of God.[4]

No account of the life of John Bosco would be complete without mention of Grigio (Gray). This was an immense gray dog. The few who saw him said he resembled a Great Dane. When John Bosco went out at night on sick calls in the city of Turin sometimes his life was in danger. Then out of nowhere Grigio materialized to escort

John Bosco safely to the oratory. At least three times Grigio saved John Bosco's life. Once the mysterious dog defended Don Bosco from a band of paid assassins.

John Bosco was troubled by Satan in much the same way as was the Cure d'Ars. In the early part of February in 1862, began what a future Salesian cardinal called a real "diabolical vexation." John Bosco was kept from getting any sleep at night. Unexplained gushes of wind blew through his bedroom, scattering papers. His pillow would shake. Then the bed would shake. Sometimes he felt a cold brush passing over his forehead. After some months this ceased. When asked about remedies, John Bosco said the Sign of the Cross availed only for a moment as did Holy Water. He was then quiet on the subject but his friends felt the remedy lay in fasting and penance.

Another work of John Bosco's was the foundation of a community for women, Daughters of Our Lady, Help of Christians. He built a church in honor of Our Lady and he built numerous other churches also.

One might think that John would enter old age with a sense of fulfillment, but only if one had not read many lives of Saints. All the Saints, in one way or another, shared in the sufferings of Jesus. They became like the Master they followed. Four years before his death, John Bosco had another dream and he wrote about it to his Salesian sons who numbered well over seven hundred in the New World and in Europe. The letter is full of sadness and reminds one of Francis of Assisi before his death, weeping over the state of his Franciscan family.

In the letter, which he wrote in Rome on May 10, 1884, John Bosco says that on a recent evening while preparing for bed and saying his prayers he fell asleep or "was carried away by a distraction." He saw the oratory as it was before 1870 with its close family spirit and the present oratory of 1884 in which the original spirit had grown cold. He closes the letter with these words:

Shall I tell you what this poor old man who has spent his whole

218

life on his beloved boys would ask of you? Simply this: so far as may be, bring back the happy days of the first Oratory. They were days of sympathy and Christian trust between the boys and those in authority, days of friendliness and forbearance towards one another for love of our Lord, days of frankness, simplicity, and candour, days of love and true joy for all.[5]

Perhaps one of the trials that caused John the most suffering was when one of his many books was conditionally assigned to the Index.[6] John Bosco, who believed firmly in the role of authority in the Christian life and who was known as a champion of the papacy, was accused of trying to undermine the authority of the pope. The controversy centered around a remark made in an appendix where John wrote that St. Peter's coming to Rome was not a truth of the faith. The ordeal of being under suspicion lasted several months. Pope Pius IX then intervened and a later edition of the book appeared, minus the "offensive" sentence!

When John Bosco died at the age of seventy-two, he was acclaimed a Saint by everyone. Huysmans called him "a matchless organizer of God's business." [7] Through St. John Bosco, God gathered to Himself sons of Italian workingmen who were being caught up in the industrial and social revolution of the nineteenth century. By his courageous love and service, St. John showed his boys that God loved them and they responded by giving their lives back to God.

Anne-Marie Javouhey

Blessed Anne-Marie Javouhey (1779-1851) was born in the French province of Burgundy on November 10, 1779. She was ten when the French Revolution began and she made her First Communion about a week before the Constituent Assembly in Paris decided to confiscate all property belonging to the Catholic Church. Schools, hospitals and orphanages conducted by the Church had to be turned over to the state. Churches were desecrated. All members of the clergy were required to take an oath of allegiance which would supersede their obedience to the pope. Those who refused, and continued to function as priests, were considered outlaws and criminals. Four of 135 bishops took the oath and about half of the priests.[8] Rome decreed that such priests automatically excommunicated themselves.

Anne-Marie became expert at hiding and assisting hunted priests. Since she was a farmer's daughter, she had a number of chores to do. What time was left over after chores were completed was spent in prayer and in catechizing her younger sisters and neighborhood children. This was done at some risk because this activity was outlawed. Anne-Marie spoke so eloquently about the love of Jesus that the suitor who asked for her hand in marriage became a Trappist monk instead. Three sisters and a brother were to follow her into religious life. On November 11, 1798, Anne-Marie made a vow of chastity and promised to devote her life to youth and the needy.

What followed next were several years of false starts and confusion. Before eventually founding the Congregation of St. Joseph of Cluny, an order of sisters caring for orphans and educating girls, Anne-Marie entered and left the Sisters of Charity, and entered and left a Swiss Trappistine Convent. It was while Anne-Marie was with the Sisters of Charity that she had an experience the meaning of which she fathomed only much later.

Anne-Marie said afterwards that she was asleep in bed and was awakened by noises in her room. The room seemed to be filled with people of every nationality and race and she heard a voice saying: "These are the children God is giving you. I am St. Teresa and I will protect your congregation." [9] At the time of this vision, Anne-Marie had no congregation. She was also puzzled because her rural education had not removed her assumption that all people in the world were white. Some of the people who seemed to be in her room were black.

Mention must be made of the role played by Anne-Marie's parents, Balthazar and Claudine Javouhey. They had ten children. The first two died in infancy. The third, Etienne, reached adulthood. The fourth child, a daughter, died in childhood. Anne-Marie was the fifth. Of the five children who followed, the four who lived, three girls and a boy, Pierre, were to join in the work God entrusted to Anne-Marie.

Some accounts of Anne-Marie's life dramatize her father as a constant opponent of God's designs. In reality he seems to have reacted to Anne-Marie as any good father with common sense would act. From the time when she began hiding hunted priests, as a young teenager, until the time in 1807 when she seemed settled in her life's work, Anne-Marie was in and out of such a variety of activities that it would have given any parent pause. Yet, despite occasional remonstrations, Balthazar and Claudine not only provided Anne-Marie with moral support, they often had to bail her out financially. When Anne-Marie left the Trappistines, she opened a small school at Souvans, in the Swiss Jura. At this juncture in his account of Anne-Marie's life, Father Joseph Mullins says: "Generously, as usual, her father, though sorely puzzled by all his daughter's apparently fruitless attempts and her seeming indecision, nevertheless came to her aid with money and provisions." [10]

It is recorded in the *Annals* of the Sisters of St. Joseph of Cluny that when she ran out of money at Souvans, Anne-Marie ran into the church and prayed in part: "My God . . . if I have erred punish me . . . but . . . do not leave the children You have confided to me without assistance. . . ." Interiorly she heard the words: "Have I ever failed you? Why importune me with your troubles and anxieties, when I have already heard your petition?" [11] When she returned to her school from the church, Anne-Marie found her father waiting with a cartload of provisions. In later years the Sisters of the Congregation of St. Joseph of Cluny presented to the Church of Souvans a silver lamp to burn perpetually before the altar where their foundress prayed for help. I like to think that when some people saw the lamp they thought kindly of Balthazar who, it seems to me, would be a great patron Saint for all fathers.

After some months Anne-Marie moved back to Burgundy and opened a school at Choisey. Then Balthazar offered her the farm-house at Chamblanc. She moved there with three young women recruits from Choisey and they were joined in their work by Anne-Marie's sisters. Father Mullins says here:

> From this moment, Balthazar and his excellent spouse may be said to have assumed a complete protectorate over the new Institute, and any concept of the foundation, which fails to take due account of their capital role in the holy work, ne-glects what was, under God, the indispensable condition of its marvelous success and rapid diffusion.[12]

In the same year that Anne-Marie centered her work in Chamblanc, Pope Pius VII passed nearby on his way to Paris for the coronation of Emperor Napoleon I. Anne-Marie had a visit with him and he gave her his blessing. About a year after this meeting, Msgr. de Fontagnes, then bishop of Autun, gave Anne-Marie's work his approval and he established her in his diocese and she placed her sisters in an unused seminary in the town of Chalon. On May 12, 1807, Anne-Marie and eight other young women made vows together and began wearing the habit [13] or dress to be worn by all Sisters of St. Joseph of Cluny. It was the parish priest of St. Pierre, the church in which they made their vows, who named the group. He placed the women under the protection of St. Joseph. St. Teresa had placed her reform houses under his protection.

The sisters had to vacate the seminary in 1809 but by that time eight new houses had been established. The work originally embraced schools and orphanages but was expanded to provide houses to care for the elderly. Many young women expressed a desire to join Anne-Marie and her sisters in the work the Lord had given them. Anne-Marie decided to set up a training house (novitiate) for the purpose of preparing women to give themselves completely to God and to the service of the kingdom. The Mother House (headquarters) and novitiate were established near the old Abbey of Cluny which by this time was in ruins.

The importance of proper training for young women before allowing them to serve in her schools and orphanages was brought home to Anne-Marie by problems arising within the community. Glen Kittler describes it this way:

> . . . new houses were opened in Autun, Rully, Couches, Provins, Donemarie, Nangis and Bray . . . the plights of over-extension arose. Some of the houses could not support themselves; money to meet their expenses had to come from more successful schools. Nuns at the successful house at Donemarie didn't like the idea of giving away the money they were earning and so they notified Nanette [a name by which Anne-Marie was familiarly known] that they were withdrawing from the congregation and going ahead on their own. The split was never repaired. In another house, burdened with bills and poverty, several nuns walked out one morning to go to Mass and they never returned. . . . Some of the nuns were proud, some of them were indifferent, some of them acted as if they had joined a sorority instead of a religious congregation.[14]

With the move of the central organization of her community to Cluny, the title "of Cluny" was added to the official title of the sisters.

Anne-Marie in 1815 established a school in Paris. She learned of a new educational method called the "Lancaster system" after Joseph Lancaster, the English educator who devised it. The method consisted of giving accelerated instruction to students of high aptitude who in turn assisted and taught slower students. This made it possible for a few professional teachers to reach a greater number of students. Anne-Marie introduced this system in her school quite successfully and people began to consider her a leading French educator.

Some Church authorities opposed the system in free state schools and all schools because they said the student-teachers or monitors were not qualified to teach religion—this despite the fact that the French minister of education agreed that religion would be taught by nuns, brothers and priests. Because of this controversy, Anne-Marie found she had some ecclesiastical enemies. However, the French government regarded her favorably. One visitor who came to Anne-Marie's school to observe the teaching methods was the Baron de Richemont, governor of Bourbon (now Reunion) in the Indian Ocean. He asked Anne-Marie if she would send some of her sisters to Bourbon to introduce their system of education. When the governor informed her that most of the children on the island were black, Anne-Marie remembered the vision in the room of the Sisters of Charity convent in Besancon and she agreed. Four sisters sailed for Bourbon on June 28, 1817.

The needs of the people in the French colonies were tremendous and Anne-Marie felt the Lord leading her to care for His people there. Not all French bishops agreed with this call. In particular, the new bishop of Autun did not wish the sisters to divide or redirect their energies. Just as the archbishop of Turin had forbidden any young men from his diocese to be ordained for John Bosco's work with boys, so too, the bishop of Autun felt there was plenty for the sisters to do in his diocese and in France, without widening their horizons. To an extent this was true and the feeling of both bishops is understandable. This was a real confrontation of the institutional and the charismatic. Real discernment is needed at such times. In John Bosco's case, as we have seen, the pope overruled the local bishops. In Anne-Marie's case, the controversy was to persist and cause her great suffering for most of her life. Final papal approval did not come until the latter half of the nineteenth century by which time the sisters had proved themselves on three continents.

With the work in Bourbon progressing, the French government asked the sisters to make a similar foundation in Senegal in West Africa. Anne-Marie sent some sisters to Senegal under the leadership of her youngest sister, Claudine. Father Mullins describes the situation on their arrival:

> They had no church; a nondescript collection of wooden shacks did duty as a hospital; . . . the only priest within a radius of fifty miles, Father Terrasse, soon tired of his ungrateful task and returned to France, abandoning the colony. . . . In a fit of pique against the civil authorities, he threw the place under interdict, so that the whole Catholic population remained the better part of two years without Mass or Sacraments.[15]

Anne-Marie suffered trials all her life from at least three sources: internal disturbances in her community, French government officials and the Bishop of Autun, Msgr. d'Hericourt, who wished to control her community. Pages could and have been written about Anne-Marie's patience, her trust in God, and her perseverence in gathering together the people the Lord called her to love and serve. Another interesting note is the crossing of Anne-Marie's path with that of Venerable Francis Libermann.

One project which led to her enemies calling Anne-Marie "the White Queen" and led her friends and admirers to thank God for her, was the work Anne-Marie did in Mana. This work will always be associated with her name.

In 1827 the French government again turned to Anne-Marie for help. The government asked her to undertake the colonization of an area on the banks of the Mana River in French Guiana. Several attempts by others had failed. The question Anne-Marie was asked was:

> What would she suggest as a means of transforming into a healthy, prosperous colony, this fever-haunted stretch of South-American coastal forest, miserably peopled with liberated or runaway slaves, on whom a handful of unscrupulous European officials and others were waxing prosperous, while the Government treasury was empty.[16]

Anne-Marie sought the Lord's guidance and in 1828 as she approached her fiftieth year, she set sail for French Guiana with thirty-six sisters and eighty-eight laymen. They were facing a disease-ridden land with a hot, wet climate. Up to that time, perhaps the only value French Guiana had for France was the location there of the prison known as Devil's Island. As she neared the work in Mana, Anne-Marie said: "I want to establish on these sparsely inhabited shores, a little haven where the Lord will be loved, served and glorified. . . ." [17]

Anne-Marie carefully organized the colony known as New Angouleme when she arrived. Her brother Pierre supervised the farm work. Workers in each trade—carpenters, shoemakers, wheelwrights, locksmiths, tinsmiths and furniture-makers—had their separate workshops. Once a week Anne-Marie visited and inspected each center of activity. In a letter sent to her sisters in France, Anne-Marie wrote:

> When I've been through all the workshops I go to the fields, where I am more at home. Here I see what is being done by the men, and then proceed to examine the work carried on by the women. . . . When time permits, I take my share in the operations by assisting in planting the different crops— maize, beans, maniocs, etc.[18]

A typical day at New Angouleme began with Mass at four in the morning. Tradesmen then went to workshops and farmers went to the fields. At seven, those who could went to the chapel for morning prayers. Because of the heat, work stopped at ten. At noon the whole colony went to the chapel for prayer followed by a meal and a siesta until two. From two until dinner, men worked on homes for their families, and children went to school. Dinner was preceded by prayer and followed by a church service [Benediction].

The government assigned twenty-five blacks [Africans] as laborers in the settlement. Some brought women with them to whom they were not actually married. And they brought children. Anne-Marie put these children into school with the white children. This did not set too well with some white European settlers who, for this and other reasons, returned to France.

Anne-Marie established a leper asylum near the colony because she found that lepers were not cared for and their suffering was intense. She discussed with the government the feasibility of transporting to New Angouleme some of the more suitable (in health and mental stability) orphans from St. Joseph of Cluny orphanages, but this plan was never realized. Anne-Marie saw the necessity of native clergy and sent some young men from one of her missions in Senegal, to France for training.

In 1829, a new governor of French Guiana, influenced by some government officials who were jealous of Anne-Marie's success and felt it contrasted with their unsuccessful attempts at colonization, withdrew the government subsidy that had been a major source of financial support for the colony. Then, the July Revolution of 1830 broke out in France and King Charles X was overthrown. He was succeeded by King Louis Philippe.

In August 1833, after five years in French Guiana, Anne-Marie returned to France. Internal affairs of her congregation were pressing. The bishop of Autun wanted sections of her community's constitution changed. At the time of Anne-Marie's return there were a little more than five hundred women in the society she had founded to care for God's "little ones": the elderly, lepers, children, orphans, and members of minority groups, blacks and Indians.

In October, Anne-Marie was again elected superior general of her society. She had a number of unpleasant interviews with the bishop of Autun who wished to control her society. The bishop was in his early thirties. Anne-Marie was fifty-four. The bishop was born a marquis and by age twenty he had a commission in the French army. After seven years of serving in various posts, he decided to become a priest. He was ordained after only two years of study ". . . not because he was brilliant, but because he had friends" writes Glenn Kittler in his biography of Anne-Marie. He continues: "He [the bishop] was about as well equipped to work as a priest as a medical student would be to practice complicated surgery after a few weeks of dissecting frogs." [19] This bishop was a source of great suffering to Anne-Marie but whether he was qualified for his post or not, Anne-Marie sensed the importance of the regulation of charisms by authority; the necessity of the institutional element of the Church. We know from her conversation and her letters that she prayed for this bishop and she did not condemn him. She, very importantly, was obedient to him. But it was an informed obedience, not a blind obedience. The bishop drew up a document which stated that the treasury of Anne-Marie's society was to be turned over to him, that he would supervise the training of her women and that he would change their uniform or habit as he didn't like it. Anne-Marie gently expressed her willingness to obey but she said she and all her sisters were bound by the constitution they had adopted and she said he would have to submit his proposed changes to the sisters. The bishop threatened Anne-Marie with an interdict of her entire congregation if she did not sign, so she signed the document.

Some months later when she was back in French Guiana Anne-Marie made a move which, in biographer Glenn Kittler's opinion, saved her society from extinction. She wrote to her sister, Rosalie, who was supervising the society's work in Bourbon, and told her to go home to France and replace her as superior general.

The revolutionists of 1830 had promised the abolition of slavery, and in March of 1831 a bill was passed freeing the slaves. They were to be put on probation for seven years. However, if they did not become "useful members of society" they were to be returned to slavery. Most slaves stayed where they were to serve their probation. In French Guiana, however, about five hundred slaves walked off their plantations and converged on the capital, Cayenne. Once again the French government turned to Anne-Marie. Would she please place the five hundred liberated slaves in her colony at New Angouleme? Yes she would—but Anne-Marie learned that most of the Cayenne probationers were men and that there were few African women there for them to marry. So, practical, holy Anne-Marie sailed to Senegal to visit the houses of service which her society had there. She came away with sixty women who crossed the Atlantic with her to be wed to the African men who had just been freed from slavery. To those who questioned her she replied: "I'm starting a colony, not a monastery. The men will be happier with a good wife." [20]

Instead of settling at New Angouleme, Anne-Marie chose a plateau called Mana nearer the sea. Anne-Marie's nephew, Louis, replaced Pierre as her assistant. At the end of 1836, 520 Africans, a good number of nuns, and a young priest from Autun were moved in.

The day at Mana resembled the schedule of New Angouleme. The women Anne-Marie brought with her were already Christian. As only Christian marriages were allowed at Mana, the men needed no urging to seek Christian instruction from the French priest. Anne-Marie devised a system of segregated classes for marriage preparation. This was highly successful. When a couple were finally married, Anne-Marie gave them a house, an acre of land and a small trousseau.

White colonists did not want the experiment at Mana to succeed as it would spell an end to cheap labor. At their instigation an attempt was made to murder Anne-Marie. Someone was to tip over the boat in which she was riding and see that she drowned. The plan failed.

The bishop of Autun was angered that Rosalie, Anne-Marie's sister, was now head of the community. The Prefect Apostolic, Bishop Guillier of Cayenne, was convinced that Anne-Marie was a member of a British and French organization of abolitionists. The bishop of Autun began a correspondence with him. Bishop Guillier visited Anne-Marie and brought with him a revised document like the one she had previously been forced to sign. She explained that her signature had no value as she was no longer superior general. Bishop Guillier's response was to excommunicate Anne-Marie. This meant that she could not receive the sacraments, and she was passed by at the Communion rail. As has been stated earlier, this was a public humiliation as well as a personal deprivation. It was to be two long years before Anne-Marie would again be able to receive her Lord in Holy Communion.

Meanwhile the colony at Mana thrived under Anne-Marie's direction. Here is one description of the town:

> The town itself had become an attractive place, neat, quiet, orderly. On the town square were a hospital, a school, a large church, the convent, the general store and shops opened by craftsmen who had learned their trades from Nanette [Anne-Marie]. There was not a policeman within miles, not any need for one. . . . All the farms were prosperous. The canals Nanette had built were a lifesaver . . . the rum distillery was operating, supervised by . . . [a] convict from De-

vil's Island to whom Nanette had promised the job ten years before.[21]

On March 15, 1838, Anne-Marie wrote in a letter: "Mana now resembles a little village in France. The streets are wide, the houses simple, but well arranged, and the gardens fairly large." [22] Anne-Marie left Mana on May 18, 1843 for France. All in Mana wept at her departure.

The people of Mana did not forget Anne-Marie. In 1848 the French government decreed that Mana was a free borough and Mana was told to elect a deputy to Parliament. Unanimously Mana voted for Mother Javouhey. When it was explained that women were not eligible to hold office, the people of Mana said they would not vote at all.

Anne-Marie was called "the White Queen" by her detractors. She once wrote in a letter about a visit to Mana of some government inspectors: "They kept repeating, with a kind of resentment: 'What a pity there is not a man at the head of such a fine enterprise!' More than ever I gratefully repeat, 'Yes, it is indeed God's work.' " [23] When she became a celebrity, King Louis Philippe, probably wishing to express the highest of compliments, said of her: "Mother Javouhey? She's a great man."

The bishop of Autun died in 1851. Anne-Marie was to die some few months later. At her death her society numbered nine hundred women serving in orphanages, schools and hospitals and places such as Mana. Upon the death of the bishop of Autun, Anne-Marie said:

We ought to think of His Lordship as one of our benefactors. God made use of him to try us when as a rule we were hearing around us nothing but praise. That was necessary, for since our congregation was succeeding so well we might have thought we were something if we hadn't had these pains and contradictions.[24]

Anne-Marie was declared "Venerable" on February 11, 1908. In 1911 her body was exhumed and was found incorrupt. She looked like she was sleeping. Forty years later her body was examined again and was once more found to be perfectly preserved. On October 15, 1950, Anne-Marie was declared "Blessed." Present at the ceremony were descendants of Anne-Marie's brothers, Etienne and Pierre. Present also were people from Mana, Cayenne and other places where Anne-Marie had served her Lord.

Notes to Chapter 15

1. F.A. Forbes, *Saint John Bosco*, Salesiana Publishers, New Rochelle, N.Y., 1962, p. 39. This resolution and others were written in "a shabby little notebook" that John kept until his death.
2. A. Auffray, S.D.B., *Saint John Bosco*, St. Dominic Savio House, Bollington, Macclesfield, 1964, p. 247.
3. Edna Beyer Phelan, *Don Bosco*, p. 209.
4. *Ibid.*, pp. 145-146.
5. A Benedictine of Stanbrook Abbey, *Letters from the Saints*, p. 115.
6. The Index Librorum Prohibitorum was a list of books Catholics were forbidden to read.
7. Phelan, *op. cit.*, p. 318.
8. Glenn D. Kittler, *The Woman God Loved*, Hanover House, Garden City, N.Y., 1959, p. 22.
9. Sister Mary de Verteuil, *The Holy Will of God One Heart and One Soul*, a paper produced as a requirement for some course work. The paper was privately circulated in 1974 by the Mother House of the Sisters of St. Joseph of Cluny in Paris, p. 3. This incident is also reported by Henri Daniel-Rops in *The Heroes of God*, by Fr. Mullins in *In Journeys Often* and by C.C. Martindale, S.J. in *The Life of Anne-Marie Javouhey*.
10. Father Joseph A. Mullins, C.S.Sp., *In Journeys Often*, Dublin The Wood Printing Works, Ltd., 1947, p. 16.
11. From the *Annals* as quoted in *Life of Venerable Mother Javouhey*, translated by J.B. Cullen, M.H. Gill & Son, Ltd., Dublin 1912, p. 73.

12. Mullins, *op. cit.*, p. 17.
13. The clothes or garb of men and women in religious orders is referred to as the "habit."
14. Kittler, *op. cit.*, p. 83.
15. Mullins, *op. cit.*, pp. 27-28.
16. *Ibid.*, p. 44.
17. de Verteuil, *op. cit.*, p. 10.
18. Cullen, *op. cit.*, p. 209.
19. Kittler, *op. cit.*, p. 176.
20. *Ibid.*, p. 196.
21. *Ibid.*, p. 211.
22. Cullen, *op. cit.*, p. 242.
23. *The Spirit Gives Life, The Spirituality of Blessed Anne-Marie Javouhey as Found in Her Letters*, compiled by the Tertianship Group of 1974, p. 69. (Library of the Sisters of St. Joseph of Cluny, Newport, Rhode Island.)
24. Kittler, *op. cit.*, p. 228.

Appendix I:
A Task for Theology

Reading lives of Saints leads one somewhat into the field of "spiritual theology." This is theological reflection on the experience of those who have lived the Christian life down through the ages. Spiritual theology is sometimes called "the science of the Saints," and is, as one theologian has said "like economics is to business."[1] Textbooks on the subject, such as Tanquerey's *The Spiritual Life* and Garrigou-Lagrange's *The Three Ages of the Interior Life*, as well as the lives of the Saints, are likely to introduce the reader to a maze of unfamiliar terminology. Those accustomed to simple expressions such as life in the Spirit, growth in the Spirit and praying in the Spirit will be baffled by terms such as: immanence, transcendence, mysticism, aridity, acquired contemplation, active life, contemplative life and state, ascetical theology, mystical theology, interior life, religious life, beginners, proficient and perfect, the purgative, illuminative and unitive ways. Any attempt to get at the meaning of some of these terms can be a frustrating experience. The reason too often given for this state of affairs is that this branch of theology is trying to express the inexpressible. However, it is my conviction that this attempt to correlate and to compare the language of charismatic renewal with the language of traditional Catholic spiritual teaching is a necessary though demanding task and an important item on the future theological agenda of the Church.

Catholic spiritual writing has made much use of the terms "mystic," "mystical" and "mysticism," and so some preliminary efforts to relate the charismatic and the traditional have been done in terms of the charismatic and the mystical.[2] I would describe mysticism in the Christian sense as the conscious awareness of the action of the Holy Spirit in one's life. In a religious sense, the term can be spoken of from a traditionally Christian or from a non-Christian viewpoint, or can be considered a sort of natural mysticism in a poetic or artistic sense. There are books such as *Three Mystics*, by a Carmelite priest, Fr. Bruno, which group together, oddly enough, Teresa of Avila, John of the Cross and El Greco. El Greco was hardly a mystic in the same way as were the two Saints! A source of confusion also is the diversity of opinion among various schools of spirituality (Franciscan, Dominican, Carmelite, Jesuit and others) and various spiritual theologians (Tanquerey, Garrigou-Lagrange, de Guibert, Poulain, Arintero) and at times it would seem even among the Saints themselves (Bonaventure, Thomas Aquinas, Teresa of Avila, John of the Cross, Francis de Sales).[3]

Remembering the counsel of Jesus to "pray always" (Luke 18:1) it is amusing to envision St. Peter out in his boat with a copy of Garrigou-Lagrange trying to figure out if he can safely leave off meditation in favor of a more simple prayer form! Sunk in a morass of terminology analyzing the spiritual life (life in the Spirit) one feels like taking the whole hundreds of years old tradition of spirituality and throwing it out as so much intellectual ballast. It is precisely here that von Hugel's construct is indispensable. If this charismatic renewal is from God, it will eventually have to acquire a sure theological foundation, to manifest its real continuity with traditional teaching (which is not to exclude an element of genuine newness) and to be integrated into the life of the institutional Church.

Not much has been written so far attempting to marry the Pentecostal experience with traditional Catholic spirituality. Fr.

O'Connor has a chapter on "Pentecost and Traditional Spirituality" in his book, *The Pentecostal Movement in the Catholic Church*. In that chapter and elsewhere in the book certain views are expressed but not developed as it would have been beyond the scope of the book. Fr. O'Connor does not see the charismatic renewal fundamentally as a new school of spirituality.[4] I would agree. There are now charismatic Franciscans, Spirit-filled Dominicans, Pentecostal Jesuits, tongues-speaking Carmelites, who seem no less true to the spirit of their order for experiencing the fullness of the Spirit. Fr. O'Connor is convinced that "some grace of infused contemplation has been given to quite a number of these people [Catholic Pentecostals]."[5] As a clue to how this might fit into the framework of traditional spirituality, Fr. O'Connor says later, ". . . I have the impression that those who have received the grace of infused contemplation without having gone through the purification which normally must precede it are often obliged afterward to take the steps which they seem to have skipped over."[6] Fr. O'Connor also feels that it is clear that the baptism in the Spirit takes different forms and has different effects from one person to another.[7]

This same view is expressed by Stephen Clark in *Baptized in the Spirit*. First Clark explains that spiritual writers have traditionally described spiritual growth in terms of the purgative way, the illuminative way and the unitive way. In the purgative way a person is purified of habitual sins. In the illuminative way a person grows in Christlike qualities and gets to know Jesus, and in the unitive way a person begins to experience the Holy Spirit working in him. Clark writes that the difference between what is happening now and what happened before, is that people are being baptized in the Spirit at the beginning of their spiritual growth. He then says that because different people have very different relationships with the Holy Spirit when they are baptized in the Spirit, different things happen to them. Being baptized in the Spirit can mean different things to different people.[8]

Perhaps another way of expressing what Clark and O'Connor are saying is that the Pentecostal experience, or the baptism in the Spirit, is a *unitive experience* which can occur at any *stage* of the spiritual life, purgative, illuminative or unitive, or even before a "spiritual life" actually begins, before one enters on the purgative way. In this last instance the unitive experience of the baptism in the Spirit perhaps serves the function of turning the person away from sin. For one in the illuminative way it teaches him what God, Father, Son and Holy Spirit, is like, and for one in the unitive way it functions to bring about union with God in pure faith. This last might fit in nicely with Clark's third category of people where he says it is probably more proper to speak of a freeing of their faith rather than a filling with the Spirit or being baptized in the Spirit.[9]

In the same book Clark makes a point that it is interesting to compare with the observation of a renowned scholar, the late Dom David Knowles in *The Nature of Mysticism*. In *Baptized in the Spirit* Clark writes: ". . . Those who have been growing according to traditional spirituality often have a great deal of spiritual maturity even if they have not been baptized in the Spirit. They are living at a higher level as Christians than many who have been baptized in the Spirit."[10] Contrast that with this by David Knowles, ". . . A mystical life in its early stages will not show the mature strength of a long life of apostolic virtue. . . ." He then opposes firmly "any suggestion that an entirely 'active,' non-mystical life of virtue may surpass in excellence the fullest mystical union."[11]

One long-standing debate with a bearing on discussions within the charismatic renewal is mentioned by the Dominican priest, Simon Tugwell, in 1972, in *Did You Receive the Spirit?*

. . . one of the great controversies of the earlier part of the twentieth century was whether the mystical and charismatic way was, in principle, proper for all christians. . . . J.G.

Arintero (1860-1928, perhaps the greatest spiritual director and writer of the period, and one of the leading figures in the revival of mystical theology) taught insistently that all christians not only *could*, but *should* aspire to the highest mystical union with God. And he warned against the tendency to fight shy of the charismatic gifts.[12]

A Jesuit, Joseph de Guibert, writing in 1946, devoted at least twelve pages of his book *The Theology of the Spiritual Life* to this controversy.[13] The question boiled down to whether every Christian could or should be a mystic. This is further complicated, with some theologians, by the equation of mysticism and infused contemplation, i.e., passive prayer, not to be obtained through one's one efforts, admitting of various degrees and marked by direct intuition of God.

My experience in the charismatic renewal supports the view of Arintero,[14] the Maritains[15] and Bouyer[16] that mysticism, far from being singular and extraordinary, is in the normal way for Christians. They are agreed that the mystical life consists in the predominance of the seven gifts of the Holy Spirit, the conscious life of grace and the experience of the touches and influences of the Holy Spirit. In fact, this debate about "the normal Christian life" is particularly relevant to the contemporary discussion as to whether or not charismatic renewal (with baptism in the Spirit and the exercise of spiritual gifts) is for all Christians.

Any relating of the charismatic renewal to traditional spiritual teaching inevitably raises questions about the connection, if any, between charisms and mystical phenomena. From within the Catholic tradition I would say that authentic mystical phenomena are an overflow into the senses of contact with God and would put them into a category distinct from charismatic gifts.[17] However, Dr. Vinson Synan, one of the classical Pentecostal participants in the Roman Catholic-Pentecostal dialogue, in his initial encounter with the Catholic mystical tradition, has failed to make any such distinctions. In writing about phenomena he says:

> Parallels to most of the miracles attributed to Catholic saints are not to be found in the literature of the modern Pentecostal-charismatic movement. In my studies, I have found no examples among Pentecostals of the following mystical phenomena: stigmata, tokens of espousal, telekinesis, luminous phenomena, the odor of sanctity, incorruption, the absence of cadaveric rigidity, blood prodigies, living without eating, and multiplication of food.[18]

Admittedly, all Dr. Synan's examples are observable phenomena, with the exception of "tokens of espousal" which can only be experienced or "seen" by the recipient, although the concomitant ecstasy could be seen by others. But it is far from obvious that all these are rightly termed mystical phenomena or indeed that they are all miraculous! In attempting some sort of classification I would at least want to distinguish paranormal activities from psychophysical accidents, even though as yet we do not have enough knowledge to assign every item to its right place on any chart, and then to distinguish all phenomena from the spiritual realities that underlie them. So I propose tentatively a classification of Dr. Synan's examples as follows:

PARANORMAL ACTIVITIES	PSYCHOPHYSICAL ACCIDENTS	MYSTICAL GRACES	CHARISMATIC GIFTS
telekinesis luminous phenomena	living without eating (inedia), blood prodigies, absence of cadaveric rigidity (no rigor mortis) incorruption, odor of sanctity stigmata luminous phenomena	spiritual betrothal (accompanied by tokens of espousal)	multiplication of food (working of miracles)

Working backwards, charismatic gifts and sanctifying graces are discussed in Chapter Two, note 16. It is easy to see that multiplication of food pertains to the charismatic gift of miracles and is a sign which upbuilds the body of Christ. It is no sign of sanctity in the one through whom God performs the miracle, and it is only sanctifying for the minister insofar as he acts in union with and in fidelity to the Lord.

Tokens of espousal pertains to entrance into a mystical state known as espousal or betrothal. Some Catholic Saints described progress in life in the Spirit in terms of increasing union with God (which it is), and they wrote in terms of a love relationship with the Lord ending in marriage. After a falling in love period, one passed through times of testing and purification called "dark nights." One then moved on to spiritual betrothal, marriage and transforming union. Catherine of Siena, for example, experienced a time of celebration at her mystical betrothal and she records that the Lord gave her a ring to seal the union, which only she could see. This ring was a "token of espousal." It pertained to a state which was a step along the way of progress of the life of sanctifying grace and so pertains to *gratia gratum faciens* although the experiential element (vision of a ring or something similar) is quite clearly an overflow into the senses.

What I call "psychophysical accidents" are concomitant phenomena which accompany and result from spiritual activity, though in no way an essential component thereof.[19] Some reflect the impact on the body of intense spiritual experience e.g., the stigmata, while others can be the by-products of a holy death, e.g., absence of cadaveric rigidity, incorruption (being immune to decay). Such phenomena do not necessarily serve much spiritual purpose and can either be shown to have a psychophysical basis or it is supposed that with the advance of science such a basis will be found. The phenomena surrounding the Saints in death has been discussed in the chapter on relics. Stigmata, which means bearing the wounds of Christ on one's body, is treated in the book *The Enigma of the Stigmata* [20] by Rene Biot.

What I classify as "paranormal activities" are extrasensory or extra-rational faculties that are not so much religious as psychic, i.e., possibly a basic human endowment.

Telekinesis, which Dr. Synan lists among Catholic mystical phenomena, is also known today as PK.[21] It is the ability to move matter with the mind alone. Soviet scientists have been seriously engaged in psychic research. In the area of telekinesis, or PK, they observed someone in particular, Nelya Mikhailova, who possessed extraordinary PK power. Dr. E. Sitkovsky, a professor at the Academy of Social Sciences attached to the Communist Party's Central Committee in Russia states: "Mikhailova's PK has nothing to do with mysticism. When a person thinks, he radiates energy and the energy is stronger in some people. PK is a physical-physiological fact."[22]

One of the occurrences in the lives of Catholic Saints (those classified as mystics) is the moving through the air of the Communion host from the priest to the mouth of the Saint.[23] This I suggest is PK.

Besides PK (telekinesis), Dr. Synan lists luminous phenomena, known in spiritual theology text books as "mystical aureoles" (Royo & Aumann) and called by those in psychic research, the "aura."[24] Royo and Aumann list these cases where a resplendent light irradiated from the body: Moses, St. Louis Bertrand, St. Ignatius Loyola, St. Francis de Paula, St. Philip Neri, St. Francis de Sales, St. Charles Borromeo, and St. John Vianney.[25]

Ostrander and Schroeder in *Psychic Discoveries Behind the Iron Curtain*, write:

The concept of a human aura, a radiating luminous cloud

surrounding the body, goes back centuries. Pictures from early Egypt, India, Greece, Rome, showed holy figures in a luminous surround long before artists in the Christian era began to paint saints with halos. This convention may actually have been based on the observations of clairvoyants who could reportedly see the radiance surrounding saints.[26]

It would seem to me that some people are particularly sensitive and possess one or more psychic endowments. Why this is so or whether all people could do the same prodigies if they knew how are questions not yet answered but being studied seriously by some investigators. It seems logical that if such a person were to be completely given to the Lord, these "powers" would also be at the service of the Lord and the Body.

In an interesting jotting in her diary, the hagiographer Ida Friederike Gorres [27] wrote in the late 1950s:

In one of the April numbers of *The Tablet* I read a very interesting review of a book by the German Cistercian Abbot Wiesinger *(Occult Phenomena in the Light of Theology*, London, 1957). He maintains that all para-psychic faculties are relics of Paradise gifts, gifts once belonging to the "spiritual" body of unfallen man. Makes very good sense to me and tallies with similar views held by Anne Catherine Emmerich. She, of course, makes a very clear distinction between the effect of these powers as used by saints and by "unredeemed" man.[28]

Karl Rahner comments on the same subject in a footnote in *Visions and Prophecies:*

Why should the natural parapsychological powers of telepathy, clairvoyance, psychometry (if these exist) not be able to apprehend religious objects, just as the "normal" powers of a religious person do, and thus occasion acts of religious value? And why should not such acts (. . .the searching of hearts, recognition of relics, etc.) be taken as "graces" of God?[29]

It should be obvious, then, that the phenomena surrounding Saints are varied in value and varied as to their causes. Some phenomena are manifestations of psychic endowments, influenced by the grace of God; others are manifestations of charisms, yet others the visible consequences or "overflow" effects from the sanctifying work of God in the heart.

Besides this confusion caused by indiscriminately mixing various categories of gifts, graces and phenomena, resulting from an insufficient familiarity with the Catholic mystical tradition, there are other theological confusions that can arise from insufficient familiarity with Pentecostalism and the charismatic renewal. One is to mix charisms with mystical phenomena by applying to gifts criteria that only properly belong to mystical phenomena. Another is to include love among a list of charisms and then to say that it is the highest charism of them all.

The misconception that treats charisms as mystical phenomena commonly appeals to the teaching of St. John of the Cross that we must be detached from such things. So, most recently, George H. Tavard says:

On the one hand, speaking in tongues, like the . . . gift of tears, has played a positive role in the life of many. On the other, the common doctrine of the great Christian mystics is to ignore such phenomena, even if they are God-given. It therefore seems that two principles ought to be kept:

1. the principle of St. Paul, that in the worship assembly one should not speak in tongues unless an interpreter can explain the meaning for the sake of the community (1 Cor. 14:28);

2. the principle of St. John of the Cross, that one should not be attached to spiritual gifts from God, for the only "proper and proportionate" means of union to God is faith (*The Ascent of Mount Carmel*, part II, chapter VIII).[30]

Likewise Robert Nowell in *What a Modern Catholic Believes*

About Mysticism states:

> . . . what can loosely be termed mystical phenomena—
> visions, trances, various phenomena that today would be
> classified under the heading of ESP or extrasensory percep-
> tion such as levitation or apparently being able to read some-
> one else's mind, as well as the manifestations associated with
> the charismatic movement. These, as mystical writers such as
> St. John of the Cross make abundantly clear, are at best
> stages on the road, and comparatively early stages at that.[31]

Even Fr. Louis Bouyer, an acknowledged authority on the
history of Catholic spiritual teaching, followed this trend in his
paper presented at the Roman Catholic-Pentecostal Dialogue
meeting in 1973.[32] While Fr. Bouyer recognizes the ministerial
character of spiritual gifts in St. Paul's teaching,[33] he also ends up
lumping together charisms and mystical phenomena, appealing to
St. John of the Cross and saying that "all, even the greatest, gifts
of God are to be freely accepted but also freely renounced if and
when God wills it."[34]

This confusion leads to charismatic gifts being considered rare
and extraordinary, because mystical phenomena are rare and
extraordinary.[35] But those who in recent times have been praying
in tongues and exercising other charisms in service to others,
consider the charisms, particularly tongues, rather ordinary. Pentecostal theologians in dialogue with Roman Catholic theologians
must wonder at the designation "extraordinary" for tongues.
Likewise, those formed by St. Paul's exhortation to seek the
spiritual gifts will not understand all the talk about detachment.[36]

To my knowledge only one theologian to date has noticed this
wrong equation of true spiritual gifts or charisms with mystical
phenomena, and that is Fr. Peter Hocken writing in *The Heythrop
Journal* in July of 1974. He remarks that the distinction of
ordinary-extraordinary never found a place in Catholic dogmatic
theology, even though it appeared in post-Reformation ascetical

writings:

> In that context, the distinction was used as a yardstick for determining what graces it was proper to seek and which it would be improper to want; thus one might without pride seek ordinary graces, but not extraordinary. This way of speaking, which seems to have been influenced by St. John of the Cross' suspicion of "supernatural phenomena," did not pass uncontested.[37]

Fr. Hocken then quotes the seventeenth century Jesuit Pere Louis Lallemant from P. Pourrat's *Christian Spirituality*, Vol. IV. Fr. Lallemant wrote that Paul's first letter to the Corinthians showed that the most extraordinary gifts of God were ordinary to the first Christians. And then Fr. Lallemant says:

> Nowadays if anyone aspires to some gift a little above the common, he is told flatly that such are extraordinary gifts which God only gives when and to whom He pleases, and that they should neither be asked for or desired; this shuts the door to them forever. This is a great abuse.[38]

Fr. Hocken then shows that the use of the phrase "extraordinary graces" does involve "a confusion between genuine spiritual gifts and accompanying phenomena treating within the same bracket true spiritual endowments and mere preternatural concomitants." He points to *The Three Ages of the Interior Life* by Garrigou-Lagrange where charisms, private revelations, visions, interior words, divine touches, stigmatization and suggestion are considered in order under the heading of "Extraordinary Graces."[39]

The second confusion seems to follow on from the first. It is to include love as a charism and then to say that it is the highest gift. Theologians as eminent as Yves Congar, Louis Bouyer and Hans Kung have fallen into this trap.[40] However, others more familiar with Pentecostalism and the charismatic renewal, e.g., Arnold Bittlinger and Kilian McDonnell, have pointed out that the term *charisma* is never used in the New Testament to describe love or charity.[41] Donald Gee, the Pentecostal leader from Britain, explained it this way:

The first and greatest *fruit* of the Spirit is Love. So marvelous is this divine Love manifested in and through the life wholly yielded to the Spirit of Christ, that Paul devotes a whole chapter (I Cor. 13) to its praises. . . .

Let us be quite clear that such love is a "Fruit" rather than a "Gift." It is distinguished from spiritual [ministry/charismatic] gifts in I Cor. 14:1. It is quite unscriptural to say, "I am seeking love, the greatest gift of all." Many say this, but Love is not mentioned among the nine gifts of the Spirit (I Cor. 12:8-11). Instead of expecting the character of I Cor. 13 to be dropped suddenly and completely into the heart as a finished gift from God, we should rather see that it is the fruit of the working out of a divine principle within. It is perfected by a life of close communion with the Lord, and in no other way.

. . . there are *nine gifts* recorded in I Cor. 12:8-11, and *nine fruits* recorded in Gal. 5:22-23.

. . . the great chapter on Love (I Cor. 13) is embedded between the two principal chapters dealing with Spiritual Gifts, and is an integral part of the subject.

The first fact teaches us that the Gifts [charisms] and the Fruit are meant to balance one another: the second that they are intimately connected with one another.

Paul's exhortation concerning "a more excellent way" in the last verse of I Cor. 12 is often interpreted as though he had written: "Don't trouble about Spiritual Gifts, only seek love." This is quite wrong; he does not write "Follow after love *instead of* spiritual gifts;" but "follow after love and *desire*

247

spiritual gifts." It is quite unbalanced and unscriptural to ignore or neglect spiritual gifts as so many do.[42]

In *Gathering a People* I have been trying to provide some helps and encouragement for those who would go back into the riches of Catholic tradition, particularly to the Saints. But the Saints were assisted by theology, whether they were conscious of it or not. St. Teresa loved theologians! To have the kind of deep and fruitful dialogue the Lord is calling His dismembered body to engage in is going to require the help of theologians who are deeply plunged into the life of the Spirit. Again I find support in von Hugel's construct. The Church, the living body of Christ needs understanding as well as balance between the three elements in the Church. Not only must we in the charismatic renewal understand the writings of theologians as they comment on the doctrine of the Saints, but we need theologians who have had experience exercising the charismatic gifts. We need theologians who are open to all the gifts not excluding tongues. We need theologians who are willing and even desirous of keeping close to those with pastoral responsibility in the charismatic renewal so that they will have a context wider than their own experience from which to write. We need theologians who pray much and we need to pray much for theologians. As Fr. Ed O'Connor said in his book *The Pentecostal Movement in the Catholic Church*, ". . . there is no reason why there cannot be even greater saints and theologians in the future than in the past."[43]

NOTES TO APPENDIX I

1. See Chapter 7, note 9.
2. E. g.V. Synan, "The Role of the Holy Spirit and the Gifts of the Spirit in the Mystical Tradition" in *One in Christ*, 1974-2, pp. 193-202; P. Hocken "Charismatics and Mystics" in *Theological Renewal*, no. 1, Nov. 1975 (published with *Renewal* magazine, no. 59), pp. 11-17.
3. A subject which seems to divide even Saints is the question of whether, at the

summit of the mystical life, the soul is led to "pure prayer" which excludes any distinct considerations, even the humanity of Jesus. The book I found most helpful on this subject was *The Crucible of Love* by E.W. Trueman Dicken.

4. E.D. O'Connor, *The Pentecostal Movement in the Catholic Church*, p. 32.

5. *Ibid.*, p. 153.

6. *Ibid.*, p. 172.

7. *Ibid.*, p. 132.

8. Stephen Clark, *Baptized in the Spirit*, pp. 65-76.

9. *Ibid.*, p. 74.

10. *Ibid.*, p. 69.

11. *The Twentieth Century Encyclopedia of Catholicism*, Vol. 38, *The Nature of Mysticism* by David Knowles, p. 37.

12. Simon Tugwell, *Did You Receive the Spirit?* p. 36.

13. E.T. New York, 1953 from Latin original *Theologia Spiritualis Ascetica et Mystica*, Rome 1946.

14. John G. Arintero, O.P., *The Mystical Evolution in the Development and Vitality of the Church*, 2 Vols., B. Herder Book Co., St. Louis, 1949.

15. Jacques and Raissa Maritain, *Prayer and Intelligence*, Sheed and Ward, London 1929, pp. 19-26.

16. Louis Bouyer, *Introduction to Spirituality*, p. 303.

17. Mystical phenomena are often divided into ordinary or concomitant (such as ecstasy) or extraordinary and gratuitous (such as locutions).

18. *Art. cit.* in note 2 above, pp. 199-200.

19. Just as phenomena, psychophysical accidents may be authentic, flowing from holiness and intimacy with God, or inauthentic, resulting from other forms of spiritual activity and contact.

20. Rene Biot, *The Enigma of the Stigmata*.

21. Ostrander/Schroeder, *Psychic Discoveries Behind the Iron Curtain*, p. 456.

22. *Ibid.*, pp. 61-62.

23. This phenomenon is discussed under the heading "Communions from a Distance" in the book cited in footnote 20, pp. 66-70

24. Ostrander and Schroeder, *op. cit.*, p. 200.

25. Royo and Aumann, pp. 672-673.

26. Ostrander and Schroeder, *op. cit.*, p. 201.

27. Ida Friederike Gorres' books include: *The Nature of Sanctity* (1933), *Mary Ward* (1939) and *The Hidden Face*, A Study of St. Therese of Lisieux (1959).

28. Gorres, *Broken Lights*, The Newman Press, Westminster, Maryland, 1964, p. 232.

29. Karl Rahner, *Visions and Prophecies*, Paulist Pub., Montreal, 1963, p. 43.

30. G. H. Tavard, *The Inner Life*, Paulist Press, New York, 1976, pp. 49-50.

31. R. Nowell, *What a Modern Catholic Believes About Mysticism*, The Thomas More Press, Chicago, 1975, p. 13.

32. This paper was entitled "Charismatic Movements in History within the Church Tradition" and published in *One in Christ*, 1974-2, pp. 148-161. It has since appeared in a slightly revised form under the title "Some Charismatic Movements in the History of the Church" in *Perspectives on Charismatic Renewal*, ed. E.D. O'Connor, University of Notre Dame Press, Notre Dame, Indiana, 1975, pp. 113-131. The references and quotations below are from this later edition.

33. "He (Paul) insists that *all* these gifts (not only the official functions) are to be considered by their possessors not, in fact, as their own, to be enjoyed freely and without regard to others, but as 'ministries' (*diakoniai*) given to them not for themselves primarily but for the good and service of all" (p.117).

34. *Ibid.*, p. 130.

35. So Bouyer describes tongues as an extraordinary gift (*op. cit.*, p. 117).

36. In the preface to *Did You Receive the Spirit?* (p. 11) Simon Tugwell exclaims that he was flabbergasted to read in an American periodical that one of the charges leveled against Teresa (of Avila) and especially against John of the Cross was that they discouraged Pentecostalism.

37. Peter Hocken, "Catholic Pentecostalism: Some Key Questions," Part II, in *The Heythrop Journal*, July 1974, p. 274.

38. *Art. cit.*, p. 274.

39. *Op. cit.*, Vol. 2, Part V.

40. Y. Congar, "Charismatiques ou quoi?" in *La Croix*, 19 Janvier 1974, as cited by Kilian McDonnell "The Holy Spirit and Christian Initiation" in *The Holy Spirit and Power*, p. 62; L. Bouyer, *art. cit.* in note 31, p. 117; H. Kung, "The Charismatic Structure of the Church" in *Concilium*, Vol. 4, Paulist Press, Glen Rock, New Jersey, 1965, p. 52.

41. A. Bittlinger, *Gifts and Graces*, p. 74; K. McDonnell, *The Holy Spirit and Power*, p. 65.

42. Donald Gee, *Concerning Spiritual Gifts*, pp. 66-67.

43. E.D. O'Connor, *op. cit.*, p. 183.

Appendix II:
Exercises and Seminars

I would like to suggest some points of similarity between the *Spiritual Exercises of St. Ignatius Loyola,* composed in the sixteenth century, and *The Life in the Spirit Seminars Team Manual* [1] a set of instructions currently enjoying widespread use in the Catholic charismatic renewal. These reflections might serve as jumping-off points for future research. My remarks will presume a familiarity with both books and will be confined to three areas: theology, psychology and history. It is my belief that St. Ignatius' *Spiritual Exercises* were and are, before anything else, primarily a tool for evangelization and initiation into the Christian life. As Ignatius gave the *Exercises,* depending on whether the exercitant (candidate) went for only one week or was allowed to complete the entire course of four weeks, the *Exercises* also provided some formation. *The Life in the Spirit Seminars Team Manual* used in our present-day charismatic renewal, consists of instructions for leaders to help them to be effective in bringing people to an experience called "baptism in the Spirit." I believe that both the *Seminars* and Ignatius' *Exercises* are pastoral tools designed to assist people in coming to a life-changing encounter with Christ, the Risen Lord, and to a fullness of Trinitarian life.

Theology

A theology of *The Life in the Spirit Seminars Team Manual* has not yet been written and perhaps cannot be written for years to come. St. Ignatius wrote the *Spiritual Exercises* over four hundred years ago and yet, according to Karl Rahner, "an account of the actual theology of the *Exercises* is something we still lack, at least on the scale we cannot but wish to have today."[2] In Rahner's opinion, the *Spiritual Exercises* "have not encountered very much understanding for their own astonishing originality."[3] This lack of theological understanding of Ignatius' *Exercises* is evidenced, according to Rahner, in at least two ways. First, there is a perpetually recurrent tendency of people to look upon the third mode of Election [4] as the normal and authentic one when, really, Ignatius seems to have considered the second mode to be the one most used, at least with regard to those affected by the *Exercises*.[5] Second, the lack of understanding of the *Exercises* over the years is further revealed in the lack of precision and the meagerness of the commentaries on the *Exercises*.[6] Rahner makes an initial move to fill this gap that he sees in a section of *The Dynamic Element in the Church* entitled "The Logic of Concrete Individual Knowledge in Ignatius Loyola."

Rahner begins by asserting that the *Spiritual Exercises* is not just ordinary pious literature. It is not a work of edification. The significance of the *Exercises*, for Rahner, is that this work of Ignatius is not derivative, it is a "marvel of a concrete and yet really new embodiment of the unchanging essence of Christianity."[7] The *Exercises* is a kind of literature "in which the Church's belief, the Word of God and the action of the Holy Spirit, which never ceases to be operative in the Church, find more authentic expression than in the treatises of theologians."[8] One of the difficulties that theologians will have with the *Exercises* arises precisely out of their significance and originality. "The *Exercises* speak a language which is a downright provocation to theological pride" says Rahner.[9] Ignatius' passages are sometimes "clumsily-worded and obscure"[10] and they contain what has long been known. Rahner exhorts theologians to destroy the appearance of platitude, to break through "tedious familiarity" and to take the *Exercises* seriously. He requests theologians to ask of the *Exercises* the kind of questions "that are not sent into the world already supplied with their complete answer."[11]

Rahner then begins to pose a central theological question for the *Exercises*, which is that "Ignatius candidly assumes that a man has to reckon, as a practical possibility of experience, that God may communicate his will to him."[12] Rahner than asks how can that happen and if it does, how do we explain it? Reflection on how knowledge of God's will is possible may strike those without an appreciation of theology as a waste of time. I would say to non-theologians what Rahner says to theologians: "the reader should not take it to be idle ingenuity."[13] Rahner also cautions theologians not to complain if ready-made answers are not supplied.[14]

Rahner reports on the progress of the theology of the *Exercises* as follows:

> In regard to the Election there is not yet clearly and explicitly enough a theology of the Exercises capable of bringing before the mind with sufficient precision the concrete ontological and gnoseological presuppositions regarding human living that are tacitly made and put into practice by Ignatius.[15]

Further on, Rahner poses the question this way:

> Is there in his [the theologian's] theology a divine impulse which within the domain in which other good impulses can occur, is so very categorically distinct from them, if the expression be permitted? Is there such a motion from God in his [the theologian's] theology as a more or less *normal** phenomenon, or only in those exceptional cases known as prophetic inspiration, visions and locutions in mysticism, the manifestation and miraculous intervention of God by an ex-

---

* Italics mine.

ceptional revelation of his will? There is no denying that the theologian of what is average theology nowadays will hesitate doubtfully over such a question. Even a present-day theologian has at heart more or less implicitly or tacitly the impression that everything that God effects (leaving aside the miraculous special cases of the public history of redemption and the like), is brought about by second causes . . . that God does not intervene within the casual connections at a distinct place with his own action. . . . [A man of the present day with the attitude to life that comes naturally to him will only with the greatest difficulty be prepared to recognize something that he discovers in his consciousness, as a highly personal influence of God, and to view his states of mind, impulses, his "consolation" and "desolation" as the effect of powers that transcend him.] It is much more likely he will think of hormones, effects of the weather, hereditary factors influencing character, repercussions of the unconscious, complexes and innumerable other things. . . .[16]

How Rahner answers some of his own questions (for example, he describes the phenomenon of the second mode of Election as the non-conceptual awareness of transcendence) [17] is not to the point here. What is to the point is that so far it seems that there have been unanswered theological questions regarding the *Exercises*. An adequate theological comparison of the *Spiritual Exercises* and *The Life in the Spirit Seminars Team Manual* will not be possible unless the present state of theological reflection on the *Exercises* improves. After eighty-five pages of text Rahner says in his concluding statement:

. . . the intention has really only been to permit the Exercises to put questions to theology. Especially the question whether it is adequately equipped to expound and explain the religious activities that are described and above all prescribed in the Exercises. If the reader surveys once again the second part of this essay he will probably rather incline to the opinion that there is still much needed before theology can assimilate and bring explicitly forward for reflection this logic of the discovering of God's will.[18]

Rahner wrote the above reflections on the *Exercises* twenty years ago. More recent writing on the same subject in 1975 and 1976 shows that Rahner has not modified his position.[19] He hails, however, the publication in 1976 of a book, *The Spiritual Exercises and the Ignatian Mystical Horizon* by a former student of his, Harvey D. Egan, S.J. In introducing Egan's book, Rahner says: "From my conviction that the real theological (and not only the spiritual) significance of Ignatius' *Spiritual Exercises* to this day has not been exhausted by their commentators, and much less by the traditional theology, but presents a not yet completed task to today's theology, it might be clear why I sincerely welcome the present book. . . ."[20]

I believe many will welcome Egan's book. Egan provides some answers to questions Rahner raised in his essay "The Logic of Concrete Individual Knowledge in Ignatius Loyola." In my opinion, Egan's book also brings into clear bold relief what Ignatius was trying to do in the *Exercises* and one who knows well how to prepare people for baptism in the Spirit will immediately see close similarities between what they are doing and what Ignatius was doing, at least in the first week. In his introduction to Egan's book I think Rahner is prophetic when he says: ". . . the results of Fr. Egan's book, if they are assimilated, could be of considerable significance for the religious, pedagogical and pastoral practices of the Church. It could mean both a positive evaluation and a critical stance with regard to today's enthusiastic movements which bring new life and, at the same time, new threats into the Church."[21]

It is my contention that *The Life in the Spirit Seminars Team*

Manual will put the same or similar questions to theology, that the *Exercises* raise. Looking back, some years from now, I believe that the *Team Manual*, and all that it signifies, will be considered the kind of literature Rahner says the *Exercises* exemplify, literature that is "an embodiment of the unchanging essence of Christianity."

Both books, the *Exercises* and the *Team Manual* are sets of instructions. Those who composed the books never intended that they be read by those making the *Exercises* or the *Seminars*. Both books contain nothing new; they contain "merely" the basic truths of Christianity.

In the article on "Concrete Individual Knowledge" which we have been discussing, Rahner reminds us that Ignatius was skilled in discerning the spirits of those making the *Exercises*. He judged them by intensity of influence, peace, darkness and so on. Without this skill, says Rahner, one may be a moral theologian but never a spiritual father.[22] Two of the reasons why there has been the paucity of theology on the *Exercises* is probably due to the loss of a sense of God's particular will and the fact that mysticism was out of favor after the condemnation of quietism in the seventeenth century.[23] A further reason might be that one has to have experienced a stirring of various spirits or must at least believe the experience to be possible [24] in order to comprehend the *Exercises*. More than that, I would say that unless one has *successfully* been involved in a directive capacity with people making the *Exercises* or if a theologian has not been in touch with that pastoral dimension, a complete understanding of the *Exercises* would be lacking.

A future theology of *The Life in the Spirit Seminars Team Manual* will, it seems to me, have to be produced by theologians "baptized in the Spirit" who have some familiarity with the pastoral dimension of the *Seminars*. Just as theologians have to break through the seemingly pious platitudes of Ignatius to get to the essence of the *Exercises*, theologians must penetrate the language of *The Life in the Spirit Seminars* to get at the reality behind the words.

History

It would seem to me that an historical approach would have to be applied in at least two fields of interest in order to produce an historical comparison of the *Spiritual Exercises* and *The Life in the Spirit Seminars Team Manual*. The first area of investigation would be the historical setting in which these works originated and then their subsequent impact on the history of the Church. The other area for study to aid the comparison would be a history of the "practice" of the *Exercises* and the *Seminars*. In other words, we could use an account of how the *Exercises* and *Seminars* were given in embryo and how they developed, the mistakes that were made and how they were rectified.

Placing the *Exercises* in their historical setting is not a difficult task and most of the works dealing with Ignatius or the *Exercises* do this, at least briefly. As for *The Life in the Spirit Seminars Team Manual* and placing it in historical perspective, we can't use hindsight yet as the institution of the *Seminars* is too close to us. We certainly seem to be at a "turning point" in history. Sociology and history could probably provide striking similarities between Ignatius' day and our own. And in both times we see God acting directly and intervening in history to gather His people to Himself.

With reference to our latter historical category, that of a history of the practice of the *Exercises* and the *Seminars*, research into the history of the practice of the *Exercises* was commented upon by Fr. Ignacio Iparraguiree S.J., in 1946 in his book on the subject. "We are not the first to labor in this field, though we must admit we do not find it too well tilled." [25]

Reading some accounts of Ignatius' life might leave one with the impression that the Holy Spirit dictated the *Exercises* to St.

Ignatius at Manresa and that miraculously they appeared on their final form. One might think that, unless one had been involved in giving *Life in the Spirit Seminars* with an attempt to adapt them to individual needs.[26] Just as one grows in pastoral wisdom in giving *Seminars*, Ignatius and the early Jesuits learned from experience in giving the *Exercises*. In what little reading I have done into the subject I have found that this is so.

From Manresa in 1522, until he entered the University of Alcala In March 1526, Ignatius spiritually instructed various people in the ways of the *Exercises*. Many or most of those he instructed during this period were women and Ignatius became the innocent victim of slanderous gossip which was to be a recurrent cross throughout his life. The period at Alcala is a very interesting one from the point of view that we see Ignatius making, what can only be called, "pastoral mistakes." Hugo Rahner says in this connection: "What Ignatius experienced at Alcala . . . forms the strangest chapter in the history of pastoral ministrations."[27]

In Alcala, Ignatius gave spiritual direction to a variety of women: widows, apprentice-girls and servants. He based his instruction on ideas basic to the *Exercises*. He spoke to them about the ten commandments, sin, and daily examination of conscience. For varying reasons, really incidental to our purpose here, Ignatius was tried in ecclesiastical court three times during this period on November 19th, 1526, on March 6th and on May 10th, 1527. Ignatius was cleared in all three cases of the charges that brought him to court but after the third appearance the judgment was that Ignatius was told to change his manner of dress (he was wearing pilgrim's garb) and he was forbidden to teach anyone, in public or in private, individually or in groups. After three years the prohibition might be lifted if the ordinary or vicar-general gave permission. The reason given for the prohibition was Ignatius' lack of learning.

The testimony given at these trials is primary source material.

Some secondary sources, based on the trial testimony which describe the Alcala period, are Hugo Rahner,[28] Michael Foss [29] and Dudon/Young.[30] Here is Dudon/Young:

> Weekly confession and Communion, examination of conscience twice a day, the practice of meditation according to the three powers of the old soul, *vocal prayer, pronounced slowly, rhythmically**—such were the exercises as taught these women of good will. . . . There was one very singular point. The greater number of them experienced attacks of melancholy, deep and inexplicable sadness, and fainting spells like epileptic seizures.[31]

Michael Foss says this of what happened at Alcala:

> Anna de Benavente, giving evidence before the inquisitor, testified that Ignatius had "expounded the articles of faith, the mortal sins, the five senses, the three faculties of the soul, and other good things concerning the service of God, and told her things out of the gospels." She was seventeen. Leonora, daughter of Anna de Menna, aged sixteen, gave much the same testimony. . . . Both Anna and Leonora were subject to fits of fainting and vomiting. Mencia de Benavente testified: "She had seen Leonora . . . after talking with Inigo [Ignatius], seized by a fainting fit, fall down, be sick, and roll on the ground. And her own daughter had sweating fits, and she had seen Anna Dias . . . in swoons. . . ." Unsurprisingly, the Inquisition was alerted by such hysteria, for the rumour had spread that Ignatius and his friends were a band of *Alumbrados*, religious enthusiasts of a particularly fanatical and unbalanced kind.[32]

Here is Hugo Rahner from his introduction to *Saint Ignatius*

---

* Italics mine.

Loyola: Letters to Women: ". . . girls swooned away, so deeply did they take Ignatius' words to heart. Only the matter-of-fact Mencia de Benavente stated in court that in her case the fainting-fits were only an hysterical manifestation."[33]

Why Ignatius' teaching and spiritual direction produced these side effects in the women of Alcala should not detain us here. We learn from the experience that Ignatius was accused of being an *alumbrado* (a member of the Illuminati movement). The further history of the practice of the *Exercises* shows us that Ignatius' methods matured as a result of the experience. Hugo Rahner points out that Ignatius "rises above his own defeats." He never forgot the pious women of Alcala, in particular the two who appeared as chief witnesses, the *beata* [34] Ramirez and the widow Mencia de Benavente. Fifteen years after the happenings at Alcala Blessed Peter Faber wrote to Ignatius the consoling news that he had just met with both women. Twenty years after Alcala Ignatius asks a friend to visit the two women.[35]

Karl Rahner in *The Dynamic Element in the Church* says that as far as he knows, "the similarities and differences between the *alumbrados* of the early sixteenth century in Spain and Ignatius have not been researched in detail, at least in German."[36] Rahner concedes a certain similarity in outlook between the two, consisting in the conviction that there is a real guidance by the Holy Spirit. But he explains that despite the similarity, Ignatius cannot be faulted for an uncontrollable mysticism or illuminism.[37] Egan in the first chapter of his recent work on the *Exercises* queries: "Is it totally unreasonable to ask if the Church of Ignatius' day was not yet ready for his Catholic and orthodox presentation of what was good in the Illuminati movement? . . ."[38]

A future history of the practice of *The Life in the Spirit Seminars* will probably show excesses such as those of Alcala. The charismatic renewal has been warned of illuminism [39] and *The Life in the Spirit Team Manual* has been faulted for what one critic believes is an overemphasis on tongues.[40] Mention of tongues in the *Team Manual* is reminiscent of the rhythmic vocal prayer Ignatius recommends.

The history of the practice of the *Exercises* shows that Ignatius and the retreat directors he trained, sometimes made the decision to hold back some people in the first week of the *Exercises*. Others completed the full four weeks. Ignatius says:

> If the director of the Exercises sees that the exercitant has little aptitude, or little natural ability or that he is one from whom little fruit could be expected, it is better to give him some of the easier exercises until he has gone to confession, and then to give him some methods of examination of conscience and a program for more frequent confession than has been his custom, so that he may preserve what he has gained, without going further into the matter of the election nor into any other exercises beyond those for the first week, especially when greater profit may be gained with others, since there is insufficient time for everything.[41]

This passage explicates the point that some did not go beyond the first week, but it is interesting also for the fact that it shows that Ignatius did not believe in wasting time as "greater profit may be gained with others." This looks like the principle of "triage." [42]

The Life in the Spirit Seminars Team Manual points out, first of all, that not all people should make the *Seminars*. "If a person is disruptive, imbalanced (i.e., has a history of 'breaks'), or if his behavior is an obstacle to other people in opening up to the Lord, we should ask him not to come to the Seminars." [43] Similarly with the *Exercises*, ". . . [they] are intended for normal personalities and there are no provisions in them for meeting and dealing with the pathological," writes Fr. Meissner in 1963 in *Woodstock Letters*.[44] Something of what Ignatius achieved by spending time individually with people making the *Exercises* is achieved in the

Seminars by means of the discussion groups. People who show "special promise for working for the Lord" are spotted and placed where they will get the most help and teaching.[45] The discussion groups are put together at the beginning of the *Seminars* with an eye to their being "reshuffled later."[46]

Another similarity we can point to briefly involves what Blessed Peter Faber called "conversations." When talking with people, Ignatius, Faber and other Jesuits would "sow . . . the truths of the *Exercises*"[47] and thereby hopefully whet the appetites of those listening for more. Faber "used this technique with St. Francis Borgia in Gandia for almost two full days, with the Princess Maria and Juana in Madrid, and with the Bishop of Speier."[48] There is a very obvious similarity between these "conversations" and the way people are evangelized prior to their signing up to take the *Life in the Spirit Seminars*.

According to Fr. Meissner in 1963, the effect of the *Exercises* is "very much diluted" in our own time. He said then that the most intense presentation of them was in the Jesuit tertian year and even then it was administered in groups.[49] That would not be so true today as there has been a resurgence of interest in the *Exercises* and in what are called "directed retreats." Although over the centuries it has become customary for some people to make some form of the *Exercises* every year,[50] I would agree with Dom John Chapman (who wrote over fifty years ago) that Ignatius meant the *Exercises* to be a once in a lifetime experience. In the same kind of way, the *Life in the Spirit Seminars* during which one is baptized in the Spirit is a once in a lifetime experience. People in the prayer community with which I am most familiar, Mother of God, are sometimes requested for one reason or another to take the *Seminars* again. Anyone who does says he benefits tremendously but it is never the same as that first time. Karl Rahner, in the introduction to his book, *Spiritual Exercises*, says: ". . . an election cannot be imposed on one from the outside, nor, especially, be repeated sincerely once a year." [52]

Psychology

A person today might very well come across Ignatius' *Exercises*, read some of his instructions, and come away with the conclusion that they consist of psychological manipulation. One making the *Exercises* is to separate himself from his friends during the period of time spent doing the *Exercises*. During the first week one is to concentrate on one's sinfulness and be led to repentance. One is "not to think of pleasant and joyful things . . . for such consideration of joy and delight will hinder the feeling of pain, sorrow, and tears" one should have for one's sins. One is not to laugh or provoke laughter. One is to restrain one's eyes except for looking to receive or dismiss the person with whom one is speaking. When the retreatant is in his room he is to close shutters and doors and deprive himself of light. In the fourth week one may feel joy and gladness and appreciate the beauties of nature. One of the methods of prayer Ignatius recommends, as we have mentioned earlier, is slow rhythmic vocal prayer associated with one's breathing.

One critique of *The Life in the Spirit Seminars Team Manual* likens the process to indoctrination by Communists:

> The technique, methodology, organization and even some of the language concur. Minute details are given concerning the conducting of the seminars, the role of the tutors and the participants and . . . no room is left for personal initiative or . . . for the inspiration of the Holy Spirit. [53]

Michael Foss discusses the psychology of the *Exercises* and makes no apologies for Ignatius. What he says could well be said of the *Team Manual:*

> The book [the *Exercises*] is a guide for spiritual directors

. . . and therefore Ignatius did not think it necessary to make it available to the general public. He knew the psychological value of surprise. Those who started the *Exercises* knowing nothing of the technique would have greater profit from the little dramas which Ignatius had in store for them. Ignatius knew that most people, however well intentioned, need a push. . . . To Ignatius, the individual soul wandered in the no-man's-land between the armies of God and the devil, and the soul must be persuaded to range itself under God's banner. If the soul was inclined towards God, but stuck in the mire of human desires and frailties, then Ignatius is prepared to intimidate and shock it, to blast it, even, into the holy ranks. He said "as the devil showed great skill in tempting men into perdition, equal skill ought to be shown in saving them." The individual psychology must be studied.[54]

My purpose will have been served if these reflections stimulate some researcher or theologian to investigate the similarities of intention and practice of both the *Exercises* and the *Seminars*. It is my conviction that the *Exercises*, like the *Seminars*, are a tool for evangelization, initiation and subsequent formation of fervent Christians.

Notes to Appendix II

1. *The Life in the Spirit Seminars Team Manual*, developed by The Word of God, Ann Arbor, Michigan, published by Charismatic Renewal Services, South Bend, Indiana, 1973.
2. Karl Rahner, "The Logic of Concrete Individual Knowledge in Ignatius Loyola" in *The Dynamic Element in the Church*, p. 84. This essay of Rahner was written twenty years ago. The fact that he has not modified his position is evident in a foreword he wrote to a new German translation of the *Exercises* by Adolph Haas (Freiburg, 1975): "The theology hidden in the simple words of the *Exercises* belongs to the most important fundamentals of contemporary western Christianity. In fact, it has yet to be fully assimilated by the Church's academic theology and

prevailing practice of piety; therefore it still has an important future" (quoted by Rahner in his foreword to *The Spiritual Exercises and the Ignatian Mystical Horizon* by Harvey D. Egan, S.J., p. xiii). In his foreword to the just-cited book by Egan, Rahner says: "Until now there has not been a book which critically synthesizes and completes past studies on the *Exercises.* Then too, there was no book which focused upon the Ignatian *Exercises* in their essence, treating this essence theologically and not 'piously' " (p. xiv).

3. *Ibid.*, p. 116.

4. An election in Ignatian terms is the making of a decision. Ignatius recognizes three ways or modes of election. The first mode in the words of Ignatius occurs "when God our Lord moves and attracts the will so that the devout soul, without question and without desire to question, follows what has been manifested to it. St. Paul and St. Matthew did this when they followed Christ our Lord" (Image Book, Mottola translation, p. 84). Ignatius describes the second mode as an occasion "when one has developed a clear understanding and knowledge through the experience of consolations and desolations and the discernment of spirits" (*Ibid.*). If God seems to be silent, Ignatius suggests the third method of election, the mode of rational reflection. This is the mode that Rahner says so many look upon as the recommended method, whereas Ignatius preferred the second mode. Rahner writes: "the third mode is regarded as an expedient if the first two are really or apparently not available. This latter case really is considered the exception not the rule for the normal Christian . . ." (*Dynamic Element*, p. 95). Even in the third mode God is requested to put His will in the soul and after the decision has been made the third way, God is asked to confirm the choice (*Ibid.*, p. 96). Therefore, "the first method is the ideal higher limiting case of the second method and the latter itself includes the rationality of the third as one of its own intrinsic elements. The third method is the less perfect mode of the second (and must be so regarded) . . ." (*Ibid.*, p. 106). In the foreword to *The Spiritual Exercises and the Ignatian Mystical Horizon* by Harvey D. Egan, S.J., Rahner writes: ". . . I agree, of course, with Father Egan when he emphasizes that in actual life the three different times for election do not appear wholly separated from each other, but signify, rather, aspects of *one* Election in which all these three aspects appear, even if in very different intensities. In Ignatius' life these 'times' were often fused. One can ask oneself whether such a fusion does not precisely make the 'ideal Election' possible" (pp. xvi-xvii).

5. Rahner, *op. cit.*, footnote 11, pp. 96-97. See also p. 116.

6. *Ibid.*, p. 116.

7. *Ibid.*, p. 88.

8. *Ibid.*, p. 85.

9. *Ibid.*, p. 88.

10. *Ibid.*

11. *Ibid.*, p. 88-89.

12. *Ibid.*, p. 94.

13. *Ibid.*, p. 89.

14. *Ibid.*

15. *Ibid.*, p. 109.

16. *Ibid.*, pp. 119-121.

17. *Ibid.*, p. 154.

18. *Ibid.*, p. 169.

19. See note #1 to this chapter.

20. Rahner in Egan, pp. xiii-xiv.

21. Rahner in Egan, p. xvi.

22. K. Rahner, *op. cit.*, p. 104.

23. Pierre Pourrat, S.S., (*Christian Spirituality*, Vol. IV, p. 264) writes: "The grief of wise and well-informed spiritual authors at this discrediting of mysticism is very understandable, but their attempts to remedy it were timid. They were afraid to write mystical works because of the public bias." In the preface to his *Institutiones theologiae mysticae*, written about 1720, the Benedictine monk Dominic Schram wrote: "Worthy reader, when you read the title *Mystical Theology* do not be disgusted or give way to the feeling of alarm which the word 'mystical' arouses in so many people!" (p. 264).

24. Aside from exceptional individuals, Rahner writing twenty years ago said that contemporary theologians would consider the impulses from good or evil spirits Ignatius talks about to be a "mediaeval personification of the causes of sudden, unforeseen psychological phenomena of which no immediate rational explanation is available" (pp. 121-122). Modern commentators on the *Exercises* having this frame of reference would judge by fruits and not discern the impulses. Such an accommodation, says Rahner, "can be accepted only by an interpreter of the *Exercises* who from the outset limits the process of Election to the method of a syllogistic deductive ethic in which it is clear from the beginning that the problem of God's will is solved by the very fact of ascertaining objectively the actual goodness of the person in question and his situation. But this view is just not that of Ignatius himself. It is only because many of his interpreters hold such a view that the question we have encountered [the problem of individual knowledge] has not been seen, or people have not been so bold as to see it, in its full acuity" (pp. 122-123).

25. Ignacio Iparraguiree, S.J., *Historia de la Practica de los Ejercicios Espirituales de San Ignacio de Loyola*, Volumen Primero, Roma, Institutum Historicum Societatis Iesu 1946. (The quotation is taken with permission from an unpublished English translation by Aloysius J. Owen, S.J., p. 24.)

26. *The Life in the Spirit Seminars* vary in quality from group to group. Older and

more established prayer groups or communities usually have more reliable and capable teachers than do newer groups. Many groups do not slavishly copy the *Team Manual* but use it as a model around which they develop their own seminars. Mother of God, the author's community in Potomac, Maryland, bases its *Life in the Spirit Seminars* on the *Exercises*.

27. Hugo Rahner, *Saint Ignatius Loyola: Letters to Women*, p. 11.

28. *Ibid.*, pp. 11-13.

29. Michael Foss, *The Founding of the Jesuits 1540*, pp. 80-92.

30. Pere Paul Dudon, *St. Ignatius of Loyola*, translation by Young, pp. 103-118.

31. *Ibid.*, pp. 113-114.

32. Foss, *op. cit.*, pp. 80-81.

33. H. Rahner, *op. cit.*, p. 12.

34. A *beata* was a woman living under religious rule in her own house. Catherine of Siena was a *beata*.

35. H. Rahner, *op. cit.*, pp. 12-13.

36. K. Rahner, *op. cit.*, pp. 93-94. Rahner writes in a footnote:

The difficulties that Ignatius had with the Inquisition in Alcala and Salamanca must be investigated one day and described not merely as the almost mythological-sounding 'crosses' such as a 'saint' has to bear, but with sober inquiry into the very understandable root of the hesitation on the part of the Inquisition. The question could then be raised whether Ignatius himself in early days, before the serenity which he certainly attained in Paris, did not, in fact, externally very much have the look of an *alumbrado*, and whether perhaps the very reason he later added this or that to the Exercises was to prevent misunderstanding and misuse of the fundamental 'mystical' idea of a divine inspiration in the making of the Election (note 8, pp. 93-94).

37. Illuminism is the claim to possess special enlightenment which frees one from submission to authority be it human or ecclesial.

38. Egan, pp. 5-6.

39. J. Massingberd Ford, "Pentecostal Poise of Docetic Charismatics?" in *Spiritual Life*, Spring, 1973, pp. 36-37.

40. Josephine Massyngberde Ford, "The Charismatic Gifts in Worship," in *The Charismatic Movement*, edited by Michael P. Hamilton, footnote 17, pp. 122-123.

41. *Exercises*, Directions #18, Mottola, Image, p. 42.

42. "Triage is the sorting of allocation of treatment to patients and especially battle and disaster victims according to a system of priorities designed to maximize the number of survivors" (*Webster's Dictionary*). There are some who feel that the Church, which engages in spiritual warfare, is like a battlefield—and that most churchgoers today, as in Ignatius' day, are dead or are in varying degrees of woundedness. The task, then, of those working to build up the Church is to base

pastoral work on the principle of triage.

43. *The Life in the Spirit Seminars Team Manual*, p. 95.

44. W.W. Meissner, S.J., "Psychological Notes on the *Spiritual Exercises*," in *Woodstock Letters* XCII 1963, p. 360.

45. *Team Manual*, p. 45.

46. *Ibid.*, p. 93.

47. Iparraguiree, p. 22.

48. *Ibid.*

49. Meissner, *op. cit.*, p. 351.

50. In the foreword to David Stanley's *A Modern Scriptural Approach to the Spiritual Exercises*, Fr. George Ganss tells us that the substance of the book was given to a group of Jesuit theological students about to be ordained. Fr. Ganss says the retreatants knew the structure of the *Exercises* well as they had already made the exercises some dozen times (p. viii).

51. In the *Downside Review*, XLVIII (1930), pp. 4-18, Dom Chapman wrote: "What St. Ignatius meant for once in a lifetime is given year by year to the same people; the preacher follows the Exercises partially and distantly; he tries to interest or startle by introducing new matter; the month is reduced to a week; the choice of a vocation is omitted."

52. K. Rahner, *Spiritual Exercises*, Herder and Herder, New York, i, 1965, p. 12.

53. J. Massingberd Ford, "Christian Prayer and the Humanizing Experience" from *Proceedings of the Catholic Theological Society of America*, September 1972, p. 127. Dr. Ford compares the *Team Manual* with a book by a former Communist, Douglas Hyde, who became a Catholic. Hyde's thesis in the book *Dedication and Leadership* is that Christians should take Christianity as seriously as Communists take Communism.

54. Foss, pp. 92-93.

GLOSSARY

(Terms frequently used in writings by or about the Saints)

Aridity

"Aridity is . . . a certain powerlessness during prayer to elicit thoughts or affections about spiritual things" (de Guibert, *The Theology of the Spiritual Life*, p. 220).

Asceticism

This term comes from a Greek word meaning exercise. St. Paul used to exhort Christians to remain in spiritual shape just as those preparing for an athletic competition needed to be in good physical condition, e.g., 1 Corinthians 9:24-27, Philippians 3:13-14, 2 Timothy 2:5. "It is clear to all that Christian holiness entails arduous and continued effort. Hence, from the very earliest days of the Church, the name 'ascetics' has been given to those who undertake in a systematic way the battle against passions and the practice of the Christian virtues. This term is found in the teachings of the Fathers and all the spiritual writers." (Thils, *Christian Holiness*, pp. XIII).

Aspirations

Aspirations are also called ejaculatory prayers. They are quick flights of the heart and mind to God, making acts of belief in His presence, or short prayers directed to the Blessed Mother or one of the Saints.

Carmelites

Members of a religious order under the patronage of Our Lady of Mount Carmel. The reforming activity of Sts. Teresa of Avila and John of the Cross resulted in two branches of the order: (a) the Calced Carmelites, or Carmelites of the Old Observance and (b) the Discalced or Teresian Carmelites.

Cenobite
A monk who lives in community, as distinguished from an anchorite or a hermit.

Cultus
Cult—veneration of God or a Saint and its public expression.

Desert Fathers
The first Christian solitaries and monks in the waste places of Syria, Palestine and Egypt, from the third to the sixth centuries.

Detachment
The relinquishing of what in one's life is not of God. "Detachment ought never to be practised for itself. I detach myself only in order to attach myself. I let go of the evil or the less good in order to seize the better or the perfect. But I never let go in order to fall into a hole." (Abbe Huvelin to Baron von Hugel, *Selected Letters* 1896-1924, J.M. Dent & Sons, Ltd., London, 1927). Detachment does not necessarily mean relinquishing. It can refer to an attitude of freedom with regard to things we must keep on using. And detachment can refer to things of God for we must not be attached to the gifts God gives us. Having a sense of detachment regarding possessions and even our life, means that God comes first and all else is seen in relation to Him.

Doctor of the Church
"A theologian of special eminence, authority, and holiness of life, formally recognized as such by the church, who by his writings taught the church or some part of it" (Donald Attwater, *The Penguin Dictionary of Saints*, p. 23). Catherine of Siena and Teresa of Avila have in recent years been proclaimed Doctors of the Church.

Dominicans

The Order of Preachers founded by St. Dominic in 1216.

Ecstasy

The alienation of the senses, a state in which the soul is wrapt in God.

Eremitical

An adjective, pertaining to hermit, or solitary.

Fathers of the Church

Writers and teachers from the second century to St. John of Damascus in the eighth century whose works are considered of special importance and are respected as interpretations of the gospel.

Franciscans

Friars Minor founded by St. Francis of Assisi in 1209. The term is also used to include Poor Clares, and many other groupings claiming St. Francis as their origin.

Hesychasts

Named after the Greek spiritual teaching of *hesychia* (quiet). They taught prayer of the heart, using the Jesus Prayer. An excellent introduction is *The Prayer of Jesus* by a monk of the Eastern Church, Desclee Company, New York, 1967.

Immanence

Opposed to transcendence. When a writer refers to the God of immanence he usually means he is viewing God from the aspect of His divine indwelling.

Inedia

Living without eating—prolonged fasting—total abstinence from food. A psychophysical phenomenon encountered in the lives of some Saints, some not saints.

Infused Contemplation

"God draws the soul gently but powerfully toward himself, enabling it to repose quietly and lovingly in His presence, as it is quite unable to do through any effort of its own" (Fr. O'Connor, *The Pentecostal Movement in the Catholic Church*, p. 204).

Jesuits

Members of the Society of Jesus founded by St. Ignatius Loyola in 1535.

Martyrology

A catalogue of martyrs and other Saints. The basic general martyrology is known as the *Hieronymianum*, first compiled before the seventh century.

Meditation

This term is used in a variety of ways but usually means discursive prayer which consists of reflections on a particular subject for the purpose of stirring the will to make acts of faith, love, humility, etc., and perhaps also to form resolutions.

Mendicants

Members of the Orders of St. Francis and St. Dominic, founded in the thirteenth century, and other orders, who subsisted by begging.

Mortification

Self-discipline, which may be physical or spiritual. Refusing to allow one's curiosity free rein is an example of spiritual mortification.

Mysticism

Experimental knowledge of God. Very general use of the

term is an awareness of God and His activity. The term is ambiguous as it is used in so many different ways by different writers. David Knowles defines theological mysticism (mystical theology) as "an incommunicable and inexpressible knowledge and love of God or of religious truth received in the spirit without precedent effort or reasoning" (*Mysticism*, p. 13). Bouyer writes "This is the meaning that mysticism should hold for us. It is nothing other than the most profound apprehension to which we can be led by grace here below—apprehension of the truths of the Gospel, the realities of the sacramental life which the Christian accepts by faith and makes his own by charity" (*Introduction to Spirituality*, p. 303).

Passion

(a) The sufferings and death of Jesus Christ. (b) The sufferings and death of a martyr. (c) A written account of a martyr's death.

Peritus

An expert serving at Vatican Council II.

Perpetual Adoration

Worship of the Blessed Sacrament continued by day and night without intermission. The practice developed in France in the seventeenth century and flourished until recently. Now the custom is diminishing.

Religious

This term in common usage is either singular (a religious) or plural and refers to a member or members of a religious order.

Religious Order

This name is reserved by Canon Law to religious institutes in which members take solemn vows.

Reparation

Jesus saved us by His death on the cross. He made reparation to His Father for the sins of mankind. But just as some Christians have felt special devotion to the "hidden life" of Jesus of Nazareth (Charles de Foucauld based the spirituality of *The Little Brothers and Little Sisters of Jesus* on the thirty years Jesus lived in obscurity) others have been drawn to join themselves to the suffering Christ in a life of reparation. "To make reparation, according to the common meaning of the word, is to compensate for a wrong, an injustice, or suffering caused to someone, whether by one's own fault or through the fault of no one at all. ... Reparation, in the sense in which it is used in the Christian vocabulary, reduces itself to this: to offer oneself in the place of all that should be offered to God, but through man's malice is withheld from him" (Raoul Plus, S.J., *Reparation*, p. 29).

Spirituality

"Christian spirituality (or any other spirituality) is distinguished from dogma by the fact that, instead of studying or describing the objects of belief as it were in the abstract, it studies the reactions which these objects arouse in the religious consciousness" (Bouyer, *The Spirituality of the New Testament and The Fathers*, p. viii). Sometimes writers will refer to a plurality of Christian spiritualities, e.g., Franciscan, Carmelite, Benedictine, Jesuit, Dominican, lay, etc. These different "schools" of Christian spirituality are but reflections of differing applications of the gospel to human life, that gospel of Jesus Christ, being "the same yesterday, today and forever."

Stigmata

Wounds of Christ imprinted on a human being.

Transcendence

> Beyond experience, beyond apprehension. The view of God as expressed by the term, "the transcendent God," usually means that the writer is referring to the unknowableness of God, the fact that He escapes and is beyond all categories and ideas.

BIBLIOGRAPHY

This bibliography is a guide to some of what is available in the field of Catholic spiritual theology, lives of Saints, and related subjects. One might wish to consult Bouyer's *Introduction to Spirituality* and his "note on great classics of the spiritual life" at the end of the book as well as suggested bibliography at the end of each chapter. Gustave Thils in *Christian Holiness* provides a bibliography arranged according to schools of spirituality. The comments are helpful. *A Guide to Catholic Reading*, an Image Book by Jack Bernard and John Delaney, has sections on lives of the Saints and one on spiritual writing.

Those familiar with books about Saints may notice obvious omissions. This list is already long and I did not want it to be overwhelming. Many of the books listed are out of print but may be found in parish libraries and, amazingly enough, in some public libraries. Religious houses and Catholic universities are sometimes willing to extend library privileges. Many of the books in this bibliography are easily attainable from distributors of secondhand Catholic books such as Christian Classics, 205 Willis Street, Westminster, Maryland, 21157, or through various book search services. Books starred with an asterisk are available through Charismatic Renewal Services, Drawer A, Notre Dame, Indiana, 46556.

SAINTS

Aigrain, Rene, *L'Hagiographie, Ses Sources, Ses Methodes, Son Histoire*, Bloud & Gay, 1953.

This book is recommended in the small selected bibliography of the 1961 edition of Delehaye's *The Legends of the Saints*. This 416-page book includes sections on such subjects as calendars and martyrologies, hagiography and history and a history of hagiography. It has not been translated into English.

Cluny, Roland, *Holiness in Action*, Hawthorn Books, New York, 1963.

In his introduction Cluny states that ". . . the real history of the Church is the history of holiness." He then treats five Saints: St. Paul, St. Augustine, St. Bernard of Clairvaux, St. Francis, and St. Ignatius. The introduction and the last chapter are excellent essays on the significance of Saints.

Delehaye, S.J., Hippolyte, *The Legends of the Saints*, University of Notre Dame Press, 1961.

Fr. Delehaye, a Bollandist who died in 1941, is the unsurpassed scholar in the field of hagiography. Unfortunately this is the only one of his works translated into English. The original French version appeared in 1905. Some of Delehaye's other important works include: *Les origines du culte des martyrs*, Paris, 1912, 2nd ed., 1933 and *Sanctus, essai sur le culte des saints dans l'antiquite*, Bruxelles, 1927.

Douillet, Jacques, *What Is A Saint?*, Hawthorn Books, New York, 1958.

If one were to read only one book on Saints this would be it even though it was written nearly twenty years ago. It includes a select bibliography. It was volume forty-six in the series *The Twentieth Century Encyclopedia of Catholicism*. Paulist Press reprinted it in a Deus Books Edition in paperback in 1963.

Kemp, Eric Waldram, *Canonization and Authority in the Western Church*, Oxford University Press, London: Geoffrey Cumberlege, 1948.

The author, at the time of the writing of this book, was a fellow of Exeter College, Oxford, and is presently Bishop of Chichester. The book was first written as a thesis for the Bachelor of Divinity degree and then rewritten in the present form. Part of Chapter V, "The Establishment of the Papal Control of Canonization, 1159-1234," was awarded the Alexander Prize of the Royal Historical Society in 1944.

Lamirande, O.M.I., Emilien, *The Communion of Saints*, Hawthorn Books, New York, 1963.

This book is volume twenty-six of *The Twentieth Century Encyclopedia of Catholicism*. It traces the doctrine of the communion of Saints from the time of its inclusion in the Apostles' Creed until the present. The author is very well-read and includes many little-known facts making this work very interesting reading. Were I to suggest two basic books on Saints, this would be one and Douillet the other.

Molinari, S.J., Paul, *Saints: Their Place in the Church*, Sheed and Ward: New York, 1965.

Fr. Molinari is Postulator for the Causes of the Servants of

God who were members of the Society of Jesus. He offers theological reflections on the function of Saints in the Church. One of the best sections in this book deals with "Extreme Tendencies in the Cult of the Saints."

Moretti, O.F.M. Conv., *The Saints Through Their Handwriting*, MacMillan, New York, 1964.

Included are illustrations of the handwriting of thirty-two Saints including Francis of Assisi and Teresa of Avila. The author also offers an analysis of the handwriting.

Rahner, Karl, "The Church of the Saints" in *Theological Investigations*, Vol. III, Darton, Longman & Todd, Ltd., 1967, pp. 91-104.

In this essay, which appeared in German in 1955, Rahner develops the idea that canonizing a Saint is a necessary part of the Church's realization of her own being.

Rahner, Karl, "Why and How Can We Venerate the Saints" and "All Saints" in *Theological Investigations*, Vol. VIII, Darton, Longman & Todd, London; Herder and Herder, New York, 1971, pp. 3-29.

In the first essay Rahner considers veneration and invocation. The second essay is a meditation on the feast of All Saints.

CHARISMATIC ELEMENT IN THE CHURCH

Aubert, Roger, editor, *Prophets in the Church*, Volume 37 of *Concilium*, Paulist Press, Glen Rock, N.J., 1968.

Some of the articles contained in this volume include: "Francis of Assisi," "St. Ignatius Loyola as Prophet," "John Wesley: Christian Prophet" and "Prophecy and Ecumenism." Two valuable articles in this book are the articles on Wesley and the one on the Russian "Startsy."

Bouyer, Louis, "Charismatic Movements in History within the Church," in *One in Christ*, 1974 Vol. 2, a Catholic Ecumenical Review, Benedictine Convent, Priory Close, London N14 4AT. This paper was presented in Rome in 1973 at the Roman Catholic-Pentecostal dialogue. It appears in revised and annotated form in *Perspectives on Charismatic Renewal* edited by Edward D. O'Connor, C.S.C., University of Notre Dame Press, 1975.

Keeping in mind the reservations expressed in Appendix I, this is an exceptionally well-written and interesting article. Fr. Bouyer gives examples to show that movements analogous to the Pentecostal movement are a quasi-permanent feature in the life of the Church.

Clark, Stephen B., *Unordained Elders and Renewal Communities*, Paulist Press, New York, 1976.

Mr. Clark, author of *Building Christian Communities*, relates the present charismatic renewal to the ascetic movement of the fourth century.

Congar, Yves, *The Mystery of the Church*, Chapter VI, "The Holy Spirit and the Apostolic Body, Continuators of the Work of Christ," Helicon Press, Baltimore, 1960.

All of the studies in this book are centered on the role of the Holy Spirit in the life of the Church. The last chapter discusses how the Holy Spirit and the apostolic institution act jointly to bring about the body of Christ.

Gerest, Claude, "Spiritual Movements and Ecclesial Institutions: An Historical Outline" in *Spiritual Revivals*, Volume 89 of *Concilium*, Herder and Herder, New York, 1973.

The author is a French Dominican on the faculty of the University of Lyons. The article is twenty pages long. Some of the points discussed in the article are: characteristics of the spiritual movement, complex relationship between spiritual movements and ecclesial institutions, four types of relationships between spiritual movements and institutions discernible in the twelfth century, and a spiritual movement integrated into the institution.

Koenker, Ernest B., "Some Charismatic Reforms in Western History" in *Communio*, Summer 1974.

This article by a Lutheran professor of history at the University of Southern California gives special emphasis to Francis of Assisi and Luther.

Kung, Hans, "The Charismatic Structure of the Church," in *Concilium*, Vol. 4, Paulist Press, Glen Rock, N.J., 1965.

This appeared two years before the charismatic renewal was a recognized movement in Roman Catholicism. In these twenty pages Kung writes that Paul accepted all gifts of the Spirit gladly, that Paul possessed tongues to an exceptional degree (1 Cor. 14, 18) and that charismata are not primarily extraordinary but common. The subject is discussed in the light of the Vatican Council documents.

Rahner, Karl, *The Dynamic Element in the Church*, "The Charismatic Element in the Church," Herder and Herder, New York, 1964.

In my opinion this is the best treatment of the subject. In this forty-page essay Rahner discusses the charisma of office, the non-institutional charismata, the teaching of the Church and spiritual gifts.

Rahner, Karl, "Observations on the Factor of the Charismatic in the Church" in *Theological Investigations*, Vol. XII, Darton, Longman & Todd Ltd., London, 1974, pp. 81-97.

This should be read in conjunction with *The Dynamic Element in the Church*.

MYSTICAL PHENOMENA AND THE MIRACULOUS

Aradi, Zsolt, *The Book of Miracles*, Farrar, Straus & Cudahy, New York, 1956.

The photographs of Saints and the bibliography give this book value.

Biot, Rene, *The Enigma of the Stigmata*, Hawthorn Books, New York, 1962.

This book is Volume 57 in *The Twentieth Century Encyclopedia of Catholicism*. Rene Biot is a Catholic physician. Besides dealing with the phenomena of stigmata, Dr. Biot examines suspension of the nutritive functions, ecstasies and visions and other prodigies.

Farges, Mgr. Albert, *Mystical Phenomena*, Burns, Oates & Washbourne Ltd., London, 1926.

Mgr. Farges was founder and first principal of the University Seminary at Angers, France in 1898. He lectured there from

1899-1905. He was a laureate of the French Academy and former director of Saint-Sulpice and of the Institut Catholique of Paris. Despite its age, it is one of two books on this subject cited by Dr. Vinson Synan as sources for his Roman Catholic-Pentecostal dialogue paper "The Role of the Holy Spirit and the Gifts of the Spirit in the Mystical Tradition."

Graef, Hilda C., *The Case of Therese Neumann*, The Newman Press, Westminster, Maryland, 1951.

Those interested in mystical phenomena should not fail to consult this book which examines the stigmata and other phenomena present in the life of a Bavarian woman who lived from 1898 to 1962. This balanced and critical study was completed in 1949 when the stigmatist was still alive. There is an excellent presentation of miraculous Communions where the host seems to move through the air (pp. 84 *et seq.*).

Helle, Jean, *Miracles*, David McKay Company, Inc., New York, 1952.

Beginning with a discussion of the Bavarian stigmatist, Therese Neumann, the author goes on to the revelations of Anne Catherine Emmerich, the miracles of the Cure of Ars, the apparitions at Lourdes, La Salette, Pontmain and Fatima. Also described are cases of fraud and the result of hysteria. In 1951 this book was selected by a jury including Etienne Gilson and Daniel-Rops as "one of the ten best religious books published since the Liberation."

Marechal, S.J., Joseph, *Studies in the Psychology of the Mystics*, Magi Books, Inc., Albany, New York, 1964.

This book was first published by Burns, Oates, and Washbourne, Ltd., London, in 1927. There are sections on

Islam and on comparative mysticism. The three chapters bearing most closely on our present subject are: "Empirical Science and Religious Psychology," "On the Feeling of Presence in Mystics and Non-Mystics" and "Some Distinctive Features of Christian Mysticism."

Monden, S.J., Louis, *Signs and Wonders, A Study of the Miraculous Element in Religion*, Desclee Company, New York, 1966.

This book first appeared in Flemish in 1958. Of this book the Hungarian Jesuit Ladislas Boros says it is "probably the most important monograph on the question of miracles." Anglican Ian T. Ramsey, one time professor of the philosophy of the Christian religion at Oxford and later Bishop of Durham, declares: "It is a most valuable contribution to the philosophy of miracles and will undoubtedly rank as a definitive work."

Thurston, S.J., Herbert, *The Physical Phenomena of Mysticism*, Henry Regnery Company, Chicago, 1952.

This book is a collection of a series of talks given by Fr. Thurston between the years of 1919 and 1938. The talks are mainly revised by Fr. Thurston himself, with the editor, Fr. Crehan, adding some notes. Fr. Thurston bases his studies on the experience he gained and information he collected in his work of revising *Butler's Lives of the Saints*, (1926-1938).

Thurston, S.J., Herbert, *Surprising Mystics*, Henry Regnery Company, Chicago, 1955.

Fr. Thurston decided to study lives of those who exhibited phenomena but not sanctity. The result was this book and a previous one, *The Physical Phenomena of Mysticism*. These books have probably not been superseded but their appearance (thanks to their editor, Fr. Crehan) in the 1950s, should not blind us to the fact that they were written in the twenties and thirties.

HISTORY OF CHRISTIAN SPIRITUALITY

Bouyer, Rev. Louis, *A History of Christian Spirituality*, Vol. I: *The Spirituality of the New Testament and the Fathers*, Desclee Company, New York, 1963.

The dust jacket, by way of introduction to the work of Bouyer and referring to the classic work of Fr. Pourrat, announces, quite truthfully: "Forty years have passed since the publication of a history of Christian spirituality that could justly lay claim to be both a readable guide for the non-specialist and a comprehensive manual and reference book for students and teachers." Vol. II, *Spirit of the Middle Ages* by Leclercq, Vandenbroucke, and Bouyer was published in 1968 (Burns & Oates, Ltd.) and Vol. III, *Orthodox Spirituality and Protestant and Anglican Spirituality* by Fr. Bouyer appeared in 1969.

Knowles, David, *From Pachomius to Ignatius*, Oxford University Press, 1966.

This is a study of the constitutional history of religious orders and should be of interest to those presently concerned with structuring Christian community.

Pourrat, Pierre, *Christian Spirituality*, four volumes, Newman Press, Westminster, Maryland, 1953-1955.

This well-known work, now perhaps superseded by *A History of Christian Spirituality* by Louis Bouyer and others, was first published in 1927. Pourrat's four books span the history of spirituality from the time of our Lord to the early twentieth century.

AUTOBIOGRAPHY

The Autobiography of St. Ignatius Loyola, translated by Joseph F. O'Callaghan, edited with introduction and notes by John C. Olin, Harper Torchbooks, Harper & Row, Publishers, New York, 1974, available 1976 from Christian Classics, 205 Willis Street, Westminster, Maryland, 21157.

Towards the end of his life, as a result of entreaties of his fellow Jesuits, Ignatius finally dictated some of his recollections to a young Portuguese Jesuit, Camara. The autobiography as told to Camara does not cover Ignatius' complete life. It begins in 1521 with his injury at Pamplona and covers the next seventeen years up to Ignatius' arrival in Rome.

The Autobiography of Saint Margaret Mary, translated and with an introduction by Vincent Kerns, The Newman Press, Westminster, Maryland, 1961.

St. Margaret Mary testified that she had a number of visions of Jesus at which time He revealed His unbounded love of men and asked her to be His messenger. This resulted in what became known as devotion to the Sacred Heart of Jesus. Of this autobiography an English Jesuit, C.C. Martindale, once wrote: "In her is no trace of originality . . . never a sense of humor. . . . Dare I suggest, with utter reverence, . . . that without overwhelming grace, she would have grown up in easy circumstances empty-headed and frivolous; in hard conditions stupid and cowed? . . . I believe Our Lord meant exactly what he said [what St. Margaret Mary recorded that Jesus said to her] when he repeated to her that by an instrument, wholly inappropriate, he meant to renew His Church. . . . This very simple, very frightened . . . girl . . . is a figure of enthralling pathos . . ." (from front and back flap of book).

The Autobiography of St. Therese of Lisieux.

There are a number of translations of this work available today. Some readers may be distracted by at times girlish expressions and at other times a rather sweet phraseology belonging to a gentler era than our own. This should not keep one from reaching the essence of the work.

*The Confessions of St. Augustine.

St. Augustine was born in 354 in North Africa. He became a Christian at the age of thirty-three and four years later he was made a priest. The *Confessions* were written in 399 after he had been a bishop three years. In this famous work Augustine describes his childhood, school days, adolescence, his relationship with his mother, St. Monica, his conversion and reception into the Church. The last chapters deal with creation. This is generally considered to be one of the world's great books.

Spiritual Autobiography of Charles de Foucauld, edited and annotated by Jean-Francois Six, Dimension Books, Denville, New Jersey, 1964.

This is a collection of letters and notes of the founder of the Little Brothers and the Little Sisters of Jesus, who was shot to death in 1916 and who will probably someday be canonized.

COLLECTED BIOGRAPHIES

Attwater, Donald A., *The Penguin Dictionary of Saints*, Penguin Books, Baltimore, Maryland, 1965.

This is a one-volume revision of Butler's *Lives of the Saints*, the standard work on this subject. Donald Attwater revised the four volumes of Butler's work in 1956, so he was well suited to produce this smaller work. This is an enjoyable and very readable little book despite the fact that it is in dictionary form.

Coulson, John, Editor, *The Saints, A Concise Biographical Dictionary*, Hawthorn Books, Inc., Publishers, New York, 1958.

Published in paperback as well as hardcover, this is an excellent book consisting of a listing of all the better known Saints and some not so well known, along with a brief biography of each.

Delany, Seldon P., *Married Saints*, Longmans, Green & Company, New York, 1935.

Perhaps a little dated, but worth reading. The chapter on Mme. Acarie is especially worth noting.

Kaye-Smith, Sheila, *Quartet in Heaven*, Harper Brothers, New York, 1952.

Catherine of Genoa, Cornelia Connelly, Rose of Lima, and Therese of Lisieux comprise the quartet. The section on Catherine of Genoa describes an experience similar to the baptism in the Spirit and the author draws on the research and writings of Baron von Hugel.

Martindale, S.J., C.C., *The Queen's Daughters: A Study of Women Saints*, Sheed & Ward, New York, 1951.

This book treats about fifty women Saints from all ages of history. It begins with St. Blandina of the martyrs of Lyons and ends with Mother Cabrini. This book is very entertaining, written with humor and verve.

Roche, Aloysius, *A Bedside Book of Saints*, Burns, Oates & Washbourne, Ltd., London, 1934.

Despite a slightly dated style, this is a wonderful little book. Topics included are: The Wit and Humour of the Saints, The Peace of the Saints, and The Littleness of the Saints. There are no footnotes and there is perhaps some legend mingled with fact but despite this, the book is to be highly recommended.

Sheed, F.J., Editor, *Saints Are Not Sad, Forty Biographical Portraits*, Sheed and Ward, New York, 1949.

The short biographies in this good collection are by well-known authors. Seven of the nine studies by Goodier in *Saints for Sinners* are here. Other authors represented are Hilaire Belloc, G.K. Chesterton, Vincent McNabb, O.P., and C.C. Martindale, S.J.

Thurston, Herbert, S.J. and Donald Attwater, Editors, *Butler's Lives of the Saints*, Vols. I-IV, Kenedy & Sons, New York, 1956.

Written in the mid-eighteenth century, Butler's work is regarded as the standard reference on the saints of the Church. It has been brought up-to-date, the 1956 edition containing 2,565 entries.

BIOGRAPHY

Auclair, Marcelle, *Teresa of Avila*, Pantheon, New York, 1953.

The biography of this Saint by Walsh is perhaps the best known life of this Saint in English but I prefer this account. Much more historical study in Spanish has been done since these books were written. See the introduction to a new translation of Teresa's works, Volume One, translated by Kieran Kavanaugh, O.C.D. and Otilio Rodriguez, O.C.D., ICS Publications, Institute of Carmelite Studies, Washington, D.C., 1976.

Boase, T.S.R. *St. Francis of Assisi*, Lithographs by Arthur Boyd, Indiana University Press, Bloomington and London, 1968.

There are probably more books on Francis of Assisi than any other Saint. This one, by the President of Magdalen College, Oxford University, is recent and well written.

Bodo, Murray, O.F.M., *Francis, The Journey and the Dream*, St. Anthony's Messenger Press, Cincinnati, Ohio, 1972.

This is an inspiring and beautiful book but not to be read by one unfamiliar with the life of Francis. It captures the mood and spirit of the Saint.

Bouyer, Louis, *Newman, His Life and Spirituality*, Meridian Books, Inc., New York, 1960.

Anything by Bouyer, author of *A History of Christian Spirituality*, deserves attention. Father Bouyer, a member of the Oratory of St. Philip Neri, is a former French Lutheran pastor. Msgr. H. Francis Davis, who wrote the preface to this work, says of this book: "He [Bouyer] is not primarily concerned with Newman's intellectual reputation. Clearly he is in full agreement with those who see in Newman one of the great modern Catholic thinkers. But his book is more concerned with Newman's personal life. He does not attempt to cover all the events of that century-long life. Rather he emphasizes those events and aspects which throw light on his inner life."

Brown, Raphael, *Franciscan Mystic*, Hanover House, Garden City, New York, 1961.

Blessed Brother Giles of Assisi, a companion of St. Francis, was beatified in 1777 and this is an account of his life. Also from the reading of this book one gets some little understanding of the struggles within the Franciscan Order after the death of Francis. It is a book that I highly recommend. The writer is a Franciscan scholar who, among other things, translated and provided introduction, notes and biographical sketches for the Image Book *The Little Flowers of St. Francis*. During the Christmas season of 1226, Giles resided in a hermitage in Cetona in Tuscany. Here he received many graces from the Lord. When someone later asked Giles if a church were to be built on the spot where he received these visitations and graces from God, what would he name the church. Giles replied: "It should be called 'Pentecost' " (p. 125).

Bruno, Fr. de J.M., O.D.C., *St. John of the Cross*, Benziger Brothers, New York, 1932.

This is a good life of St. John of the Cross. It is not as historically accurate as Fr. Crisogono's life of the Saint but some prefer it. Against the background of sixteenth-century Spain, we see the great mystical theologian and friend of St. Teresa of Avila kidnapped and imprisoned by monks who refuse to be reformed.

Carrouges, Michel, *Soldier of the Spirit, The Life of Charles de Foucauld*, (1858-1916), translated from the French by Marie-Christine Hellin, G.P. Putnam's Sons, New York, 1956.

This is one of the many biographies of de Foucauld. It is written by a Catholic journalist who visited the places in North Africa where de Foucauld lived and worked. This biography is one which the Little Sisters of Jesus in Washington, D.C. recommended to me.

Clasen, Sophronius, O.F.M., *St. Anthony, Doctor of the Gospel*, translated from the German by Ignatius Brady, O.F.M., Franciscan Herald Press, Chicago, 1961.

Here is an excellent little work on Anthony of Padua containing many photographs. The text quotes liberally from Anthony's sermons and writings. This book has recently been reissued in paperback, same publisher, 1973.

Crisogono de Jesus, O.C.D., *The Life of St. John of the Cross*, Longmans, London; Harper & Brothers, New York, 1958.

This is the best life of this Saint in English. Scholars should consult the Spanish edition (Crisogono de Jesus, O.C.D., San Juan de la Cruz, Vida y Obras, Biblioteca de Autores Cristianos, ed. 3a, Madrid, 1955) because the English edition did not include most of the critical apparatus.

Daniel-Rops, Henri, *The Call of St. Clare*, translated from the French by Salvator Attanasio, Hawthorn Books, Inc., New York, 1963.

The author of this book wrote over seventy historical studies, children's books and works of poetry and fiction. He was the youngest man ever to be elected to the Academie Francaise. This is a beautiful book. The text includes letters of St. Clare, some of her prayers and the testament which she wrote to pass on spiritual lessons to her sisters in the Lord. More than thirty pages of photographs illustrate the text.

Daniel-Rops, Henri, *Monsieur Vincent*, Hawthorn Books, Inc., New York, 1961.

This is the story of the seventeenth-century Saint Vincent de Paul, founder of two religious orders. The text is illustrated on nearly every page with color line drawings and there are twenty pages of photographs of paintings depicting St. Vincent and scenes from his life.

De la Bedoyere, Michael, *Francis, A Biography of the Saint of Assisi*, Image Books, Doubleday & Company, Garden City, New York, 1964.

Of this book, Fr. David Knowles, author of a book on *Mysticism*, wrote: ". . . as near to the living Francis as ordinary mortals can hope to get with ordinary words."

De la Bedoyere, Michael, *Francis de Sales*, Harper & Brothers, Publishers, New York, 1960.

The author of this and other biographies, for many years editor of the London *Catholic Herald*, seems to have the ability to blend good scholarship with readability. This is an excellent account of the holy bishop of Geneva.

De la Bedoyere, Michael, *The Greatest Catherine, The Life of Catherine Benincasa, Saint of Siena*, The Bruce Publishing Company, Milwaukee, Wisconsin, 1947.

Michael de la Bedoyere, the author, married Catherine, the daughter of Algar Thorold, who translated Catherine of Siena's *Dialogue* into English. Devotion to St. Catherine runs deep in de la Bedoyere and in this book. The author comments on prior works on Catherine of Siena and then describes his sources. Catherine seems to come alive with his presentation and nine illustrations enhance the work.

De la Bedoyere, Michael, *The Life of Baron von Hugel*, Charles Scribner's Sons, New York, 1951.

The author makes use of diaries and of letters to von Hugel's wife. This work marked the first book on the baron's complete life, although many studies had previously been published. The baron and Cardinal Newman are considered the two greatest influences on modern English Catholicism.

Dirvin, Joseph I., C.M., *Mrs. Seton, Foundress of the American Sisters of Charity*, Farrar, Straus and Cudahy, New York, 1962.

Father Dirvin here provides a wonderful account of the life of Elizabeth Bayley Seton (1774-1821) who, in her forty-seven years lived New York society life, mothered five children, and founded the American Sisters of Charity.

Dirvin, Joseph I., C.M., *Saint Catherine Laboure of the Miraculous Medal*, Farrar, Straus and Cudahy, New York, 1958.

This biography was the result of ten years of research, and it is quite readable.

Dudon, S.J., Paul, *St. Ignatius of Loyola*, translated by William J. Young, S.J., The Bruce Publishing Company, Milwaukee, Wisconsin, 1949.

This is the best biography of Ignatius in English, although one by James Brodrick, S.J., is better known. Another book to consult would be *Ignatius the Theologian* and *The Spirituality of St. Ignatius Loyola*, both by Hugo Rahner.

Englebert, Omer, *Saint Francis of Assisi*, second English Edition revised and augmented by Ignatius Brady, O.F.M. and Raphael Brown, Franciscan Herald Press, Chicago, Illinois, 1965.

This is a definitive biography of Francis. If one were to read only one book on this Saint, I would recommend this one. This work includes a one thousand item bibliography, arranged by topics, a chronology of Francis' life and other important research aids.

Farnum, Mabel, *St. Gabriel*, Society of St. Paul, Youngstown, Ohio, 1950.

This is not a book on the Archangel Gabriel. It is the life of Saint Gabriel of the Sorrowful Virgin. In 1856 Francis Possenti entered the Passionist Novitiate in Monovalle, Italy. Five years and five months later he died a holy death and was acclaimed a Saint. St. Gabriel was baptized and he was christened Francis. The monastery in which he died, Isola, had originally been Franciscan before being abandoned and then given to the Passionists. Francis Possenti's name in religion became Gabriel of the Sorrowful Virgin. All his short life Gabriel was devoted to the Mother of God, especially under her title "Sorrowful Virgin."

Foss, Michael, *The Founding of the Jesuits 1540*, Weybright and Talley, New York, n.d.

This book, published around 1969, will not replace standard

biographies, but it offers a fresh approach to the subject and has some good insights. I include it here not only because I benefited from reading it, but because many scholars have never heard about the book. The book was reviewed in *America*, Dec. 27, 1969 by Joseph Brusher and in *Catholic World*, April 1970 by C.J. McNaspy, S.J., who says: "Foss . . . is quite subjective and (at least to a Jesuit) fairly gripping in a dramatic way."

Franciscan Institute, *The Legend and Writings of St. Clare of Assisi*, St. Bonaventure, N.Y., 1953.

This book contains Celano's legend of St. Clare and Clare's writings. The book is still available from the institute.

Gorres, Ida Friederike, *The Hidden Face, A Study of St. Therese of Lisieux*, Pantheon, New York, 1959.

There are perhaps more biographies of this Saint than any other except St. Francis of Assisi. Therese was originally presented to the world with writings and photographs which had been "touched up" and altered to bring them more in line with "traditional" notions of sanctity. This study by Frau Gorres should be read by those seeking to know this Saint better. Many consider this to be the best life of St. Therese. It is considered a controversial work by some of the Saint's other biographers. Peter-Thomas Rohrbach in his *The Search for Saint Therese* accuses Frau Gorres of projecting "traditional Franco-German tensions into the literary arena" (p. 23) and he reminds readers that Hans Urs von Balthasar, a German theologian, evaluated this book in this manner: ". . . she (Gorres) has to resort to depth psychology in order to bring out her heroine's greatness. This leads to obvious misinterpretations, so that in spite of her brilliant account of

Therese's personal life and milieu, Gorres' work is inadequate on the theological side" (p. 30).

St. Gregory the Great, Pope, *The Life and Miracles of St. Benedict*, The Liturgical Press, St. John's Abbey, Collegeville, Minnesota, 1956.

This is the basic source for all lives of Benedict as it is by the only contemporary witness. The book is available in various editions from various sources.

Habig, Marion A., editor, *St. Francis of Assisi's Writings and early Biographies*, Franciscan Herald Press, Chicago, Illinois, 1973.

This book is also subtitled, "English Omnibus of the Sources for the Life of St. Francis." The book includes the writings of St. Francis, the two lives by Celano, major and minor lives by St. Bonaventure, the *Legend of the Three Companions*, *Mirror of Perfection*, *Little Flowers of St. Francis*, other writings and several indices. An indispensable source book.

Henry-Couannier, Maurice, *Saint Francis de Sales and His Friends*, Scepter, Chicago, Dublin, London, 1964, available in 1976 through Christian Classics, 205 Willis Street, Westminster, Maryland 21157.

De Sales' friends included many Saints, particularly St. Jane Frances de Chantal and Mme. Acarie. Other Saints who move through the pages of this book are St. Robert Bellarmine, St. Charles Borromeo and St. Vincent de Paul.

Homan, Helen Walker, *Star of Jacob, The Story of the Venerable Francis Libermann*, David McKay Company, Inc., New York, 1953.

This story traces the life of Jacob Libermann, son of a rabbi, born in 1802, and destined to become a Catholic priest and founder of the Congregation of the Holy Ghost and of the Immaculate Heart of Mary. On July 1, 1876, Rome bestowed upon him the title "The Venerable Servant of God." This is a sensitive portrayal and is easy to read.

*Jorgensen, Johannes, *St. Francis of Assisi*, McKay, 1912, Image, 1955.

This is perhaps the best known biography of Francis. The text is accompanied by many notes.

Lindsay, T.F., *St. Benedict: His Life and Works*, Burns & Oates, London, 1949.

This is one of the best lives of Benedict in English.

Magaret, Helene, *A Kingdom and a Cross, St. Alphonsus Liguori*, The Bruce Publishing Company, Milwaukee, Wisconsin, 1958.

This biography of the founder of the Redemptorists follows Alphonsus through the ninety-one years of his life. It begins with Alphonsus learning how to obey his parents. It follows him as he learns to discern movements of grace. He writes more than a hundred books and becomes a bishop. In his last years he is excluded from the society he founded. Alphonsus' life does not lack religious experiences but, when one puts down this book, one is overwhelmed, not with the memory of prophetic dreams or visions, but with the beauty of a holy life.

Sister Mary Fidelis, S.N.D., *As Gold in the Furnace, The Life of Blessed Julie Billiart, Foundress of the Sisters of Notre*

297

Dame de Namur, The Bruce Publishing Company, Milwaukee, Wisconsin, 1957.

For twenty-two years, from age thirty-one to fifty-three, Julie Billiart was crippled. One day a priest commanded her to take one step for the love of the Sacred Heart of Jesus. Julie did, and her paralysis was cured. In the remaining twelve years of her life she founded many convents and went on long journeys for the Lord.

Sister Mary Francis, P.C., *Walled In Light: St. Colette*, Sheed and Ward, New York, 1959.

Written by a Colettine Poor Clare, this is a book I would highly recommend. Against the background of the fifteenth century and Colette's efforts to reform the Poor Clares, we see Colette restore a dead child to life, prophesy to St. Vincent Ferrer that he will die in less than two years, and lead her sisters in three days of prayer and going about the cloister on their knees to implore God to enlighten St. John Capistran on a matter affecting the Poor Clares' mode of life. St. John Capistran sees a vision of Christ and all is well.

Mead, Jude, C.P., *Shepherd of The Second Spring, The Life of Blessed Dominic Barberi, C.P.*, St. Anthony Guild Press, Paterson, New Jersey, 1968.

Dominic was an Italian shepherd boy who became a Passionist priest. He had a special love for England and spent the last eight years of his life there. It was Dominic whom John Henry Newman chose to hear his confession and receive him into the Catholic Church. This book gives good background on the Oxford Movement, St. Paul of the Cross, founder of the Passionists, and on beatification and canonization processes.

Merton, Thomas, *What Are These Wounds? The Life of a Cistercian Mystic, Saint Lutgarde of Aywieres*. The Bruce Publishing Company, Milwaukee, Wisconsin, 1950.

This is one of my favorite books by Thomas Merton. It contains the delightful story of Lutgarde's finger.

O'Mahony, O.C.D., Christopher, editor and translator, *St. Therese of Lisieux by Those Who Knew Her*, Our Sunday Visitor, Inc., Huntington, Indiana, 1975.

This is a translation from the French of the testimonies given by fifteen witnesses at the diocesan inquiry into the life and virtues of Therese of Lisieux which was held in Lisieux in 1910 and 1911. This is a particularly valuable book since thirteen of the witnesses knew St. Therese very well and their testimonies show clearly the substance of her sanctity and how singleminded was her love of God.

Pernoud, Regine, *Joan of Arc by Herself and Her Witness*, Stein and Day, Publishers, New York, 1966. Paperback, 1969.

Mlle. Pernoud bases this work on the letters, chronicles and testimony at Joan's trial.

Petitot, Father Henry, O.P., *The True Story of St. Bernadette*, translated by a Benedictine of Stanbrook Abbey, The Newman Press, Westminster, Maryland, 1950.

Most books about Saint Bernadette deal with the apparitions at Lourdes. Many people assume that Bernadette was canonized because the Blessed Mother appeared to her. Most of this book deals with Bernadette after the apparitions. We learn that Bernadette was stubborn and that she was impatient when opposed. We learn how, during the years from the time the apparitions ceased until her death, Bernadette became purified and sanctified, and emerged a great woman from whom we can learn how to please the Lord.

Phelan, Edna Beyer, *Don Bosco: A Spiritual Portrait*, Doubleday and Company, Inc., Garden City, New York, 1963.

This is an excellent biography with a good bibliography appended.

Raymond of Capua, Blessed, *The Life of St. Catherine of Siena*, P.J. Kenedy & Sons, New York, 1960.

This is a famous life of a Saint by a Saint.

Robo, Etienne, *Two Portraits of St. Teresa of Lisieux*, The Newman Press, Westminster, Maryland, 1955, revised and enlarged in 1957.

Father Robo here presents a controversial biography of the Saint. This is one of the two books on Therese, the other being the work of Frau Gorres, singled out for refutation by Peter-Thomas Rohrbach in *The Search for St. Therese*, and in which Goures says: "Both books are well-written and stimulating, and they have both enjoyed a wide reading here in America. Father Robo's book is more polemic and argumentative, written with the fire and occasional irascibility which make that kind of reading exciting and absorbing" (p. 231).

Father Robo attempts to show us, as does Ida Gorres in her book, that a false St. Therese was foisted upon the believing public by the Carmel of Lisieux who "touched up" photographs of Therese and "edited" her autobiography. The 1957 edition of this book includes a chapter entitled "The Neurosis of St. Teresa." Father Robo makes a case for his conjecture

300

that Therese was neurotic and her greatness lay in the fact
that with God's grace she overcame her overly-sensitive and
idiosyncratic nature. If nothing else, this and the book by P.T.
Rohrbach serve as a good introduction to the world of hagiography.

Rohrbach, Peter-Thomas, O.C.D., *The Search for St. Therese*,
Hanover House, New York, 1961.

This book by a former Carmelite priest, author of the excellent little book *Conversation With Christ*, examines Therese's life in the light of modern psychology and historical criticism. The author evaluates various books on Therese. He
describes the process of her canonization and he provides an
interesting point of view. This book should perhaps be read
along with more traditional biographies of the Saint to whose
tomb Pope John made five pilgrimages in the course of his life.

Sheppard, Lancelot C., *Barbe Acarie, Wife and Mystic*, Burns,
Oates, London, and McKay, New York, 1953.

Mr. Sheppard was the General Editor of *The Twentieth Century Encyclopedia of Catholicism.* Here he presents us with
an account of Mme. Acarie, Blessed Mary of the Incarnation
(1566-1618) who was instrumental in bringing the Teresian
Carmelites to France in 1606.

Sheppard, Lancelot C., *Don Bosco*, Burns, Oates, London, 1957.

Here is another good biography by Mr. Sheppard who also
authored Vol. 42 of the above mentioned encyclopedia entitled "Spiritual Writers in Modern Times."

Trochu, Francis, *The Cure D'Ars, St. Jean-Marie-Baptiste Vianney*, translated by Dom Ernest Graf, O.S.B., Newman Press,
Westminster, Maryland, 1953.

For years this has been considered the best life of the Cure whose dates were 1786-1859. Abbe Trochu drew on the *Acts of the Process of Canonization* when preparing this book.

Trouncer, Margaret, *The Nun*, Sheed & Ward, New York, 1955.

Margaret Trouncer wrote several readable biographies of Saints, including ones on St. Bernadette and St. John Vianney. This one deals with St. Margaret Mary Alacoque, the French sister associated with revelations leading to devotion to the Sacred Heart of Jesus.

Van der Meer, F., *Augustine the Bishop*, Sheed & Ward, London and New York, 1961, distributed in the United States as of 1976 by Christian Classics, 205 Willis Street, Westminster, Maryland 21157.

The front flap of this book reads: "Most people who know Augustine do so chiefly from the *Confessions*. This is understandable, but still curious; for it means that the greater part of his life and activity are left out. Probably most people feel that once Augustine had finished sowing his wild oats the excitement was all over; the rest cannot be more than a colorless routine of plodding clerical piety—admirable, of course, but not very interesting. . . . In fact his long life at Hippo Regius, first as priest and then as bishop, was so packed with variety, activity and incident that one wonders how on earth he managed to get it all in." Anyone interested in this period of Church history and/or in Augustine should make this book a must. Accompanying the text are sixty-six pages of notes, two indices, twenty-four plates and a map.

Van Kaam, Adrian, *A Light to the Gentiles: The Life Story of the Venerable Francis Libermann*, Duquesne University Press, Pittsburgh, 1959.

The author of this very good biography has also produced *Religion and Personality, Personality Fulfillment in the Spiritual Life, The Art of Existential Counseling* and others.

Vicaire, O.P., M.-H., *Saint Dominic and His Times*, McGraw-Hill Book Company, New York, 1964.

Marie-Humbert Vicaire's biography is a definitive study of Saint Dominic.

Von Balthasar, Hans Urs, *Therese of Lisieux*, Sheed & Ward, New York, 1954.

By a German theologian, this is an excellent account of the life of the "Saint of the Little Way." Pentecostals familiar with Watchman Nee's pamphlet, "Why This Waste," which is a chapter from *The Normal Christian Life*, will appreciate this quote of Saint Therese with which Von Balthasar chose to introduce his book: "The most fervent Christians, the priests, consider we are too extreme, that we ought to serve with Martha instead of consecrating to Jesus the vessels of our lives with the perfumes contained in them. . . . But after all, what matter that our vessels are broken, since Jesus is consoled and since, in spite of itself, the world is forced to awareness of the perfumes they breathe forth, perfumes which serve to purify the poisoned air the world is ever breathing."

Von Matt and Rahner, *St. Ignatius of Loyola*, Henry Regnery Company, Chicago, 1956.

Photographer Leonard von Matt produced magnificent pictorial biographies of a number of Saints including: St. Francis of Assisi, St. Pius X, St. Bernadette, St. Benedict, St. Dominic and St. Vincent de Paul. The text of the book on Ignatius was written by Hugo Rahner and the texts of the other books were done by authoritative writers on that particular Saint. These books are magnificent. They are hard to locate outside of libraries because people usually do not want to part with them.

Waldham, Juliana, *The Case of Cornelia Connelly*, Image Books, Doubleday & Company, Inc., Garden City, New York, 1960.

This is an excellent treatment of the unusual life of Cornelia Peacock Connelly (1809-1879) a wife, mother, nun, foundress of the Society of the Holy Child Jesus and, perhaps someday, canonized saint.

Walsh, William Thomas, *Saint Teresa of Avila, A Biography*, The Bruce Publishing Company, Milwaukee, Wisconsin, 1943.

This is a very good, and lengthy (592 pages) biography of the great Saint Teresa, recently declared a Doctor of the Church.

Weisheipl, O.P., James A. *Friar Thomas d'Aquino*, Doubleday and Company, Garden City, New York, 1974.

Father Weisheipl, priest of the Order of St. Dominic, is a recognized authority on the life and works of Thomas Aquinas. Included is a summary chronology of Aquinas' life and "A Brief Catalogue of Authentic Works" which encompasses fifty pages. This is an excellent example of modern hagiography combining scholarship with readability.

304

CLASSICS OF THE SPIRITUAL LIFE

(These are available in many editions and translations, so with a few exceptions, bibliographical information will be omitted.)

*St. Benedict, *Rule for Monasteries*.

This should be of especial interest to those involved in forming and living Christian community. Composed in the sixth century, this rule has influenced the life of many communities in the West. This rule formed the basis of Western monasticism.

St. Catherine of Siena, *Dialogue*.

The *Dialogue* of Catherine of Siena (1347-1380), is considered a masterpiece of Italian religious literature and one of the best examples of mystical writing.

Chautard, O.C.S.O., Dom Jean-Baptiste, *The Soul of the Apostolate*.

Written in 1912 by a Trappist, this work enjoys widespread renown, though it may appear a little dated. The word "apostolate" itself has no meaning for many Christians today. It seems to be passing out of the vocabulary of Catholic conversation. However, this should be no impediment to extracting the wisdom contained in this wonderful little book. Dom Chautard wrote a prayer as a prologue to the book from which we quote in part:

"O Jesus, Emmanuel, Thou dost return, ascending to Thy apostles, Thy Gospel, Thy Cross, Thy Eucharist, and givest them the mission to go forth and beget for Thy Father, sons of adoption.

"And then Thou dost return, ascending to Thy Father.

"Thine, henceforth, O Holy Spirit, is the care of sanctifying and directing the Mystical Body of the God-man.

"Thou deignest to take unto Thyself fellow-workers, in Thy

function of bringing, from the Head, divine life into the members.

"Burning with Pentecostal fires, they will go forth to sow broadcast in the minds of all, the word that enlightens, and in all hearts the grace that enkindles. . . .

"O Divine Fire, stir up in all those who have part in Thy apostolate, the flames that transformed those fortunate retreatants in the Upper Room. Then they will be no longer mere preachers of dogma or moral theology, but men living to transfuse the Blood of God into the souls of men. . . ."

*Cloud of Unknowing.

This is an anonymous work from a time when English mysticism flourished. Other well-known spiritual writers of that period were Richard Rolle (1300-1349), Walter Hilton (d. 1396, *The Scale of Perfection**) and Julian of Norwich (1343-1413). The main theme of this work is that God cannot be grasped by man's intellect, and that only love can pierce the "cloud of unknowing" which is between them. This is not a book for beginners in the spiritual life.

Desert Fathers: *The Wisdom of the Desert* by Thomas Merton, New Directions, N.Y., 1960.
This is a collection of sayings from the Desert Fathers of the fourth century. It is perhaps less scholarly but a little more readable than Helen Waddell's book (see following note). A sample "Abbot Hyperichius said: 'It is better to eat meat and drink wine, than by detraction to devour the flesh of your brother' " (Saying XIX).

Desert Fathers: *The Desert Fathers*, tr. and ed. by Helen Waddell, Henry Holt, N.Y., and in paperback.
This has historical as well as spiritual interest and is a classic work on the subject.

St. Francis de Sales, *Introduction to the Devout Life and Treatise on the Love of God.*
Written three centuries ago these are considered some of the best writing by any Saint.

*St. Ignatius, *Spiritual Exercises.*
This work by the founder of the Jesuits, St. Ignatius of Loyola (d. 1556), is divided into four weeks of meditations. Ignatius intended that this book be read by spiritual directors who were to work one to one to bring an individual into a deep relationship with Jesus over a period of thirty days. The most readily available translation is one by Mottola, but most Jesuits I know use Puhl.

St. John of the Cross, *Dark Night of the Soul* and other works.
The four major works of this Doctor of the Church who died in 1591, and who cooperated with Teresa of Avila in the reform of the Carmelite Order, are: *The Ascent of Mount Carmel, The Dark Night, The Living Flame of Love,* and *The Spiritual Canticle.* Mr. Allison Peers, an authority on Spanish mysticism, has translated the works of Teresa of Avila and John of the Cross. It is important to read his introductions and notes. A more recent version of St. John's works is by Fr. Kieran Kavanaugh, O.C.D. and Fr. Otilio Rodrigues, O.C.D. This translation includes all of the Saint's poems in the original Spanish with parallel English translations. St. John has much to teach souls but is often read and quoted by beginners in the life of the Spirit who really don't understand him. Many Catholics say, "I'm in the Dark Night" when they encounter their first trial. As St. John says, people who really have this experience are few.

*Brother Lawrence, *The Practice of the Presence of God.*
Brother Lawrence (1611-1691) was a Carmelite friar. This

work is widely known among Christians of every denomination.

Little Flowers of St. Francis.
The *Fioretti* or Little Flowers captures the spirit of early Franciscanism.

St. Louis de Montfort, *True Devotion to the Blessed Virgin.*
In this treatise, de Montfort wrote the prophecy: "I clearly foresee that raging brutes will come in fury to tear with their diabolical teeth this little writing and him whom the Holy Ghost has made use of to write it; or at least to envelop it in the silence of a coffer, in order that it may not appear."
The saintly author died in 1716 and the manuscript wasn't found until 1842. The work met with great success and went through many editions. This work should have special interest for Pentecostals because de Montfort, in writing on the nature of perfect devotion to the Blessed Virgin which he equates with perfect consecration to Jesus Christ, stresses a renewal of the vows of Baptism. The only drawback, also mentioned by Thils in *Christian Holiness*, is the frequent use of the word "slave" which may grate on the modern ear. This can be overcome by substituting the word "servant" in place of "slave." So, for example, a paragraph of the final act of consecration to Jesus would read:
"I give Thee thanks for that Thou hast annihilated Thyself, taking the form of a slave [servant] in order to rescue me from the cruel slavery [servitude] of the devil."

Scupoli, Lawrence, *The Spiritual Combat.*
The Spiritual Combat is considered by Louis Bouyer to be one of the most important works of the Counter-Reformation. The first edition was published in Venice in 1589. St. Francis

de Sales called it a "golden book." The first chapter states the purpose of the book which is to lead souls to the summit of spiritual perfection. For eighteen years St. Francis de Sales carried a copy of this little book in his pocket. It was reissued in paperback by Newman Press in 1945.

St. Teresa of Avila, *Way of Perfection*, *Interior Castle*, and other works.
St. Teresa's complete works include her *Autobiography*, *The Way of Perfection*, *The The Interior Castle*, the *Foundations*, and *Letters*. *The Autobiography of St. Teresa of Avila* (d. 1582), written in obedience to her confessors, gives Teresa's account of her progress in seeking God's will. The next two works listed above deal with successive stages of prayer and tell of her adventures in founding convents or communities in various towns in Spain.

*Thomas a Kempis, *The Imitation of Christ*.
The Imitation of Christ is probably the most widely read Christian work next to the Bible. Written in the fifteenth century, the work has been attributed over the years to various authors, including John Gerson and Gerard Groote. The book was written by a monk for monks. This should be kept in mind lest some views expressed by the author seem narrow or negative. However, much of the wisdom counseled in this work can safely be taken to heart by those presently living in Christian community. The author counsels avoiding the kind of exclusive friendships which will hinder the love of the brethren in community. On another subject, the sentence: "I would rather feel compunction of heart for my sins than only know the definition of compunction" is one of the most famous and well-remembered phrases of the book. To say, as some do, that the book is anti-intellectual, is like saying St.

Francis of Assisi was anti-intellectual because he counseled his friars to have few books, besides the Bible. There is always a creative tension between the mystical and the intellectual in the Church and books such as the *Imitation* and Saints like Francis help to keep the scale in balance.

LETTERS

Combes, Abbe, editor, *Collected Letters of Saint Therese of Lisieux*, translated by F. J. Sheed, Sheed & Ward, New York, 1949.

A 1972 edition has been published by Sheed & Ward, London. Here are two hundred and forty-six letters arranged in the order of their writing. They are perhaps more revealing than the *Autobiography* because Therese wrote them with no notion of distribution or publication. Abbe Combes supplies a biographical framework so one can know, for example, that a very cheerful letter was written at a time when Therese was suffering and in pain from the disease which killed her.

De la Colombiere, Blessed Claude, *Faithful Servant, Spiritual Retreats and Letters of Blessed Claude*, translated by William J. Young, S.J., B. Herder Book Company, Book Craftsmen Associates, Inc., New York, 1960.

These are the letters of the man who, with St. Margaret Mary, popularized devotion to the Sacred Heart of Jesus.

Letters from the Saints, arranged and selected by a Benedictine of Stanbrook Abbey, Hawthorn Books, Inc., New York, 1964.

A wonderful collection of letters of well-known Saints and one I especially recommend.

Rahner, Hugo, *St. Ignatius Loyola–Letters to Women*. Herder and Herder, New York, 1960.

In this book, Hugo Rahner, brother of Karl Rahner, has collected all the letters which Ignatius wrote to or received from women. Since this in an annotated edition of the correspondence it could well be considered a biography.

Saint Teresa, *The Letters of St. Teresa*, 4 Vols., translated by the Benedictines of Stanbrook, London: Thomas Baker, 1926, *The Letters of Saint Teresa of Jesus*, 2 Vols., translated and edited by E. Allison Peers. Burns, Oates and Washbourne, Ltd., London, 1951. (Westminster, Maryland, 1950)

The letters of the great reformer, St. Teresa.

Scudder, Vida D., *Saint Catherine of Siena as Seen in Her Letters*, London: J.M. Dent & Sons, Ltd., New York: E.P. Dutton and Company, 1927.

We are indebted to Vida Scudder, an Anglican, for this translation into English of some of Catherine's letters. To my knowledge there are four volumes of her letters in Italian which no one has translated into English.

Spiritual Letters of St. Francis De Sales, The, Rivingtons, London, Oxford and Cambridge, 1871.

Any collection of letters of St. Francis de Sales is worth reading. They are out of print and hard to find, but worth the search.

Vann, O.P., Gerald, *To Heaven With Diana*, Henry Regnery Company, Chicago, Illinois, 1965.

This is a study of the letters of Blessed Jordan of Saxony to Diana d'Andalo, the letters having been written between 1222 and 1237. Blessed Jordan succeeded St. Dominic as master general of the Dominican Order. Diana d'Andalo was a Dominican nun who had known St. Dominic.

SPIRITUAL THEOLOGY

Father Garrigou-Lagrange devoted nearly twenty pages of *The Three Ages of the Interior Life* to a discussion of the difference between spiritual theology and spiritual writing. Just as mathematics or physics have their special set of terms, so too the spiritual life and its study has a terminology supplied by theologians. However, many spiritual writers and Saints had a limited knowledge of theology and sometimes their writing seems to clash with that of theologians. This should be only an apparent conflict but in particular cases it may be that the difference is one of terminology and not of doctrine or it may be that the theologians need correction from those living the Christian life at greater depth. Spiritual theology and spiritual writing should complement one another—von Hugel's construct again. A good example of this taken from two Saints writing about the same thing from different points of view would be St. John of the Cross defining contemplation as a nonactivity, and St. Thomas calling it the highest possible activity. This is because the suspension of all human activity *seems* to the soul like nonactivity and St. John of the Cross was writing from an experiential point of view and St. Thomas was writing as a theologian. Lest we be tempted to dismiss the writing of theologians because, for one thing, it is more difficult to read, we might consider two quotes here. Fr. Donald Gelpi, S.J., in Pentecostalism: *A Theological Viewpoint* reminds us: "Enthusiasm is a charismatic experience gone awry for want of adequate theological

312

reflection." The charismatic, mystic and Saint, Francis of Assisi, said in his *Testament:* "We should honor and venerate theologians. . . ."

This category is included in my listing of books pertaining to Saints because books such as these can help to put Saints' lives in perspective.

Bouyer, Louis, *Introduction to Spirituality*, Liturgical Press, Collegeville, Minnesota, 1961.

This is a book I especially recommend. There is a useful reading list at the end of the book containing notes on the great classics of the spiritual life.

Dicken, E.W. Trueman, *The Crucible of Love*, Sheed and Ward, New York, 1963.

This is a comparative study of the teaching of Sts. Teresa of Avila and John of the Cross, by an Anglican pastor of two rural agricultural villages in the English midlands. It is the only book that for me answered the question of how to harmonize Teresa saying not to abandon the humanity of Jesus when at prayer and John saying one has to get beyond all thoughts and sense impressions.

Fr. Gabriel of St. Mary Magdalen, O.C.D., *Divine Intimacy*, Desclee, N.Y., 1964.

This work consists of meditations on the interior life for every day of the year by a renowned Belgian Carmelite, an authority on the lives of Teresa of Avila and John of the Cross. Fr. Gabriel, in this, his last book, deals with some fundamental

313

problems encountered in living in the Spirit. Each meditation is followed by passages from Scripture or from the writings of some Saint or holy person. Of this book Pope John said: "This book of meditations is meant for all priests, seminarians, religious, the devout laity. . ." that is, all who seek union with God.

Garrigou-Lagrange, O.P., Rev. R., *Christian Perfection and Contemplation*, B. Herder Book Company, St. Louis, 1937.

In a note at the end of the chapter on "The Mystical Life" in *Introduction to Spirituality*, Bouyer says of the above work: "Following a Thomistic line of thought, nourished by the Carmelite spiritual tradition and especially that of St. John of the Cross, Fr. Garrigou-Lagrange has provided a synthesis as yet unsurpassed . . ." (p. 307).

Garrigou-Lagrange, O.P., *The Three Ages of the Spiritual Life*, 2 vols., Herder, 1948.
Fr. Garrigou-Lagrange here develops the conclusions reached earlier in *Christian Perfection and Contemplation*.

Tanquerey, S.S., Adolphe, *The Spiritual Life*, Desclee & Company, Tournai, Belgium, 1930.

This has been a standard reference text for years.

Garrigou-Lagrange, O.P., *The Three Ways of the Spiritual Life*, Newman Press, Westminster, Maryland, 1955.

This is a small book which condenses much of what was said at length in the above-mentioned works.

de Guibert, S.J., Joseph, *The Theology of the Spiritual Life*, Sheed and Ward, New York, 1953.

This has been a standard text in many seminaries.

Knowles, David, "The Nature of Mysticism," Vol. 38 of the *Twentieth Century Encyclopedia of Catholicism*, Hawthorn Book Publishers, New York, 1966.

This is an excellent book. In describing the climate of sixteenth-century Spain, Knowles comments, "There had been an almost Pentecostal effusion of graces . . . ." The author treats the nature of mystical experiences and includes chapters on spiritual growth and prayer.

Thils, Gustave, *Christian Holiness, A Precis of Ascetical Theology*, Lannoo Publishers, Tielt, Belgium.

The appendix to this work is a thirty-two page bibliography of spiritual writings arranged according to chronology and schools of spirituality.

Underhill, Evelyn, *Mysticism*, Meridian Books, New York, 1955.

This book, which originally appeared in 1911, is considered a classic work on the subject. The appendix to this book is a twenty-one page historical sketch of European "mysticism" from the beginning of Christianity to the death of William Blake, the poet. The essay includes poets and "natural" mystics as well as Saints, but it is well worth reading. There are thirty pages of bibliography. Evelyn Underhill (1875-1941), an Anglican, was a married woman whose spiritual director was Baron Friedrich von Hugel, a Catholic. Some of her other

315

works include *The Mystic Way* (1913) and *The Life of the Spirit and the Life of Today* (1922).

Von Hugel, Baron Friedrich, *The Mystical Element of Religion as Studied in St. Catherine of Genoa and Her Friends*, Vols. I and II, J.M. Dent & Sons, London, 1928.

This great work by a Catholic layman appeared in 1908. The first eighty pages deal with three basic elements in religion: institutional, intellectual and mystical. The work is out of print but can be found in most university libraries. Portions of the work are contained in *Spiritual Counsel and Letters of Baron Friedrich von Hugel*, edited by Douglas V. Steere, the Quaker observer at the second Vatican Council.

BOOKS ON MARY, THE MOTHER OF GOD

Attwater, Donald A., *A Dictionary of Mary*, Kenedy, 1956.

The book follows a dictionary format, explaining and listing facts of the life of the Blessed Mother, theology of Mary, her feasts and her shrines. The author was editor of the revised *Butler's Lives of the Saints*.

Bouyer, Louis, *The Seat of Wisdom*, Henry Regnery Company, Chicago, Illinois, 1965.

Fr. Bouyer calls his book an essay on the place of the Virgin Mary in Christian theology. There is a chapter devoted to "Mary and the Holy Ghost."

Delaney, John J., Editor, *A Woman Clothed with the Sun*, Hanover House, Garden City, New York, 1959.

Contained in this work are accounts of eight apparitions of Our Lady in modern times written by various writers. The events included are: Guadalupe, the Miraculous Medal, La Salette, Lourdes, Knock, Fatima, Beauraing and Banneaux. The section on the Miraculous Medal is by Fr. Joseph Dirvin, author of the definitive biography of St. Catherine Laboure. Whether one accepts these visions or not (see chapter on "Voices and Visions") this book covers well this aspect of Catholic piety.

Dollen, Rev. Charles, *A Voice Said Ave!*, St. Paul Editons, Boston, Massachusetts, 1963.

Here in this volume are included passages from the writings of the Fathers, Doctors, and theologians that deal with Our Lady. The free translations are by Father Charles Dollen, Library Director of the University of San Diego. This book can be for devotional use as well as being instructive. The illustrations and layout of the entire book show that it was a labor of love for the author. Writings from some of the following are represented: St. Bernard, St. Bonaventure, St. Bernardine of Siena and St. Thomas Aquinas.

Garrigou-Lagrange, Rev. R., O.P., *The Mother of the Saviour and Our Interior Life*, B. Herder Book Company, St. Louis, Missouri, 1954.

In his preface, Fr. Garrigou-Lagrange expresses his purpose in writing the book. He says it is to be "an exposition of the principal theses of Mariology in their bearing on our interior life." Also in the preface, the author, who was an eminent spiritual theologian, noted that theologians often went through three periods in coping with Marian doctrine. First

317

there is a period when under the influence of piety, the theologian admits some prerogative of Our Lady. Then follows a period of seeing doctrinal difficulties and the theologian becomes more reserved in judgment. In the third period there is a return to the first position, not now, however, because of sentiment, but due to a more profound grasp of tradition and theology. The author then draws an analogy between this and three periods in the soul's growth in devotion. The first is based on sense-perceptible devotion, then follows a stage of aridity, then finally a stage of perfect spiritual devotion.

Graef, Hilda, *Mary: A History of Doctrine and Devotion*, Two Vols., Sheed and Ward, New York, 1963.

The title of this work adequately indicates the contents.

National Conference of Catholic Bishops, *Behold Your Mother*, Nov. 21, 1973, United States Catholic Conference, 1312 Massachusetts Avenue, N.W., Washington, D.C. 20005

Behold Your Mother is a pastoral letter of the American Bishops on the Blessed Virgin Mary. Along with the Bible and the Vatican Council documents and certain other books, this should be required reading for all those seeking to understand Catholic tradition. On p. 59 of this pastoral letter there is a suggested bibliography.

Rahner, S.J., Hugo, *Our Lady and the Church*, Henry Regnery Company, Chicago, Illinois, 1965.

Fr. Hugo Rahner tries to help us to see the Church in Our Lady and Our Lady in the Church. The book is based on writings of the Fathers of the Church.

Rahner, Karl, *Mary, Mother of the Lord,* Herder and Herder, New York, 1962.

These are theological meditations. As it says on the back flap, "because of . . . sound doctrinal basis, the present book is preserved from the emotional and sentimental excesses that have occasionally obscured the devotion to Mary. In a style which is marked by the simplicity and clarity of the liturgy, Father Rahner discusses Mary in theology, the basic concept of Mariology, the Immaculate Conception, the Divine Motherhood, the Assumption, and the mission of Mary as Mediatrix of all graces." This is a book I especially recommend.

Thurian, Max, *Mary, Mother of All Christians,* Herder and Herder, N.Y., 1964. The American edition is out of print, but the book can still be had under the title, *Mary, Mother of the Lord, Figure of the Church,* Faith Press, 7 Tufton Street, London SW 1, England.

Of this book, the American bishops' pastoral, *Behold Your Mother,* says: "Brother Max Thurian of the French Calvinist monastery of Taize has put all Christians in his debt with a valuable book on the Mary of the gospels: *Mary, Mother of the Lord, Figure of the Church.*"

Ward, J. Neville, *Five for Sorrow Ten for Joy,* Doubleday and Company, Garden City, New York, 1973.

J. Neville Ward, a Methodist minister of Bath, England, offers us an approach to the rosary with a collection of meditations. As one reason for writing the book, Rev. Ward says in his preface, ". . . in Methodism the silence about the Mother of Jesus is positively deafening. It is so complete that during a ministry of over thirty years I have begun to wonder what anxiety is behind this surprising mental hang-up." While admitting initial nervousness, Rev. Ward tells how he overcame it and in so doing has produced a beautiful book. I would draw special attention to his mention of von Hugel in the chapter on "Coming to Church."

MISCELLANY

Bainton, Roland, *Women of the Reformation in Germany and Italy*, Augsburg Publishing House, Minneapolis, 1971. *Women of the Reformation in France and England*, Augsburg Publishing House, Minneapolis, 1973.

The author taught church history at Yale Divinity School for 42 years until his retirement. In his preface to the first volume Dr. Bainton says of these two volumes: "The term 'Reformation' is used in the title because it designates a recognizable reform, but the word is here employed in a broad sense to include not only Protestantism but also evangelical Catholicism." These books contain valuable bibliographical listings.

de Bles, Major Arthur, *How to Distinguish the Saints in Art*, Art Culture Publications, Inc., New York, 1925.

According to the author, ". . . almost seventy percent of all pictures painted, at least up to the end of the fifteenth century, at the zenith of the High Renaissance, were painted for churches or the private chapels of the powerful rulers of the small states, into which Italy, France and Flanders were then divided." The author contends that in order to appreciate this religious art one needs to understand symbolism—that is, the emblems and/or attributes that distinguish the saintly personage portrayed by the artist. Nearly a thousand pictures and more than three hundred artists are included in this book. Although none of the reproductions are in color, this book (which was published over fifty years ago) is beautiful to look at as well as being very informative.

Foxe, John, *History of the Christian Martyrs*, edited by Marie Gentert King, Pyramid Books, New York, 1968, 1971.

According to *The Oxford Dictionary of the Christian Church*, (ed. Cross & Livingstone, 2nd edition revised, Oxford University Press, 1974) which has a reputation for impartial scholarship the historical value of Foxe's book, whose object was to extol the virtues of the Protestant martyrs of Queen Mary's reign, "is impaired by the author's credulity and bitterness." I have included this book because it is presently enjoying some circulation. It is a good example of the kind of naive and polemical work that must be avoided as we approach learning about and sharing our common Christian heritage.

Hodgkin, L.V., *A Book of Quaker Saints*, Macmillan and Company, Ltd., London, 1922.

This quaint and charming book about "Early Quaker Saints" was intended for Quaker children but it is the kind of book that appeals to all ages. This work is 548 pages long and has eight pages of notes. Seven lovely water-colors by F. Cayley-Robinson illustrate the text.

Kepler, Thomas S., *The Fellowship of the Saints*, Abingdon-Cokesbury Press, New York, 1948.

This is an excellent anthology of Christian devotional literature. The compiler in his preface credits two writers with having helped him appreciate "the standards by which a 'saint' should be judged" and these two were Baron von Hugel and Douglas Steere. An appendix contains a chronology of devotional writings with a parallel chronology of events in Church history. Another appendix is a list of suggested readings.

Marx, O.S.B., Michael, *Protestants and Catholics on the Spiritual Life*, The Liturgical Press, Collegeville, Minnesota, 1965.

I consider this a prophetic book. Published more than ten years ago, it is a collection of papers given at an Ecumenical Institute on the Spiritual Life held at St. John's Abbey in Collegeville from August 31 to September 6, 1965. Participants in the conference were from Orthodox, Protestant and Roman Catholic traditions. The chief initiator of the conference was the Quaker observer at the Second Vatican Council, Dr. Douglas V. Steere. Papers by Bernard Haring and Barnabas Ahern are among those included in this book. It concludes with an epilogue, an evaluation of the papers by Kilian McDonnell, O.S.B.

Saints in Season: Companion to the Lectionary, Dominican Publications, St. Saviour's, Dublin 1, Ireland, 1976.

This book includes an introduction by Austin Flannery, O.P., short biographies of Saints by Vincent Ryan, O.S.B., articles on "Honouring the Saints Today" and "The Communion of Saints." A section devoted to "Documentation" includes: "How the proper of the Saints was reformed," decrees from councils and "Joy in the Hearts of the Saints" by Pope Paul VI.

Index ac Status Causarum Beatificationis Servorum Dei ex Canonizationis Beatorum, Sacred Congregation for the Causes of Saints, Rome 1975.
This book is a directory listing all causes for beatification and canonization whether in process or dormant.

MOTION PICTURES

Film Code

FCE

Film Classic Exchange
1914 South Vermont Ave.
Los Angeles, Calif. 90007

FI

Films Incorporated
1144 Wilmette Ave.
Wilmette, Il. 60091
(FI has offices in Atlanta, Hollywood, Honolulu, New York, Salt Lake City and San Diego. Write to Wilmette for addresses.)

ROA Films
1696 N. Astor St.
Milwaukee, Wis. 53202

SWANK

Swank Motion Pictures, Inc.
201 S. Jefferson Ave.
St. Louis, Mo. 63166
(SWANK has offices in New York, Boston, Chicago and Houston. Write to St. Louis for addresses.)

TWYMAN

Twyman Films, Inc.
329 Salem Ave.
Dayton, Ohio 45401

UNITED

United Films
1425 South Main
Tulsa, Oklahoma 74119

BECKET

Richard Burton and Peter O'Toole star in this film about Thomas a Becket.*

BROTHER SUN, SISTER MOON

This 1973 film by Zeffirelli, remembered for his beautiful *Romeo and Juliet*, received generally poor reviews. In fact, several critics termed it a disaster. Only the first part of Francis' life is covered and it is marred by historical inaccuracies. The only redeeming feature of the film is the photography which is magnificent. The camera captures the red-flowered fields of Assisi and the atmosphere of that part of Italy. Having had experience with students of varying age groups viewing this film I would suggest that it is useful for pre-teens or for those adults who love good photography. Those who know and love Francis should avoid the film. High school and college students leave the movie with the impression that Francis and his followers were dropout flower children.

Color/$150.00 + $5.00 shipping charge   FI

DON BOSCO

This is the life story of the "apostle of youth."
B&W/90 min./$25.00   ROA

FRANCIS OF ASSISI

Made in 1961, this filmed account of the life of Francis stars Bradford Dillman, Dolores Hart, Stuart Whitman and Cecil Kellaway. *The Washington Post*, December 1974, gave this film a two

* indicates author has been unable to locate the film.

star (out of four) rating in their list of TV movies. Historical accuracy is not a strength of this film.

Color/105 min.   **FI**

JOAN OF ARC

This 1950 film stars Ingrid Bergman in the title role. Jose Ferrer made his film debut in this triple Academy Award winner.

Color/100 min./$50.00   **UNITED**

THE LITTLE FLOWER OF ST. THERESE

I hesitate to list this film as I have not viewed it. The film is in French with English subtitles. The fact that St. Therese's name is misspelled in FCE's film list does not give one confidence.

$75.00   **FCE**

A MAN FOR ALL SEASONS

Winner of six Academy Awards, this film stars Paul Scofield as St. Thomas More. Other stars include Wendy Hiller, Robert Shaw and Orson Welles.

Color/120 min./$125.00   **SWANK**

MONSIEUR VINCENT
(French Language/English Subtitles)

This 1945 film, made by Jean Anouilh and Bernard Luc, based on the life of St. Vincent de Paul, stars Pierre Fresnay and Aime Clariond and was directed by Maurice Cloche. *Monsieur Vincent* won an Academy Award for Best Foreign Films and 8 International Film Festival Awards including Best Actor at the Venice International Film Festival.

B&W/112 min./$50.00 (Lent and Easter $75.00)   TWYMAN

MONSIEUR VINCENT

Same as above in English.

B&W/ 112 min./$45.00   ROA

THE RELUCTANT SAINT

Maximilian Schell stars as St. Joseph of Cupertino, the Saint renowned for the phenomenon of levitation. Others in the cast include Ricardo Montalban, Akim Tamiroff and Lea Padovani.

B&W/105 min./$22.50   ROA

THE SECRET CONCLAVE

This is the life story of Pope St. Pius X. Among other things it depicts a conclave summoned in the Sistine Chapel of the Vatican, for the election of a pope.

90 min./$25.00   ROA

SONG OF BERNADETTE

This 1944 inspirational classic won an Academy Award for Jennifer Jones who portrays St. Bernadette. The cast includes Gladys Cooper as the nun, Mother Vazous, Charles Bickford as the local parish priest, Anne Revere as Bernadette's mother and Vincent Price as the imperial prosecutor. The movie is based on the novel by Franz Werfel.

B&W/$40.00   FI

CASSETTES

Burgess, Stanley M., *"Lesser Known Sources in the Roman Catholic Tradition for Charismatic Piety,"* Logos Tapes, 201 Church Street, Plainfield, New Jersey 07060.

This is a recording of a paper presented at the Society for Pentecostal Studies in November 1973. Burgess is a classical Pentecostal and an historian. He suggests the above title of his talk for classical Pentecostals. For Catholics he says an appropriate title would be: "Long-neglected Sources. . . ." This talk is evidence of the interest of Pentecostal scholars in Catholic mystical tradition. At the beginning of the talk Burgess says "so much of what I have is within the footnotes." And he doesn't read the footnotes so we are left guessing about a number of things. The paper is flawed by some factual errors also. See footnote 9 in Chapter 11 for a discussion of this talk.

Hardon, S.J., John A., *Saints as Doctrinal Patterns of Sanctity*, produced by The Daughters of St. Paul, 50 St. Paul's Avenue, Jamaica Plain, Boston, Mass. 02130.

In writing the conference Fr. Hardon drew upon the official teaching of the Church regarding the process of canonization. This talk is valuable for its discussion of heroic virtue. The emphasis on "attaining perfection" may grate on some ears.